Conversations with Audre Lorde

Literary Conversations Series

Peggy Whitman Prenshaw
General Editor

D1519392

Photo credit: © Dagmar Schultz

Conversations with
Audre Lorde

Edited by Joan Wylie Hall

8|07
University Press of Mississippi
Jackson

Books by Audre Lorde

The First Cities. New York: Poets Press, 1968.
Cables to Rage. London: Paul Breman, 1970.
From a Land Where Other People Live. Detroit: Broadside Press, 1973.
The New York Head Shop and Museum. Detroit: Broadside Press, 1974.
Between Our Selves. Point Reyes, California: Eidolon Editions, 1976.
Coal. New York: W. W. Norton, 1976.
The Black Unicorn. New York: W. W. Norton, 1978.
The Cancer Journals. San Francisco: Spinsters Ink, 1980.
Chosen Poems Old and New. New York: W. W. Norton, 1982.
Zami: A New Spelling of My Name. Watertown, Massachusetts: Persephone Press, 1982.
Sister Outsider: Essays and Speeches. Trumansburg, New York: The Crossing Press, 1984.
Our Dead Behind Us. New York: W. W. Norton, 1986.
A Burst of Light: Essays. Ithaca, New York: Firebrand Books, 1988.
Undersong: Chosen Poems Old and New. Revised Edition. New York: W. W. Norton, 1992.
The Marvelous Arithmetics of Distance: Poems 1987–1992. New York: W. W. Norton, 1993.
The Collected Poems of Audre Lorde. New York: W. W. Norton, 1997.

www.upress.state.ms.us

The University Press of Mississippi is a member of the Association of American University Presses.

12 11 10 09 08 07 06 05 04   4 3 2 1
∞
Library of Congress Cataloging-in-Publication Data

Conversations with Audre Lorde / edited by Joan Wylie Hall.
    p. cm
    Includes index.
    ISBN 1-57806-642-5 (cloth : alk. paper) — ISBN 1-57806-643-3 (pbk. : alk. paper)
    1. Lorde, Audre—Interviews. 2. Poets, American—20th century—Interviews.
    3. Feminists—United States—Interviews. 4. Lesbians—United States—Interviews.
    5. African American lesbians—Interviews. 6. African American poets—Interviews.
    7. African American women—Interviews. I. Lorde, Audre. II. Hall, Joan Wylie.

PS3562.O75Z64 2004

                                                      2003062103

British Library Cataloging-in-Publication Data available

Contents

Introduction   vii

Chronology   xix

Interview with Audre Lorde   *Margaret Kaminski*   3

Audre Lorde   *Nina Winter*   9

Audre Lorde   *Ellen Shapiro*   18

Audre Lorde: Interview   *Karla M. Hammond*   26

An Interview with Audre Lorde   *Adrienne Rich*   45

My Words Will Be There   *Mari Evans*   71

Interview: Audre Lorde Advocates Unity among Women   *Shelley Savren
    and Cheryl Robinson*   79

Audre Lorde   *Claudia Tate*   85

An Interview with Audre Lorde   *Susan Cavin*   101

Speaking the Unspeakable: Poet Audre Lorde   *Karla Jay*   109

Poetry, Nature, and Childhood: An Interview with Audre Lorde
    Louise Chawla   115

An Interview with Audre Lorde   *Joseph F. Beam*   128

Audre Lorde on Her Cancer Illness   *Dagmar Schultz*   132

The Law Is Male and White: Meeting with the Black Author,
    Audre Lorde   *Dorothee Nolte*   143

The Creative Use of Difference   *Marion Kraft*   146

Poetry and Day-by-Day Experience: Excerpts from a Conversation
    on 12 June 1986 in Berlin   *Karen Nölle-Fischer*   154

Audre Lorde: A Radio Profile   *Jennifer Abod*   158

An Interview with Audre Lorde   *Ilona Pache and Regina-Maria Dackweiler*   164

Frontiers   *Pratibha Parmar and Jackie Kay*   171

Breaking the Barriers of Silence   *Laureen A. Greene*   181

Above the Wind: An Interview with Audre Lorde   *Charles H. Rowell*   184

Index   201

Introduction

Born in Depression-era Harlem to West Indian parents, Audre Lorde described herself as a "Black lesbian feminist poet warrior mother." When Dorothee Nolte interviewed her for *Der Tagesspiegel*, Lorde laughed that some part of this description was sure to irritate everyone. Her lifelong outsider status, she told Mari Evans in *Black Women Writers*, was "both my weakness and my strength." Not surprisingly, the word "differences" recurs in her fifteen books and also in the twenty-one interviews gathered here, whether she is talking with a journalist from San Diego or a Detroit librarian. Yet Lorde speaks just as often of the necessity to "bridge," "arc," "cross" the barriers of race, class, nationality, sex, politics, and even—in *The Cancer Journals* (1980)—the gap between the sick and the healthy.

Conversations with Audre Lorde includes a newly transcribed interview on nature, taped in 1984; translations from the German media; dialogue from a 1987 radio program aired in Boston; Lorde's previously unpublished interview about her cancer; articles from the 1970s and 1980s feminist, lesbian, and gay media; interviews from book collections and from scholarly journals like *Signs* and *Callaloo*; and other primary material for exploring an author who is receiving increased attention from academics and general audiences in Europe, the Caribbean and South America, the United States, and the World Wide Web. While Lorde's interviews with Adrienne Rich, Charles Rowell, Mari Evans, Karla Hammond, and Claudia Tate (all included here) are familiar to researchers, this collection offers many resources that are difficult or impossible to find anywhere else; and endnotes will point readers to additional interviews that are omitted for lack of space.

The title of Audre Lorde's 1984 essay collection *Sister Outsider* suggests the continuing relevance—she would prefer the word "usefulness"—of her interviews and her writings in a world where differences explode at terrible cost. According to Lorde, the outsider whom we reject is, in fact, a member of the family. "How do we organize around our differences, neither denying them nor blowing them up out of proportion?" she asks at Medgar Evers College in the speech "I Am Your Sister: Black Women Organizing Across Sexualities,"

reprinted in *A Burst of Light* (1988). Frequently invited to speak at universities, conferences, and women's centers, Lorde carried this message to white
audiences too; but her struggles with cancer, along with her frustration at the
seeming racial insensitivity of some white feminists, increased her awareness
of the limits to her time and energy. As Lorde tells her fellow poet Adrienne
Rich in a long interview from *Signs*, black and white women face different
choices and different "pitfalls." Lorde and Rich are open about the misunderstandings in their own interracial friendship; yet their ongoing conversation
is a model of what Lorde calls "meeting across our differences."

Years earlier, when Lorde, Rich, and Alice Walker were all nominees for the
National Book Award in 1974, Rich—as winner—read a statement the three
had prepared jointly, acknowledging those women whose voices are not heard.
In New York, where she was one of the few Black students at her Catholic
grade school, at Hunter High School, and at Hunter College, Lorde was conscious of her minority status and the difficulty of making herself heard. But,
as early as 1953, when she went to Mexico to study briefly at the National
University, she was invigorated by experiences with the larger community of
people of color. "All of these brown people in the majority was very very
wonderful for me," she remarks to psychologist and environmental scholar
Louise Chawla in a previously unpublished interview that appears below.

Lorde explains to Adrienne Rich that, even though she had been writing
poetry since childhood, the months in Mexico resulted in "a kind of releasing
of my work, a real releasing of myself." Twenty years later, in 1974, her first
trip to Africa also had a major impact on her writing. The legends and land-
scapes of Dahomey are prominent in *The Black Unicorn* (1978), which many
critics consider her best volume of poetry. Lorde tells Karen Nölle-Fischer,
who translated her autobiographical *Zami: A New Spelling of My Name*
into German, that her encounter with African mythologies proved "very productive and wonderful and very validating." And in one of her last interviews,
Lorde comments to *Callaloo* editor Charles H. Rowell that the *Black Unicorn*
poems "have always felt to me like a conversation between myself and an
ancestor Audre." Interviewed by the literary critic Claudia Tate, she reflects
upon Afro-American literature as a definite part of the African tradition,
which views human life in "a kind of correspondence with the rest of the
world as a whole." Lorde cites many contemporary African authors for teaching her to see living as an "experience" instead of a "problem"; and she recognizes a typically African transcendence of pain and suffering in works by
several African Americans.

During the 1980s, Lorde often visited the Caribbean homeland to which her parents never returned, spending winters in the Virgin Islands as a relief from the harsh cold of New York. After she settled permanently in St. Croix with her companion, Gloria I. Joseph, she told Rowell that "there is a large and ever present Blackfullness to the days here that is very refreshing for me, although frustrating sometimes, because as in so many places, we have so many problems with how we treat each other." Again, the immersion in "Blackfullness" seemed to take her writing in new directions. Speaking with *HOT WIRE* interviewers Jorjet Harper and Toni L. Armstrong Jr. after Hurricane Gilbert hit St. Croix in 1988, Lorde remarked that she was working on her first novel, about a Black lesbian mother who is "really attempting to survive in the late '60s and '70s."[1]

In the Virgin Islands, Lorde and Gloria Joseph were extremely active in the Woman's Coalition, Sisters in Support of Sisters in South Africa, and other groups for the betterment of women's lives. When Helga Lukoschat and Ulrike Helwerth asked them about these activities in an interview for the German newspaper *taz, Die Tageszeitung*, Lorde described the "cultural imperialism" of the United States in the Islands and the negative impact of tourism on the ecology and the Caribbean people.[2]

Lorde's sense of responsibility toward the Black Diaspora extended to women of African descent in Germany, where she underwent alternative therapies for cancer. In 1984, she was teaching a poetry workshop and a course on Black American women poets at the Free University of Berlin when the editor and scholar Dagmar Schultz conducted an interview on her cancer, published below for the first time. In a contemporaneous interview for the newspaper *taz*, Lorde and Schultz discuss Lorde's work with the Kitchen Table Women of Color Press in the United States—a venture she describes further in an interview with Shelley Savren and Cheryl Robinson for *The Longest Revolution*, a California feminist newspaper. In *taz*, Schultz and Lorde outline plans for Schultz's sub rosa Press (later renamed Orlanda Women's Press) to publish a book of writing by Afro-German women. Lorde stresses "how important it is that the voices of these women be heard and that their special situation and the racism to which they are subjected become public knowledge, and that the white women's movement discuss this."[3]

The resulting volume, *Farbe bekennen*, edited by Schultz, May Opitz, and Katharina Oguntoye, appeared in 1986, the same year that Heidrun Schmidt interviewed Lorde for *taz* on the "biomythography" *Zami*.[4] In 1991, *Farbe bekennen* was translated as *Showing Our Colors: Afro-German Women Speak Out*. Introducing the volume, Lorde summarizes its significance, both to the contributors and their readers: "In the interest of all our survivals and the survival of our children, these Black German women claim their color and their voices." To examine our connections, she says, we must "listen carefully to each other's stories."

Many interviews indicate that Lorde did a great deal of listening on her several journeys to Germany and other parts of Europe. In 1987, she told Ilona Pache and Regina-Maria Dackweiler that, as an African American, she had little prior knowledge about Afro-Germans: "There are many, many differences—those I am learning." Discovering that the word "Afro-German" was not in common use, Lorde encouraged her Berlin students and other Afro-Europeans to acknowledge the whole of their background. In an interview with Marion Kraft for the German magazine *EAST*, she says she is excited to make contact with other people of color, learning from each other's differences in order to battle oppression creatively and "really move toward change, toward that future we can share."

Lorde's invitation to participate in the June 1984 International Feminist Bookfair in London seemed the ideal chance for her to talk with British members of the African Diaspora. But the poet was frustrated that the conference organizers provided few opportunities for her to meet at length with Black feminists and lesbians. A notable exception was her conversation with three women of color who interviewed Lorde for the feminist journal *Spare Rib*: Dorothea [Smartt], Jackie Kay, and Uma [Kali Shakti]. Lorde emphasizes her need to hear their reaction to her work: "I existed in a vacuum for so many years. I wrote the stuff and sent it out into the ether, and had no idea who was relating to it."[5]

Subsequently, the Afro-Scots poet Jackie Kay and film maker Pratibha Parmar invited her to participate in a transatlantic interview by tape for a 1988 collection of writing by Black and Third World women. As she does in her German interviews, Lorde notes differences and similarities between Afro-Europeans and African Americans. She considers an "international network" of Black and Third World women to be "absolutely essential," and she urges feminists who are angry with a "strong right-wing turn" in world politics—a recurring concern of her 1980s interviews—to articulate their anger.

"Your silence will not protect you," Audre Lorde famously states in "The Transformation of Silence into Language and Action," collected in *Sister Outsider*. In "the mouth of the dragon we call america," says Lorde, "it is not difference which immobilizes us, but silence. And there are so many silences to be broken." In an interview for *The Progressive*, she tells the journalist William Steif that she uses the lower case A because she is "angry about the pretenses of america," a country that she believes is "on the wrong side of every liberation struggle on Earth." Criticizing Jesse Helms, the Pentagon, and the Reagan-Bush administrations, Lorde notes the exclusion of American Indians and many others from the American dream, and she emphasizes to Steif the need first to recognize such problems and then to "speak up."[6]

Audre Lorde's recollections of childhood in several interviews help to explain her dread of silences. She tells Anita Cornwell that her parents "spoke a language that for some reason I couldn't hear. Or didn't want to hear." Admitting she was a "difficult child," she adds that she was "silent when I should have spoken, and loud when I should have kept my mouth shut."[7] Interviewed by Deborah Wood at Howard University's 1976 National Conference of Afro-American Writers, Lorde says her mother feared that a daughter who wanted to write would not get work with the civil service: "Out of her fears and silences, 'good' meant establishment."[8]

Lorde's father, Frederic Byron Lorde, read widely, allowed her to read whatever she wanted (sometimes over her mother's objections), and valued her poetry; but Lorde tells *Christopher Street* interviewer Ellen Shapiro that "absolute terror" was her usual response to the man who "felt many emotions deeply, for which he had no name, and to which he gave no expression."

In a conversation with Nina Winter evoking many childhood memories, Lorde recalls that her parents "never discussed color, really, in our house— or, to be exact, they never discussed *race*." Identifying her parents' silences with fear and suppressed emotions, Lorde identified poetry with a release of ideas and feelings and an impetus to activity. In "Poetry Is Not a Luxury," an often-quoted essay from *Sister Outsider*, she asserts that poetry is "a vital necessity of our existence. It forms the quality of the light within which we predicate our hopes and dreams toward survival and change, first made into language, then into idea, then into more tangible action." Interviews with Karla Hammond and Margaret Kaminski make frequent reference to Lorde's own poems and offer important commentaries on the transformative role of literature. Speaking with Hammond in *The American Poetry Review*, Lorde praises the leadership of the "philosopher/Queen, the poet warrior," and states that, "For me, 'woman' is synonymous with 'poet' because poetry is about feeling."[9]

Hammond's *Denver Quarterly* interview reveals a surprising variety of poetic influences on Lorde, from the English Romantics and American lyricists to T. S. Eliot. She speculates that she had a "very emotional relationship with poetry when I was young because I was very inarticulate. I didn't speak, probably because I was left handed and had been taught to write with my right hand. I couldn't stutter because I got hit if I stuttered. So writing was the next best thing." Questioned by Margaret Kaminski about a "feminist aesthetic," Lorde replies that in "alternative aesthetics," including the black aesthetic and the feminist aesthetic, "art and poetry become part and parcel of one's daily living, one's daily expression, the need to communicate, the need to share one's feelings, to develop within oneself the best that is possible. And the definition of art as betterment, I think, is a mainstay of the alternative aesthetics."

In a late interview for *BLK* with Alycee J. Lane, Lorde is even more emphatic in discussing the ends of artistic expression: "I think all art by its nature must be revolutionary. In times that are as sick and as critical as the time that we live in, how can any art not be revolutionary?"[10] Rejecting a value in "art for art's sake," she stresses that the function of art is "empowerment in one way or another. As a poet I choose to do that with words." Lorde's remarks come in the midst of a serious conversation on world events, but she concludes with lighter observations on her favorite television shows (*Bill Cosby*, the old *Kung Fu*, and Black Entertainment Television), her vices (mangoes, oatmeal cookies, and impatience), and even the joy of wearing dreadlocks. Like several other interviews, Lane's article for *BLK* is punctuated with Lorde's laughter.

Audre Lorde's many pleasures have an important place in the philosophy she outlines in the *Sister Outsider* essay "Uses of the Erotic: The Erotic as Power." Men have "misnamed" the erotic, she says, equating it with the sexual and sometimes confusing it with "its opposite, the pornographic." Lorde's erotic is "an assertion of the lifeforce of women; of that creative energy empowered, the knowledge and use of which we are now reclaiming in our language, our history, our dancing, our loving, our work, our lives." These remarks are echoed in several interviews. Speaking with Jennifer Abod for a radio profile, she remembers dancing her "lungs loose" so late one night that she failed to prepare a presentation for a women's group the next day. She tells *off our backs* interviewers Fran Moira and Lorraine Sorrel that "If we listen to poetry in the same way we listen to music, it should be an enveloping, a mantle, something that strokes you, something soft."[11] Women have a greater ability than men to express a "primal force through our work," she adds, because "our bodies have an imprint of the connection between work and life."

Lorde distinguishes destructive acts of the body from creative ones in an interview with Susan Leigh Star for the collection *Against Sadomasochism: A Radical Feminist Analysis* (1982), where she argues that sadomasochism "feeds the belief that domination is inevitable."[12] Speaking with Susan Cavin for the *Big Apple Dyke News*, Lorde comments further on the healthy exercise of power: "I see that political liberation is not possible until each one of us begins to think of ourselves as power principles, as a nest of power relative to other people's power, of course."

When Jil Clark of Boston's *Gay Community News* asks Audre Lorde how she was "empowered" by breast cancer, she answers: "That sense of death at our shoulders becomes, not something that renders me impotent, but rather something that renders me more able to touch my power because I reckon less with my fear."[13] For Lorde, *The Cancer Journals* is a crucial weapon in breaking the silence surrounding the disease; and the mythic figure of the one-breasted Amazon inspires her to fight her battles. In Germany for cancer treatments, she tells Dagmar Schultz that "We meet breast cancer like we meet every other crisis, out of a composite of who we are."

Motherhood constitutes an essential part of Lorde's composite identity. In an unusually dramatic interview with James Baldwin, Lorde charges him and other Black men with providing responsible models for her son's relationships with Black women "so our kids will not have to repeat that waste of themselves."[14] She frequently refers with pride to both of her children, Elizabeth and Jonathan, born in the financially stressful early years of her marriage to Edwin Rollins, a legal aid lawyer who encouraged her to accept a life-changing invitation to teach creative writing at Tougaloo College in Mississippi. "It was a difficult time for a black woman and a white man to be married," she remarks to Steif.[15] And she acknowledges, in a *Blacklight* conversation with Joseph Beam, that racial differences made her subsequent partnership with Frances Clayton "an issue" in the gay and lesbian communities and in the larger "racist society." After Lorde's 1970 divorce, she and Clayton raised the children to adulthood. Interviewed by Dania and Vera of Berlin's lesbian Spinnboden-Archiv, Lorde affirms the value of institutes like Spinnboden and New York's Lesbian Herstory Archive, and she observes that lesbian mothers are typically a "silent minority."[16]

Lorde's dreams for the future often center in children (her own and others), whose vulnerability she portrays especially in her first five volumes, in
such poems as "Suffer the Children" and "To My Daughter the Junkie on a
Train." Many interviews emphasize the need for drastic changes in the conditions she exposes in the poetry. Speaking with Jewelle Gomez in conjunction
with the filming of "Before Stonewall: The Making of a Gay and Lesbian
Community," Lorde asserts that "The Black power and the civil rights movement of the late '50s and early '60s was the prototype of every single liberation movement in this country that we are still dealing with today."[17]

In an interview with the feminist writer Karla Jay, however, she points out
that the vision of the 1960s was an "incomplete" one and that some "real
challenges" have yet to be met. Outspokenly critical of U.S. involvement in
Grenada, for example, she tells J. F. Beam in the Philadelphia *Gay News* that
the invasion involved "very grave errors and injustices."[18] Interviews with Lee
Chiaramonte and Laureen A. Greene further delineate the work that needs to
be done to guarantee a more just future. In "Letter from Berlin," Lorde
describes to Chiaramonte her efforts to perfect the sort of writing "that can
start others feeling and thinking and moving in the directions I travel."[19]

Audre Lorde's interviews comprise a major record of her own feelings,
thoughts, and movements. Readers of *Zami* will recognize some key scenes
(with added details) from Lorde's early years. As oral history, the interview
collection complements Alexis De Veaux's *Poet Warrior: A Biography of Audre
Lorde*, currently in press and the first book-length study of Lorde. Audre
Lorde's authoritative voice is nearly as audible in her printed remarks as it is
in conversations recorded in two valuable film documentaries: Ada Gay
Griffin and Michelle Parkerson's "A Litany for Survival: The Life and Work of
Audre Lorde" (1995) and Jennifer Abod's "The Edge of Each Other's Battles:
The Vision of Audre Lorde" (2002).

This introductory essay refers to thirty-nine interviews with Audre Lorde
from the United States, the United Kingdom, and Germany. (An article for
Contact that Lorde mentions in the Chawla interview contains only a few of
her direct remarks and is thus not cited here.) The twenty-one interviews
selected for *Conversations with Audre Lorde* represent a variety of themes, occa-
sions, interviewers, media, and time periods, from Kaminski's Detroit Public
Library radio program in 1975 to Rowell's 1990 phone call to the Virgin
Islands. Following conventions of the Literary Conversations Series, interviews
are not edited to eliminate occasional repetition; such repetitions, in fact,

underscore Audre Lorde's abiding concerns and her sometimes aphoristic expression. She rarely repeats herself as closely as she does in the exchanges with Mari Evans and Claudia Tate, however; and Lorde seldom contradicts herself, but close readers will observe occasional discrepancies. A few interviews originally appeared with footnotes, which have been omitted or incorporated in brackets. Obvious misspellings and typographical errors are silently corrected. Although Audre Lorde preferred that the word Black be capitalized, the interviews vary in this respect. To avoid copyright infringement, I omit the passages of poetry that appear in some interviews, indicating the omission.

A special and appropriate strength of the collection is the presence of several European interviews, including one from England and five from Germany; three of the German interviews were translated specifically for this book. Several contributors deserve particular mention and thanks for their help with the international material. Jackie Kay corresponded with me about British interviews and described a large commemoration in London in 2002 of the tenth anniversary of Audre Lorde's death. Wilfried Raussert's close translation allowed me to read the Pache-Dackweiler interview from *Listen* before Ilona Pache kindly contributed the transcription of her audiotape published below, an expansion of the German version. With great dispatch and faithfulness to the originals, Francis J. Devlin translated interviews from *taz, Der Tagesspiegel,* and *Virginia* and allowed me to make slight revisions consistent with Lorde's dialogue in her English-language interviews; no one could hope for a better collaboration. Dagmar Schultz, whose photograph of Audre Lorde graces the cover, also contributed an English text of her previously unpublished interview, an insightful supplement to *The Cancer Journals.* Without her knowledge, her generosity, and her help with permissions, this collection would not reflect Lorde's deep bonds with Afro-German women and with other women's communities in Germany. Marion Kraft, who participated with Dagmar Schultz at Berlin's 2002 commemoration of Audre Lorde, sent me a copy of her English-language interview, which appeared in *EAST. Englisch Amerikanische Studien,* a hard-to-find journal that ceased publication in 1986.

Many U.S. interviewers made unusual contributions that enhance the value of this book. Louise Chawla transcribed the long interview she conducted with Audre Lorde for her study of five New York poets, *In the First Country of Places: Nature, Poetry, and Childhood Memory.* With Lorde's remarks on the energy of the city and the appeal of nature (including her hopes to move to the West), the Chawla interview stands out for its lyricism.

Jennifer Abod gave me permission to transcribe "Audre Lorde: An Audio Profile," a CD recording of the radio program that features Lorde and several other prominent writers and scholars; I very much appreciate her careful corrections of my transcript. Karla Jay took the time to find the printed version of her conversation with Audre Lorde after I discovered her taped interview in the New York Public Library's Karla Jay Papers.

I thank each interviewer, publisher, translator, editor, literary agent, and interviewer's estate—with particular gratitude to those who waived fees or granted nominal charges to make this book a reality, and with apologies to those whose interviews appear in endnotes because of hard choices imposed by space constraints.

I owe a large debt to Lester C. Olson for sending copies of several interviews that he discovered in his research on Audre Lorde's speeches at the Lesbian Herstory Archives. Special thanks too to Catherine Ann Wiley, Jennifer Browdy de Hernandez, and Jyl Lynn Felman for their enthusiastic participation in the 2002 MLA special session I organized on "Audre Lorde, New Yorker." The University of Mississippi helped to fund my travel to New York; I am grateful to Joseph R. Urgo, English Department chair. The University's interlibrary loan department was a crucial resource for locating interviews, thanks to Martha E. Swan, Lisa Harrison, and Anne Johnson.

At the University Press of Mississippi, Seetha Srinivasan and Peggy Whitman Prenshaw were unusually supportive from the start; and Anne Stascavage provided expert, reassuring, and resourceful guidance to the end. Thanks also to Kathy Burgess, Alison Sullenberger, and all others from the Press who helped this book to reach its readers. I am very grateful to friends at the University of Mississippi who encouraged my research on Audre Lorde, especially Anne R. Gowdy, Shirley James Hanshaw, Jack Barbera, Susan Major, David Galef, Deborah Barker, Annette Trefzer, and—above all—Colby H. Kullman.

Others corresponded and assisted, from San Juan to Berlin: Alexandrina Deschamps, Norma Valle Ferrer, Daniel Fogel, Ann Holder, Joan Larkin, Leslie Adelson, Jennifer Michaels, Donald W. Faulkner, Liz Di Novella, Kevin Everod Quashie, Alexis De Veaux, Gloria I. Joseph, Sidney Brinkley, Ekpenyong Ani and the Orlanda Press, Mary A. Tate, Barbara C. Ewell, Susanne Dietzel, Audrey Wolf, Jerry W. Ward Jr., Mairead Byrne, Barbara Grier, Alan Bell, Anne Kent Rush, Marianne Novy, Sheila Harris, Priya Jha, Philip C. Kolin,

Michelle Parkerson, Barbara J. Butler, and many more. Thanks, finally, to my family—J. R. Hall, Jennifer Hall, and Justin Hall—whose requests for progress reports were a major factor in the completion of this book.

JWH
August 2003

Notes

1. Jorjet Harper and Toni L. Armstrong Jr., "Audre Lorde," *HOT WIRE: The Journal of Women's Music and Culture*, January 1989, 2.

2. Helga Lukoschat and Ulrike Helwerth, " 'The Caribbean Is No Paradise' " [" 'Die Karibik ist kein Paradies' "], trans. Francis J. Devlin, (Berlin) *taz, Die Tageszeitung*, Women's section, 5 August 1989, 11. Devlin's unpublished translations of Audre Lorde's three *taz* interviews were of major help to the volume editor.

3. Dagmar Schultz, "Interview with Audre Lorde, Poetry: A Weapon and a Way" ["Interview mit Audre Lorde, Dictung: eine Waffe und ein Weg"], trans. Francis J. Devlin, (Berlin) *taz, Die Tageszeitung*, Women's section, 19 July 1984, 10.

4. Heidrun Schmidt, "The Passionate Poet" ["Die leidenschaftliche Poetin"], trans. Francis J. Devlin, (Berlin) *taz, Die Tageszeitung*, Women's section, 18 June 1986.

5. Dorothea [Smartt], Jackie Kay, and Uma [Kali Shakti], " '. . . No, we never go out of fashion . . . for each other!,' " (London) *Spare Rib*, November 1984, 29.

6. William Steif, "The *Progressive* Interview: Audre Lorde," *The Progressive*, January 1991, 33.

7. Anita Cornwell, " 'I Am Black, Woman, and Poet': An Interview with Audre Lorde," in Cornwell's *Black Lesbian in White America* (Tallahassee, FL: Naiad Press, 1983), 41. An earlier and shorter version of Cornwell's interview was published as " 'So Who's Giving Guarantees?': An Interview with Audre Lorde," *Sinister Wisdom*, Fall 1977, 15–21.

8. Deborah Wood, "Interview with Audre Lorde," *In the Memory and Spirit of Frances, Zora, and Lorraine: Essays and Interviews on Black Women and Writing*, ed. Juliette Bowles (Washington, DC: Institute for the Arts and the Humanities, Howard University, 1979), 13.

9. Karla Hammond, "An Interview with Audre Lorde," *The American Poetry Review*, March/April 1980, 19.

10. Alycee J. Lane, "Audre Lorde: The Celebrated Author on Everything from Black Germans to 2 Live Crew," *BLK*, September 1990, 13.

11. Fran Moira and Lorraine Sorrel, "interview, audre lorde: lit from within," *off our backs*, April 1982, 2.

12. Audre Lorde and Susan Leigh Star, "Interview with Audre Lorde," *Against Sadomasochism: A Radical Feminist Analysis*, ed. Robin Ruth Linden, Darlene R. Pagano, Diana E. H. Russell, and Susan Leigh Star (East Palo Alto, CA: Frog in the Well, 1982), 68.

13. Jil Clark, "Inside and Out: The Struggle Against Silence, An Interview with Audre Lorde," (Boston) *Gay Community News*, 10 October 1981, 8.

14. James Baldwin and Audre Lorde, "Revolutionary Hope: A Conversation between James Baldwin and Audre Lorde," *Essence*, December 1984, 74.

15. Steif, 32.

16. Dania and Vera, "Audre Lorde: Schwarze lesbische Dichterin und Kämpferin, Interview von Dania und Vera am 15.6.84" ["Audre Lorde: Black Lesbian Poet and Warrior, Interview with Dania and Vera on 15 June 1984"], *Spinnboden*, June 1984, 8.

17. Jewelle Gomez, "Audre Lorde & Maua Adele Ajanaku: An Interview," *"Before Stonewall": The Making of a Gay and Lesbian Community* [illustrated guide to the film *Before Stonewall*], by Andrea Weiss and Greta Schiller (Tallahassee, FL: Naiad Press, 1988), 55.

18. J. F. Beam, "Facing the Unfaceable," (Philadelphia) *Gay News*, 15 March 1984, 14.

19. Lee Chiaramonte, "Letter from Berlin: Audre Lorde Answers Questions on Writing, Voice and Being a Woman Warrior," *Visibilities*, September/October 1988, 5.

Chronology

1934   Audrey Geraldine Lorde is born in New York City on February 18, youngest of three daughters of Linda Belmar Lorde and Frederic Byron Lorde, immigrants who never achieve their dream of returning to the West Indies. Her mother is a former hotel maid; her father, a laborer and later a real estate broker in Harlem.

1938   Lorde drops the "y" from her first name because she dislikes the sight of the letter projecting beneath the lines of her writing paper. She learns to read and begins to communicate verbally after an early childhood in which she is considered mute. She often recites poetry to express her emotions.

1939   Extremely nearsighted, Lorde starts school in a sight-conservation class at a Harlem public school. Later attends Catholic grade school and feels isolated as the only student in her sixth-grade class who is not white.

1946   Begins to write poetry.

1951   Graduates from Hunter College High School in New York, where she begins a lifelong friendship with poet Diane Di Prima. During high school, Lorde publishes poetry in *Seventeen* and the *Harlem Writers' Quarterly* and attends meetings of the Harlem Writers' Guild, where she meets Langston Hughes. After graduation, she moves away from home, becomes self-supporting, and begins coursework at Hunter College.

1951–52   Nurse's aide at Bellevue Hospital.

1952–53   Works at factories in Stamford, Connecticut, saving money for a long trip to Mexico. Is fired from a ribbon factory after three weeks because the union is reluctant to admit African Americans.

1953   Works as a clinic clerk in a New York health center. Active in the Committee to Free the Rosenbergs, she goes to Washington, D.C., in June to picket the White House.

1953–54   Attends the National University of Mexico and, on her return to New York, publishes the story "La Llorona" in *Venture* magazine under the pseudonym Rey Domini. Lorde becomes part of Greenwich Village's "gay-girl" culture and works as a clerk-typist in the accounting office of a hospital.

1955–58 Library clerk for New York Public Library Children's Services.

1959   Graduates with a B.A. in literature and philosophy from Hunter College.

1959–60 Social investigator with the Bureau of Child Welfare.

1960–62 Young adult librarian at Mount Vernon Public Library, Mount Vernon, New York.

1961   Graduates from Columbia University with a master's in library science, a degree she pursued to learn how to access information that might help her effect social change.

1961–63 Librarian at Mount Vernon Public Library.

1962   Marries Edwin Ashley Rollins, a legal aid attorney, on March 31. She is anthologized in *Beyond the Blues: New Poems by American Negroes*, edited by Rosey Poole and published in England. Langston Hughes includes her work in his anthology *New Negro Poets, USA*.

1963   Daughter Elizabeth (Beth) Lorde Rollins is born.

1964   Son Jonathan (Jonno) Rollins is born.

1966–68 Head librarian at the private Town School in New York City. In December 1967, suffers a near-fatal case of flu, which she considers life-altering.

1968   With editorial help from Diane Di Prima, who also wrote the introduction, Lorde publishes her first volume of poetry, *The First Cities*, at Poets Press. This collection is considered more introspective and less socially engaged than her later work. Winner of a National Endowment for the Arts residency grant, she teaches her first creative writing course for six weeks at Tougaloo College in Jackson, Mississippi, where she edits her students' work in the literary magazine *Pound*. At Tougaloo, meets the psychotherapist Frances Clayton (a visiting assistant professor from Brown University). Lorde becomes a lecturer at City College of the University of New York and is a distinguished visiting professor at Atlanta University.

1969–70 Lecturer in the Education Department at Herbert H. Lehman College in New York.

1970   Divorces Edwin Rollins and establishes a household on Staten Island with her children and her partner Frances Clayton. Dedicates her second book of poetry, *Cables to Rage*, to her children; the poem "Martha" is viewed by some commentators as an early statement of her lesbianism. Appointed associate professor of English at John Jay College of Criminal Justice in the City University of New York.

1972   Receives a Creative Artists Public Service grant.

1973   Publishes a third book of poetry, *From a Land Where Other People Live*, including "The Day They Eulogized Mahalia," about singer Mahalia Jackson. Visits Barbados.

1974   Lorde first travels to Africa, accompanied by her children. Receives a Creative Arts Public Service Book Award for poetry. A National Book Award nominee for poetry for *From a Land Where Other People Live*, she publishes a fourth volume, *The New York Head Shop and Museum*, including "Viet-Nam Addenda" and "Blackstudies" (at five pages, one of her longest poems). Reading a joint statement prepared with Lorde and their fellow nominee Alice Walker, the NBA winner Adrienne Rich accepts the prize on behalf of all "unheard" women.

1975   Receives the Broadside Press Poet's Award and the Staten Island Community College Woman of the Year Award.

1976   Publication of Lorde's fifth and sixth poetry collections: *Coal*, her first book published by a major press (W. W. Norton), and *Between Our Selves* (Eidolon Press). Appears at the second National Conference of Afro-American Writers, sponsored by Howard University's Institute for the Arts and the Humanities in Washington, D.C. Awarded a second Creative Artists Public Service grant. Travels to Russia for two weeks in September as the invited American observer to the Union of Soviet Writers' African-Asian Writers Conference.

1977   Lorde speaks on "The Transformation of Silence into Language and Action" for a panel on lesbian literature at the Modern Language Association conference in Chicago.

1978   Publication of Lorde's seventh poetry collection, *The Black Unicorn*, which extensively incorporates African mythology. Attends the Women against Violence and Pornography in Media Conference in San Francisco. Diagnosed with breast cancer, she undergoes a mastectomy. "Uses of the Erotic: The Erotic as Power," her talk for the

Fourth Berkshire Conference on the History of Women at
Mt. Holyoke College on August 25, is published by Out & Out
Pamphlet, distributed by Crossing Press.

1979   Lorde is a featured speaker at the first national march for gay and
        lesbian liberation in Washington, D.C. In April, makes her first trip
        to Grenada, her mother's birthplace. Reads in Boston with poet
        Kate Rushin and others in the summer to raise funds for the
        Women's Safety Committee after the murders of twelve Black
        women; the following night, reads at Harvard's Sanders Theater
        with poet Adrienne Rich. Participates in "The Personal and the
        Political" panel at the Second Sex Conference in New York on
        September 29, reading "The Master's Tools Will Never Dismantle
        the Master's House," later included in *The Cancer Journals* and in
        Sister Outsider.

1980   Delivers the paper "Age, Race, Class, and Sex: Women Redefining
        Difference" in April at Amherst College's Copeland Colloquium.
        Publishes her first nonfiction book, *The Cancer Journals.* Reads and
        speaks at the United Nations World Women's Conference in
        Copenhagen, where she first meets editor and scholar Dagmar
        Schultz, who will later translate and publish her work in Germany.
        Lorde is appointed professor of English at Hunter College, where
        she is elected to the Hunter College Hall of Fame.

1981   Receives a second National Endowment for the Arts grant. The
        American Library Association names *The Cancer Journals* Gay
        Caucus Book of the Year. Gives the keynote presentation, "The Uses
        of Anger: Women Responding to Racism," in June at the National
        Women's Studies Association in Storrs, Connecticut.

1982   Publication of *Chosen Poems Old and New,* her eighth poetry col-
        lection, dedicated to Frances Louise Clayton. Most of the selections
        are reprinted from her first five collections; the seven new poems
        include "Afterimages," her poem about the murder of Emmett Till
        in Mississippi in 1955. Lorde edits *Lesbian Poetry: An Anthology* and
        publishes the autobiographical *Zami: A New Spelling of My Name,*
        which she describes as a "biomythography" of "dreams/myths/his-
        tories." "Zami" is a Caribbean Carriacou name for "women who
        work together as friends and lovers." Delivers the keynote presenta-
        tion, "Learning from the 60s," at Harvard in February for the

Malcolm X Weekend; the same month, she gives a reading at the Library of Congress with Marge Piercy. Spends a week in Grenada in late December, two months after the U.S. military invasion, which she severely criticizes.

1983   Lorde speaks on the twentieth anniversary of the 1963 March on Washington for Jobs and Justice. *Macht und Sinnlichkeit* (*Power and Sensuality*), lectures by Lorde and Adrienne Rich, is published in Germany.

1984   Publication of *Sister Outsider: Essays and Speeches*, which reprints Adrienne Rich's interview with Audre Lorde from the Summer 1981 issue of *Signs*. The collection includes "Poetry Is Not a Luxury," "Uses of the Erotic: The Erotic as Power," "The Master's Tools Will Never Dismantle the Master's House," and other pieces written between 1976 and 1984. On her first "teaching trip" to Europe, Lorde is weakened by liver cancer. Guest professor for three months at the Free University of Berlin's John F. Kennedy Institute for North American Studies. Speaks at the First International Feminist Bookfair in London in June but calls it a "monstrosity of racism." Edits the anthology *Woman Poet—The East*. Gloria I. Joseph, social scientist from the Caribbean, founds Sisters in Support of Sisters in South Africa, an organization in which Lorde becomes active from the start.

1985   Travels to Cuba in March in a delegation of Black women writers, including Toni Cade Bambara, Mari Evans, Rosa Guy, Gloria Joseph, Alexis De Veaux, and others. In Melbourne, Australia, gives keynote address on "The Language of Difference" at the Women's Writing Conference. Undergoes alternative therapy for liver cancer at Lukas Klinik in Arlesheim, Switzerland, in December. Kitchen Table: Women of Color Press, which she helped found as an outlet for women of many ethnicities, publishes "I Am Your Sister: Black Women Organizing Across Sexualities," Lorde's speech at Medgar Evers College's Women's Center in New York. The Audre Lorde Women's Poetry Center is dedicated at Hunter College.

1986   Publication of Lorde's ninth poetry collection, *Our Dead Behind Us*, dedicated to Gloria I. Joseph. The impact of Lorde's travels to Germany is seen in "Berlin Is Hard on Colored Girls" and "This Urn Contains Earth from German Concentration Campus." With

Merle Woo, publishes "Apartheid USA and Our Common Cause in the Eighties," a Freedom Organizing Pamphlet from Kitchen Table Press. In April, speaks at "The Ties That Bind," a Virgin Islands conference on Caribbean women, organized by Gloria Joseph. In London on June 16, anniversary of the Soweto Uprising in South Africa. Later in June, Lorde meets with the Zamani Soweto in Bonnieux, France.

1987   Lorde is named Thomas Hunter Professor at Hunter College. Works with the Afro-German Women's Group in Berlin and speaks at the "Dream of Europe" conference, where she says that Black Europeans, the "hyphenated people," offer Europe a last chance for dealing with differences. Moves to St. Croix, U.S. Virgin Islands, initially for the winters and later as a permanent home. On St. Croix, she receives the name Gambda Adisa, or Warrior: She Who Makes Her Meaning Known.

1988   Receives the Manhattan Borough President's Award for Excellence in the Arts. *A Burst of Light*, her second essay collection, reprints Susan Leigh Star's interview "Sadomasochism: Not about Condemnation," three of Lorde's earlier essays, and her new essay "A Burst of Light: Living with Cancer."

1989   *A Burst of Light* wins a Before Columbus Foundation American Book Award. Lorde receives an honorary degree from Oberlin College. Helps organize relief efforts for St. Croix, Virgin Islands, after Hurricane Hugo destroys or seriously damages most homes, including the house she shares with Gloria Joseph. Lorde and Joseph travel to Berlin.

1990   "I Am Your Sister: Forging Global Connections Across Difference," a conference honoring Lorde, draws over two thousand people from twenty-three countries to Boston in October. With Gloria I. Joseph and Hortense M. Rose, publishes *Hell under God's Orders: Hurricane Hugo in St. Croix—Disaster and Survival* (Winds of Change Press) on the personal, social, and ecological effects of the storm. Receives the Bill Whitehead Memorial Award for Lifetime Achievement in Gay and Lesbian Literature from the Publishing Triangle. Haverford College awards Lorde an honorary degree.

1991   Travels again to Germany. Receives an honorary doctorate from Hunter College. Awarded the Walt Whitman Citation of Merit as poet-laureate of New York State, a two-year appointment announced by Governor Mario Cuomo and the New York State Writers Institute. At a November 13 ceremony in Albany, Lorde accepts the $10,000 cash prize and criticizes national politics in an address that is followed by a standing ovation.

1992   Publication of her tenth poetry collection, *Undersong: Chosen Poems Old and New*, a revision of the 1982 volume. Lorde spends the summer in Berlin with Gloria Joseph at the home of Dagmar Schultz and Ika Hügel, where she gives her last reading; a recording, dedicated to Soweto women, is sent to South Africa. In Germany, reads and discusses with Orlanda Press many books that the publisher is considering for translation. Lorde sends a protest letter, published in German newspapers, to Chancellor Helmut Kohl after racially motivated attacks occur in Rostock. At home in the Caribbean, Lorde and Joseph are joined for Lorde's final days by Schultz, Hügel, and the Afro-German poet May Ayim. Dies of cancer on November 17 at Christiansted, St. Croix, Virgin Islands. Lorde leaves many of her personal papers to Spelman College in Atlanta.

1993   January 17 memorial service brings thousands of mourners to the Cathedral of Saint John the Divine in New York. Eulogists include Lorde's two children, with Angela Davis, Sonia Sanchez, Barbara Smith, and others. Posthumous publication of her eleventh book of poetry, *The Marvelous Arithmetics of Distance: Poems 1987–1992*, including "Thanks to Jesse Jackson" and "Jessehelms."

1997   *The Collected Poems of Audre Lorde* is published by W.W. Norton.

Conversations with Audre Lorde

Interview with Audre Lorde

Margaret Kaminski / 1975

From *Chomo-Uri: a women's multi-arts magazine* (University of Massachusetts at Amherst), 3.3 (Spring 1977), 14–21. Internal evidence suggests the interview was conducted in 1975 or late in 1974. Reprinted by permission.

[*This interview was originally done as part of the Detroit Public Library's "Meet the Author" radio series.*]

Margaret Kaminski: Your book of poetry, *From a Land Where Other People Live*, was nominated for the National Book Award in poetry, along with Adrienne Rich's book, *Diving into the Wreck*, and another woman poet's book, whose name escapes me at the moment. I remember the three of you issued a joint statement on that occasion which appeared in feminist magazines. Would you like to comment on this?

Audre Lorde: The other woman who received the nomination for poetry in 1974 was Alice Walker, and she received it for her book *Revolutionary Petunias*. Most of what I have to say was included in that statement. I could add, though, that we published it because we felt very strongly about not wanting to be caught up in the male competitive aspect of poetry, that poetry as competition, as opposed to poetry as feeling, sharing—evocative, was not something that we wanted to further.

MK: Was this—people talk about the feminist aesthetic—do you think that this is the main difference?

AL: I think that it's part of, I hope that it's part of the feminist aesthetic. I know certainly, for instance, it's part of the black aesthetic, the whole concept of art as business, art for art's sake, art as the competitive gesture, I connect with a very male-oriented concept of living, as opposed to, and we could call them alternate aesthetics, which include the black aesthetic, the feminist aesthetic, where art and poetry become part and parcel of one's daily living, one's daily expression, the need to communicate, the need to share one's feelings, to develop within oneself the best that is possible. And the definition of art as betterment, I think, is a mainstay of the alternative aesthetics.

MK: Were you surprised when your book, *From a Land Where Other People Live*, was nominated for the National Book Award and when it was so widely reviewed?—it was in *Ms.* magazine, and so on.

AL: Well, I guess I should, since this is a public interview, I should be a shrinking violet and say, yes I was shocked, but actually no, I wasn't. I've always felt that if I could have a voice, if I could get work published, if it could get out, that it would be recognized because the things I have to say I feel are terribly important. And I think that I'm learning to say them better and better all the time. I think they are things that are essential to my living, to your living, to the living of all involved, engaged human beings. In addition to that: Margaret, I've been writing a long time: I've been writing a long time. I've been out there, you know, really hustling, and it sharpened me in some ways, but it's also removed a lot of the elements of surprise. I'm surprised by very little these days.

MK: I can see what you mean, that it might almost be an anticlimax, that you're already working on something else by the time you get the award, and so on.

AL: That's a very good point; yes. You must remember that by the time a book of poetry comes out, by the time it sees the light, it may see your light and be new, but I've already gone through it. I've already gone past it into the next book that I'm working on. It's almost retrograde, you know, although, of course, they stand for themselves. I stand behind every work I've ever written.

MK: I have a quote here from that book:

[quotes from "Who Said It Was Simple"].

Why is it, do you think, that some black women do not seem as conscious as they could be of sexism, even when the statistics show that women of both races, say, in full-time jobs, get on the average of $5,000 per year less than their male counterparts?

AL: Well, I disagree with you, Margaret. I think that black women are very aware of sexism. I think they are terribly, tragically aware of sexism because I think that we probably, you know, are destroyed by it as much as and sometimes even more. I mean that not only do we have our own men, not only do we have black men, right, sitting on us, but we've got a whole white male establishment. So I think that we are very aware of sexism. I think what is operative here is that we're also aware of racism and the ways in which those two things mesh. And this is the point I was trying to make in the poem, "Who Said It Was Simple?"

that racism and sexism fed each other, that if we removed sexism tomorrow, I have no reason to believe that the white female establishment would be any less racist than the white male establishment. And this is why I think it's absolutely necessary for women, black and white women, to get together and to begin to recognize some of the ways in which liberation is sucked away from us all, that we cannot separate the struggles for liberation because it is, eventually, all human liberation. And until we come into that concept, until we broaden our viewpoints so that liberation doesn't remain the private province of any one particular group, until we do that, we're going to be working against each other, and working against ourselves. So I don't think that black women are unaware of sexism, I think that they see it in a context which is that it is part and parcel of the kind of racism, the kind of ism that is destroying us all, and of which sexism is only a part.

MK: Both of your books, the 1973 one and your new book, *New York Head Shop and Museum*, deal with a very powerful mother figure and reveal that you are very conscious of your motherhood. When one out of four black women are heads of families, do you see the mother aspect as an even stronger issue?
AL: It's really hard for me to relate to that question, Margaret. I see the nurturing principle as also one of the saviors of the human race, whether it occurs in women or whether it occurs in men. I am very much in touch with mine. I think we are all mothers in that sense. You see, what we have done essentially, is relegate to that word "mother" a whole set of feelings and patterns of relationships with other human beings that are basically nurturing, that are basically helpful. We've said, those belong to mother and nowhere else. I believe that that word "mother" needs to be fed into the grinder and come out M-H-T, whatever, come out initials, or come out just pap which we can then spread, because I believe it is part and parcel of us all, and I think that it's one of the saving principles of human relationships, that we do help each other, that we do respond in terms of survival and teaching. And that's what motherhood is all about.

MK: I've read that in anthropology books, that some anthropologists consider this as the first humanizing, or the first socializing instinct, that brought us out of barbarism. And hopefully will be the thing that . . .
AL: . . . that saves us.

MK: . . . that saves us. Again, on this theme of motherhood in your poetry, what do you foresee as the future of the family in the United States, and particularly of the black family?

AL: That's another question, Margaret, that I *really* can't relate to. I don't foresee families. I foresee, again, varying patterns of relationships. I think it will probably vary from group to group. I think that some of the taboos that we suffer under now, that a family must be made up of male/female plus children, all locked into a kind of an authoritarian, blind, give or take, I think that that will hopefully disintegrate. I think that if we begin to think of families in a wider context, groups of people relating to each other in a give-and-take manner, then our definitions of families will broaden so that we have groups of people, sustain groups, support groups, in whatever period of life, whatever time, whatever place, right, that come together and remain. I think families in that sense, human beings, are basically social and we will always find some way of grouping together, and our children need to be protected.

MK: I didn't mean "family" in the strict sense, that it is changing. You have published a poem, too, in *Moving Out*, Detroit's feminist literary magazine. What do you think of the women's small press phenomena?

AL: I say bully for it. I think that it needs to be encouraged and I certainly hope it continues. I think that any small press movement is very good, and I think in particular because women have suffered so much from the kinds of public silence that have been imposed upon us, in terms of being unable to publish in a large literary magazine, being unable to get things that we really feel very strongly about having said. I think that the women's press movement is a very healthy aspect of the movement. And I think it will expose, also, much of what *is* being said to a wider group.

MK: I think one of the most interesting poems in your latest book *New York Head Shop* is called "The American Cancer Society or There Is More Than One Way to Skin a Coon," which talks about the new commercials on television which show black people as consumers. Although these commercials are obviously to make money, don't you think that there might be something good about having more black people on television, even if it is in this way?

AL: There's something good about having more black people on television, yes, but I think that is taking part in something that I consider very, very dangerous to the black community, which is mistaking the images of success.

That was once a line in that poem which I took out, but, very much so. If we relive the mistakes of white America, we will be doomed to perhaps the same kind of self-destruction that I think white America is taking part in. And in order to avoid that, we must not mistake the symbols of success. It is not successful to have a hundred million black machines because, although black is beautiful, a black machine is a black machine. I am not interested in seeing my children grow up to become American consumers. I am interested to see them grow up to be human beings who are black.

MK: This poem brings up all sorts of questions to me, like, all of a sudden, black people need Gleem instead of believing that all black people have perfect teeth, which is a stereotype. And I can see inconsistencies like this in the treatment of women, like on one hand, women "of healthy peasant stock" can supposedly take more pain, but on the other hand, rich women need smelling salts and all kinds of pills and so on. I see this as kind of the same thing. Is this something of what you had in mind while writing the poem?

AL: Well, yes. Sojourner Truth said it very well. You know, after the Civil War in the large women's meeting in 1898 which took place with Elizabeth Cady Stanton and all the rest, the woman's rights, feminists' rights meeting at which Sojourner Truth spoke. She said that they say that women need to be helped, that they cannot drive horses, they cannot work, they cannot walk, but I have walked so many miles; I have worked as a blacksmith; I have drawn carriages, never mind driven them, and am I not a woman? right? So, the economic basis of the kinds of prejudices and stereotypes of racism, of sexism, are very obvious. When we need strong, pioneer women to cut down forests, to work beside "their men" that's fine. But on the other hand, when that need passes, we tie them into girdles, if they're white. We set them in a drawing room, and we say they have vapors.

MK: The same poem mentions that there has never been a black astronaut. Do you think this is going to change? And, to take it a step further—everyone asks this question—when will there be a black president?

AL: Well, there again those are very seductive questions, Marge, those are very seductive questions. I'm not concerned with having a black astronaut. I recognize, I note that there is not one. I note that there are women in training. Interestingly enough, a black woman—did you know that?—is in training, and was in training at the time when that poem was written, in the space program, right? That kills two birds with one stone, right? She's female and she's black. I'm not really interested in having black astronauts. I recognize that there are none. I'm not even really interested in having a black president. I am interested in having black people and women in positions of power where they can perhaps guide or effect the shapes in which our power travels. The whole concept of presidencies, of spending millions and millions of dollars in getting people to that satellite up there when we can't even move them through Detroit, or through New York without, you know, killing people. Two hundred and fifty people were killed in the New York subways in the last three months, and that is a fact: pushed, fallen, or jumped. Now, that doesn't hit most of the newspapers. I don't know how it is here (in Detroit). I don't know how many people are killed in your back alleys. But when we consider the amount of money we're spending, or that we have spent in the last ten years, in a war that we were not concerned with, or getting people to the moon, it's as if the powers that be in this country have already given up on this country. Well, I'm not willing to do it and it is black input and the input of women that I am interested in developing into that system. So when you say having black astronauts and black presidents, that I have difficulty with.

MK: In the same poem, the same book, rather, in "One Year to Life on the Grand Central Shuttle" you write, "But hope is counter-revolutionary." What do you mean by that?

AL: Well, I think we seduce ourselves with hope, we seduce ourselves with "Tomorrow it will be better, so of course I won't fight today; I'll wait until tomorrow." And when tomorrow comes and it is, of course, worse, I say, "Well maybe next week." Hope in that sense has always been a tool of oppressors. You give people just enough hope. Either you completely dehumanize them, which is what we have done with black people for the last 400 years, or, for middle and lower-middle white America, which is what is happening now, I think very very much on this whole, that silent majority; they're not silent, they're just white with rage. It is my opinion, OK, what you say, "Tomorrow it will be better. Don't revolt; don't recognize where your true interests are. It will get eventually better. We get rid of the blacks, we get rid of the spics, we get rid of all of those agitators, then you'll come into your own." So meanwhile, you seduce this fury and redirect it against people who are suffering, too, because they believe that that is their hope. In that sense, I think hope is counter-revolutionary.

Audre Lorde

Nina Winter / 1976

From Nina Winter, *Interview with the Muse: Remarkable Women Speak on Creativity and Power* (Berkeley, California: Moon Books, 1978), 72–81. The interview was conducted in November 1976. Reprinted by permission.

I think we are all very much alone and very unlike anyone else. Of course I think this and if I didn't I probably wouldn't be writing poetry. There is a mistake that a lot of us make: the belief that we can all merge into one gigantic unit. It just doesn't happen that way. There is a difference between unity and amalgamation, and that difference is enormous.

I was a very difficult child. I was a rebel from the time I can remember and I can remember fairly far back. My earliest memories are of war between Me and Them. "Them" were my two sisters and my parents. It was their camp against mine, and since there were always more of them, I knew very early that I would have to be smarter than all of them put together. I don't know exactly *how* I knew this but I did. This was in New York, in Manhattan, in the middle of Harlem on 142nd Street and Lennox Avenue.

My parents were West Indian and very, very strict. We never went out to play; we never went anywhere down the street by ourselves. We were over-protected. But raising Black children in New York City in the 1930s was just as hard or harder than it is today. I didn't talk until I was five. My mother took me to doctors for checkups and they thought maybe I was mute, but actually I was just sensible, because who could ever get a word in edgewise between my mother, my father and my two sisters? There was a rigid familial structure in that house, arranged by my mother, and I was low woman on the totem pole, at least until I learned to read. Then I became absolutely insufferable because all I ever said was, "Why, why, why?" In addition to that it had been established that I was legally blind, though actually that meant I was extremely nearsighted. My mother made arrangements for me to start kindergarten early in a special sight conservation class in a public school. It was very exciting to be starting school. When I came to class I already knew how to read and write because I had learned about all that from a librarian at the Countee Cullen Library.

I was reading fairly early and how it started was this: My mother used to take my two older sisters and me to a library club at what is now the Schomburg Collection, but at that time it was the old 135th St. Library. Here, I was the enfant terrible again, lying on the floor screaming, having tantrums and so on. But then a woman, a huge woman with strange hooded eyes like a hawk's, I thought, came over to me and said, "What's wrong, little girl?" This was Augusta Baker. She was the children's librarian and everyone else knew who she was, but I didn't. She impressed me with her manner, which was very stern, and with her eyes and her hugeness and her presence. I remember my mother picking me up by the ears (I was a chunky little kid) and Augusta Baker saying, "Well, would you like me to read you a story?" Now my household was such that my mother never read to us. Reading and books were something my parents valued, but it was just not a part of our family culture for the children to be read to. So Augusta Baker sat me down at a table and she read *Horton Hatches the Egg* and *Madeline*, and *Hubert* which has gone out of print. But these three classics had me hooked. I remember thinking that reading was something I was going to do. What she did, I was going to do too and was going to have it for my own.

I was four and I didn't know at the time whether *that* meant reading it, writing it or telling it. I knew that was something I was going to do. And it went from there. I learned how to read, I learned how to talk, I learned how to write. Later I became a librarian.

In school they gave us something that looked like music books to write in, with big yellow paths and big heavy black crayons because this was supposed to be a sight conservation class. It wasn't right. I knew it, and I said, "You can't write with these crayons." I was distraught and crying all morning long. I knew it was all wrong to write with crayons. With crayons you color, you don't write. It was very unusual for me to cry. My mother had raised us not to. It was, we thought, a sign of weakness. But I couldn't stop and wouldn't stop. Finally they sent for my mother and I was taken out of there and put into the first grade in Catholic School.

I was a trouble-maker from the start. First, because I was a rebel by nature, and then because I didn't recognize my numbers. I could read and write, but I didn't know page nineteen when the teacher said "Turn to page nineteen." So I sat next to Alvin; Alvin was in the Brownies and did know numbers but he didn't know how to read. When Alvin turned to the right pages, I read, and when it was his turn to read I would cue him, and together we got out of the

Brownies and into the Angels. But it didn't last very long because he got sick and died of tuberculosis. I wrote a poem about Alvin. I didn't know that he was sick and then he didn't come back after Thanksgiving. There was a memorial mass for him, and by the end of January I was back in the Brownies again. But I remember Alvin because he was my first ally.

Augusta Baker left that branch after a couple of years. Still, libraries from that time on were where I went. Books were where I found sustenance, and from telling myself stories at night to writing them down was a very short space. They all went together. When I thought about dealing with young people, dealing with any people, and the ways that I wanted to do it, I knew that it was with writing.

I was writing seriously by the time I was in high school, and I knew it was something I would always want to do. But how was I to earn a living? I didn't especially want to teach. I did want to give other people that kind of joy that I found from books, and libraries were the places I knew and felt good in, so it was natural enough that I should become a librarian. For about two years, in Mt. Vernon and Manhattan, I set up libraries and worked with young people. It was innovative and stimulating at first, but once I had done it, it wasn't creative any more and I had to find something else. All the time of course I was writing.

That spring I decided I really had to find something else to do. My friend Diane Di Prima said, "Now, we really have to do this book of yours, so get your things together and we'll get them out." So I did. That was my first book of poems, called *First Cities*. At the time it felt very daring and brave to throw them out into the world because they were all I had and once they were out, I felt like I had nothing.

Diane was the head of the Poet's Press. She and Alan Marlow were running the American Theatre and the Poet's Press. She and Alan were both writing and printing a lot of the literary understuff that went on in the Village and getting a number of the National Endowment grants. Diane and Alan were living in the Hotel Albert on 12th Street with their press and their four kids and the dogs and cats. One night just before Christmas, Alan called me up and said, "For God's sake Diane has gone into labor." My friend, Yolanda, and I went down to deliver the baby. My husband, Ed, said, "Don't you think you ought to read up about it?" I have always collected medical books because I believe in being self-sufficient. So I looked in one, and under "Home Delivery" it said, "Not advised." I thought, "All right, I've read enough medical books, and what about all those novels I've been reading about delivering children in the Ozarks and Africa? I know you don't really need boiled water and I know you really need sterile scissors, and I will play it by ear." Diane had had four children and I'd had two. I figured between the two of us we should be able to deliver this child. So I put on my silver amulet, met Yolanda in the parking lot, and we went down there a little after midnight.

There was very little to do. Child-birth does itself. Especially with a woman who has had children. Tara came out with lots of dark hair. It was very beautiful. When she came around I remember bending over her. The amulet touched her head and the skin is so incredibly tender there that there is still the faintest little mark right on the top of her forehead, yes. And then we cut the cord and tied it with the scissors I had brought.

When you see a baby being born you can understand what many people believe, which is that we are a process. We are only a stage. Because babies, when they are born, are as if they are from another world. Just another complete world, aligned to human beings but not quite human. They are so beautiful and so completely themselves. It is a very wonderful thing to see and to be a part of, and it makes me think sometimes I would like to be a mid-wife because it is mystic and spiritual and erotic and empowering. There is a special connection with a baby you helped to be born and with the mother.

There are a few of us—not many—who are still connected from the time we were girls. What we believe now we believed, more or less, when we were twelve, thirteen, fourteen. We used to communicate with Keats. We called him up. And Shelley too. We had our wars, and some of us died. But we never lost. We never lost the sense of what it was to be connected. There was a period of war in the late 40s' and early 50s' when things were bleak, and there was very little trust around and there were so few of us. We were women-identified women, and it was us against the world. Again there were people—women— we couldn't talk to. We left home. Some girls went away to school and some of us ran away from school. We clashed in various ways and went apart. We married and had children and came together again, and always there has been a lot of connection and contact—touching in all ways. We were the only black and white women really talking to each other in New York City in those days: Joan, Diane, Maryon, Lori, Felicia, Mephi and I. We shared a vision and I have since found other people who share it. It is a vision that we are complete.

By "we" I mean not just the chosen few but all of us who are human. We share the vision that we are complete in ourselves and that as we move into a knowledge of that completeness, we will be able to deal with the worlds in which we live. What we call "evil" is motivated by those things that are *not human*. And there are people who are not human, I do believe, I do believe. Check out the Leakey discoveries in Ethiopia about parallel development. What we call humanness is a stage in the life process. What was before or who was before we do not know completely, but it is less important to find that out than it is to unravel our piece—elegantly, and see how it fits into the whole and be about our business, which is basically to survive and teach. I wrote a poem about my friends which was published by Broadside Press in 1973 in my book, *From a Land Where Other People Live*:

[quotes "Neighbors"].

A lot of those women didn't make it. A lot. I count myself as lucky. Every one of us who survived that period did it through luck and love, and there were a lot of people who didn't get enough of either. This feels like a part of *me* not making it because all of our destinies are entwined. We are connected to each other to the extent that we are aware of who we are and what we can do.

Sometimes I resent what I see as a push these days for the trappings of "sisterhood," because it is a sisterhood which has no real meaning in the terms that I see it being pushed. I think that some of the people who shout sisterhood most strongly have no concept of what real connectedness between women is all about. I have a debt which is first of all to myself and to the earth of which I am a part for this time. And that is a debt which all women must come to feel deeply. That is a debt I think we are all paying, in one way or another. It is one we pay consciously or unconsciously, but I would choose consciously. Because it is more interesting that way. Of course, having children, you are confronted constantly with unanswerable questions. My son once picked up a chicken heart at dinner and said, "Does this thing love?"

I have many poems to people I have loved and to people who have died. When I was in high school, a friend of mine killed herself. I never really came to terms with death until I had Beth, my oldest child. Beth was about ten when she started dealing with her death fears the way children do. She wept a lot and said, "I don't ever want to die," and I had to deal with it, and not on a false level. I had to get all the way down deep and roll around in it with her and and come up with something that could work for me and work for her too. I found out a lot of things for myself that helped and fit into place with the over-all vision, things that had until then been left out or not integrated. Words that I had thrown away cropped up and took on a new meaning.

"Grant me the grace of a happy death." This was part of a prayer which
I had to say as a kid. These are Catholic words and I have no patience with
Catholicism, except those pieces which are real and not Catholic pieces but
human pieces. "A happy death," it occurred to me, is a real thing. This prayer
says, 'When I come to die, may I be ready; May I be happy to die, because
I am at a time when I can.'

Looking closely at other people who are dying and thinking about it, and
talking to Beth about it, I realize that the fear of death is that you are dying
too *soon*. Nobody wants to, but at the point that you die you can pray that you
are no longer the same person. I pray that when I am about to die I will not
be the same person that I am now. What this does is place another kind of responsibility upon us to enjoy. Not just to live, but to *savor* our living, for Beth to
savor being ten, and for me to savor the things I must do for her and myself.
It would not have been so clear if I hadn't had to say it to her in a language she could understand. Which is the very same process as making a
poem.

When you reach out and touch other human beings, it doesn't matter
whether you call it therapy or teaching or poetry. Sometimes it is not touch but
a mass assault. The ads on color television are brilliant. A spectacular image
flashes on the screen: the word "L'Eggs. . . ." Legs. The French "Le Eggs." And
there you have it. The legs. The egg. Woman. The display in the supermarket
creates the same *process* as poetry. The words enter you and resound in your
head consciously and unconsciously. In response to ads you think, "Goddamn
we are condemned." The impetus for this Madison Avenue creation is similar
to the impetus for creating poetry. It creates connections, but they are what I
call destructive creation—creation that prostitutes our very substance. We have
to live with it; we have to deal with it. We must. We can deal with it by turning
it into a concept of connectedness. This is hard to accept, but I think we have to
or die early.

I do not mean to suggest an idealistic, all-encompassing love because we
are not always *given* to love. Love is a part of something *else*: relatedness, and
this is what I am talking about. Of course I want to be connected with people
I like, with people who satisfy me, who may share even a little piece of my vision.
But what about being connected to the people who may not even be aware
of humanness? Who have no connection with their own humanity? This is
much harder. When I become more aware of myself as thinking and feeling
and acting all the time, then all the time it is painful.

One pays a lot, we all pay a lot, for awareness. When I develop that sense of awareness, I develop, by extension, a sense concerning *you*. That does not dictate why my relationship *is* with you. I may have to fight you, but as soon as I am aware of you, I must relate to you. I must take you in. This is engagement. It is a prerequisite to any kind of love, and it is difficult and necessary.

We are talking about survival, which is half of our work. One chooses the conscious route not only because it is more interesting, but because it is the only way to be in control of events. When I was little, for example, I believed that my parents controlled the universe, because I was little and I was a daughter. But later I learned that it was not true because I discovered that I could get around them. I had to find out for myself that they were fallible. The moment I realized this, their power was broken.

My parents never discussed color, really, in our house—or, to be exact, they never discussed *race*. But we knew it was important. My mother would tell us that we must never trust white people, but not *why*. While we were growing up in Harlem, our contacts were with other black people. White was that thing out there that you never trusted, though of course white nuns and the priests, again, were supposed to be special. They were supposed to believe in God. I knew they weren't special but my mother warned me that Sister So-and-So and Father So-and-So were different from other white people—somehow immune from the racist disease. So there were all these double messages, and what was clear was that everybody lies and nobody will tell you the truth. You have to listen and you have to look because no one is going to tell you.

In 1947 or so when I was thirteen, I went to Washington with my family as a graduation present. There were my father and my mother and the three of us. Washington was still segregated. My father had a huge sense of history. He would bring us American Heritage books and talk to us all the time about our history, our country, Washington, the Capitol and the Supreme Court. The Sunday we arrived we went to look at the Federal buildings, and afterward, as a special treat my father took us to an ice cream parlor across the street from the Supreme Court. We walked in and sat down at the counter (because it wouldn't cost as much as if you sat in a booth), and the waiter came over and said in a whisper, "I can't serve you here but I can give it to you to take out." *Right?* And there we sat as if we had never been black before. That is something I will never forget. Never. I was outraged. Because nobody had *told* me.

I went home and on my father's typewriter I typed an impassioned plea for justice filled with every cliché you can imagine. But this terrible thing had happened, and I wondered why no one got upset about it. My father had never gotten upset, never gotten embarrassed. This is what I thought: "You've been telling me all these wonderful things about American history, and we can't be served in that store." It made a profound impression. It was my first great betrayal. And the sense of outrage never leaves.

Pain is important: how we evade it, how we succumb to it, how we deal with it, how we transcend it. I always thought I had a very low threshhold for physical pain, that I could not take it and that was that. I did not know how to stand still gracefully when I got beaten, which was every day. I passed out in dentists' offices. And there was always the secret fear of it. Recently, I had a physical experience that was ghastly and terrible—and wonderful, because it taught me about pain.

Not too long ago I unlocked the old window of my very old Victorian house on Staten Island. Somehow the chain broke and the window fell down immediately and caught my hand. There was no way to pull it out and everyone was gone for the weekend. I broke the window and called for help, and it was seven minutes before someone came. I have the scars to remind me. It was crucial, that seven minutes. In it I lived the whole history of pain from start to finish. The genesis of pain, where you put it, how you channel it and how you end it. The choice was immediate: to die, or to bear the pain. And what does bearing mean? It means changing or going through. It is not death. It is an experience encapsulated. It could stop. It could be ended. By chewing off my arm, for example. But this was not possible for me. So the pain is transformed. The intensity changes. It has to stop or it has to change. This was a physical knowledge that I had not had before, that pain has a mutability. That is very, very important, and that is just as true about emotional pain: it will change or stop. And the worst thing that can happen is death, but that is a whole different thing to involve yourself in. I felt at that point that there was nothing I could not do, nothing that I could not deal with, because pain will always either change or stop. Always. I have tested this since then, and it is always clear and workable.

With writing, for example. All writers have periods when they stop writing, when they cannot write, and this is always painful and terrible because writing is like breathing: when you can't, something goes dead, something stops moving inside you. But you know that it will change. The confidence that it will change is what makes *bearing* possible. So pain is fluid. It is only when you conceive of it as something static that it is unbearable.

In the old days, when we were children, our hero used to be Simon Templar, "The Saint." "The Saint" books were marvelous swashbuckling stories. There was Leslie Charteris, the Asian doctor, and one of his favorite drugs was Scopolamine—which was also called "twilight sleep" because it doesn't put you totally out. What it does—I have found out since—is block. It does not stop the experience of pain, but it blocks your memory. It can be used only for certain kinds of recurrent pain, like childbirth or dentistry. This is a very fascinating concept for me: you can experience pain without remembering it. It means that pain is only in your memory of it or your anticipation. The same as pleasure.

There are two sides to this drug, Scopolamine. It relieves pain because you can neither anticipate nor remember, but by the same token you cannot *learn* from it. It does not inform the mind. Sometimes I look at groups of people, and this phrase "Twilight Sleep" comes to mind. It is what happens to a system, to a movement, as soon as the people in it begin to believe in the movement more than in the individual. When you have individuals believing that you can start with the movement first and *then* the people, or that liberation belongs to one private group, then you have people moving en masse through their pain in a twilight sleep, and this is always harmful and destructive because it is emotional blindness. Nothing is learned. We can help each other to move, to grow, to become more human, but finally one does whatever one does alone. To do it with the mind and the heart and the eyes open is to feel . . . *more*. Sometimes this means to feel more pain, but this way is never dull. It is never a Twilight Sleep. *I choose to be awake.*

Audre Lorde

Ellen Shapiro / 1977

From Ellen Shapiro, "Interviews: Three Women on Lesbians and Fathers" [Joan Larkin, Audre Lorde, and Kate Millet], *Christopher Street*, 1.10 April 1977, 24–40 [28–33 on Lorde]. Reprinted by permission.

Ellen Shapiro: What were some of the positive aspects of being your father's daughter?

Audre Lorde: My father was a good, strong, West Indian man; 6′4″ and very powerful. He had once been a constable in Grenada. And he dreamed of a dynasty, really; he thought of himself as a start of a line. So he had three daughters—it didn't matter if we were girls or boys—we were going to follow in his footsteps. He used to talk about having a doctor, a lawyer, and a teacher.

My mother's household was characterized by an incredible amount of emotional interaction. My mother was an angelic and maniacal hysteric, fed by endless furies. And so am I. My father lived in the center of it, but didn't participate very much. First of all, one word out of his mouth and that was it, but he also worked twenty hours a day, so he was never around a lot. He'd come in around 9 o'clock and the food would be kept warm on the stove. And I guess if I had to think of the nicest times, the closest times with my father, I'd think of getting a bite off his plate at dinner when he came home late. And pulling his white hairs out when he was balding. That's about the closest positive contact I ever had with him.

Except, I remember that when we moved uptown, I was enrolled in a predominantly white school; my teachers were terribly bigoted, and I wanted to take a test for a specialized high school. Or, to be more exact, my father wanted his children to take the test. Well, for all the usual reasons, my teachers avoided telling me about the examination date. Now my father, because of his work, didn't really get involved with school affairs. But Monday morning, he did not go to the office, but went to school with me. And he laid down the line: "When was the test? My daughter was going to take it." And I felt, "Well, that's it." And I took the test and I passed. That's one of the few times I remember my father moving in concert with me.

18

ES: What did he want for his daughters?

AL: I think he wanted his children to excel. And he had those visions regardless of our sex. Now I may be missing something, because I heard from my aunts that they both had once wanted boys very much. But my experience, in terms of growing up, was that there wasn't anything I couldn't do with my life, if I set my mind to it.

He was the only person who responded to my poetry. I don't think he understood it any more than my mother did, but it had a value to him. And books had a value; reading. I remember once I had joined a book club and I sent for *Forever Amber* by Catherine Windsor. And my mother, of course, opened all my mail and was horrified; she wanted to prohibit me from reading it. But my father took a very interesting position. He said that if it was written, I could handle it. That you must not stop someone from reading any book. You see, he would buy books in lots, at auctions. And they were half-garbage and half-classics, but they were there.

There were a lot of ideals in my house, and I always felt they came most strongly from him. If I knew that no matter how far I transgressed, if I really wrote, if I really distinguished myself—he might not like it, but he'd respect it. And that's very different from my mother. I could have gotten the Pulitzer Prize at age thirteen and it wouldn't have meant much to her if I came home late. But it would have to him.

ES: How did he and your mother interact?

AL: My parents had an interesting relationship. They moved in concert, and it was a concert that really shut us out. It was very painful. Everything they did was supposedly for the children, but they met, they decided things, and they spoke to us and the world with one voice. There was never such a thing as asking my mother or father to do something without also knowing it would be shared with the other. We couldn't split them, they were the united front.

He concentrated his power on the rational, determination business, the logical approaches. And here's my mother—who's all over the wall, who brought all these twenty-one emotional guns to bear—whatever she felt, that was it. Mow them down! And the two of them together seemed to cover the whole territory; analyze and attack. And that's one of the losses: I was never able to deal individually with one of my parents or the other directly, and I always felt I had to out-think and out-run this huge, all-powerful parent machine.

ES: The sense I got from your poetry is that, while you viewed your mother with intense emotion, your father is often described as if he were in a picture frame.

AL: I was very emotionally involved with my mother, but the one emotion I can speak of concerning my dad was terror. Absolute terror. There was a legend that if my father ever hit you, you'd be killed. So of course he didn't do the disciplining—it was always my mother. My cousins called my other uncles "Uncle Dave" or "Uncle Ned." But my father was "Uncle Lorde." That'll tell you more about him than anything else.

I used to steal money from him when I was eleven or twelve. I would arrange the most elaborate schemes, the least of which was boring holes through doors. My father had a license to carry a gun because he carried the money home from his office. And when he would miss money, he'd line the three of us up, take out his gun and start cleaning it. I would be terrified. I mean, I knew my father wasn't going to shoot me, but he was a great dramatist. His voice would get lower and lower the angrier he got. He never shouted, but his voice became incredibly intense. And it would be an absolute nightmare.

And of course they would know that *I* had done it; my two sweetheart sisters would never think of such a thing. But fairness would require that I would have to admit it. And I knew it, so I would *never* say anything. I would just hang on; I kept saying no. And he would take me into a dark room, turn out all the lights and talk about sending me to reform school. When I talk about it now, it's still so frightening to me. I used to think, "He's really going to torture me, he's really going to send me to reform school." But I absolutely refused to admit anything. The idea of having a daughter who was a thief and a liar was more intolerable to him than the money loss, and that was one of my endless ways of rebellion.

It was my life at stake. Somehow I was stealing from him all the things I never had, you know, emotion, demonstrative love, whatever. This had escalated past my mother. She could beat me if she found the money, with no need for the niceties of an admission of guilt, but getting the admittances somehow moved into his territory. I know my mother wouldn't get involved in "Did you do it?": she would *decide* that I did it, and beat the shit out of me. But with my father, it became a whole trial and test of wills and admitting and the dark lights and the gun and voice and I was determined to win or die.

I believe my father felt many emotions deeply, for which he had no name, and to which he gave no expression. But I had no knowledge of this as a child. I only thought he was aloof, all-powerful, and unfeeling. My mother seemed pretty all-powerful also, but at least I had once seen her cry, in a dentist's office, and at least she got angry and yelled. I have no real proofs of my father's depth of unexpressed emotion. I have only the fact that he came from a West Indian culture that allowed him a certain amount of self-definition, to live thirty years as a black man in a white man's world. I have only his silence, awesome intensity, the headlong life which he lived, and the fact that he was a burned out husk of a man at fifty-five.

He came to this country a poor man and died thirty years later only slightly less so, leaving behind three daughters who never knew him (and so had come to hate him), a wife who loved him desperately, and a business that supported that wife for another twenty-five years. She would much rather have had him. He bought the American dream and it killed him.

Together with my mother, my father managed to convince us as children that they were in total charge of our universe. That was a tragic deception. When we three girls went to bed without supper, I did not know it was because there was no money for food that day. I thought it was because we had been disobedient, or late, or too noisy, or whatever my mother chose to accuse us of. And my father was silent, or not there. He had managed to project the image of a powerful black man in charge of his half of the sky at a time when white America's response to that image was total destruction, whether or not the image was true. And he was totally destroyed. Not only by the overt oppression of a system he was too proud to question—and so could only fight within—he was also destroyed by his programmed inability to give voice to his own powerlessness, his own fury, his own grief, and fear, and his love.

ES: How old were you when he died?
AL: My father died when I was nineteen. I had left home after high school and didn't see my parents for a year, until he was ill. He had a series of strokes and my mother had assumed the business. I went to the hospital, and as I was getting off the elevator, I could hear his voice. He was delirious, and with his deep voice was reciting the 23rd Psalm, which he used for his real estate business: "I will dwell in the house of the Lord . . ." And he was saying this over and over.

I remember being enveloped in a deep sense of sadness. Not grief, just an overwhelming sense of sadness that this man should come to this end, that he was not old, yet he was dying an old man's death. There was also rage and fury, but not as if it was someone I loved, but a symbolic man that I had been close to. And I've often thought about that. I used to stand in his hospital room, when he was in the oxygen tent and I could see him dwindling day by day. And I had a feeling of a cosmic mistake happening, but very little emotional involvement. It was years before I could feel an emotional loss, because I couldn't mourn something I never had. I could only feel a once-removed grief for who he was, for what I couldn't ever have again: a father. I felt that I was being robbed directly of a father; a parent—no, because we never had *that* relationship.

ES: Thinking back to your childhood, can you remember instances of sexual tension between you and your father?
AL: I discovered I had a body, which was pretty hard in my household, because we were supposed to be disembodied spirits. When I was thirteen, I was full of sexuality. That's part of what used to come out in the juicy, gorgeous poems I wrote then. And of course, I was conscious of the little things. My father was always clothed around us. And I thought that was strange because other men walked around without their shirts on. But there was always something secret and special about his body. And I always wondered, "what does he look like?"

I had my own room. My two sisters didn't, but I was so crazy that I couldn't live with anybody. But my father had his wardrobe in there because there wasn't enough space. I used to take off my pajamas, because it was so hot, and I would sleep in the nude. Well, my father had to come in early in the morning to get his clothes for the office. And evidently he said something to my mother about my sleeping habits. So my mother took me aside and said that it really was not nice of me to expose myself in front of my father. He had to go in there every morning and he had no idea if I was sleeping in my pajamas or not. So when I slept without my pajamas, I'd pin them up on the outside of the door to announce to him that I had no clothes on. He was infuriated by it. When he told my mother, the first thing I knew, I was awakened early one morning with a beating, by mother, for my impertinence. But I really felt that if he was bothered by my body, he should not come in, because it was *my* room.

I always felt my mother was the guardian of my father's sexuality. She was the one who always went around saying, "Don't leave your sanitary napkins wrapped in paper, because your father will see it." I knew there was something wrong with that, because, first of all, it was wrapped up, and besides, she had said there was nothing dirty about menstruating. So there were a lot of prohibitions. He never dealt with a lot of parts of himself—that's what he kept mother around for. And I can only say that I picked up sexual feelings from him on a level that was never expressed.

ES: How did he contribute to your lesbian identity?

AL: Well, we were brought up largely outside this whole feminine stereotype. It was black-white, rather than girl-boy. Not that my parents thought of our upbringing in feminist terms, but rather that their children, male or female, were going to be "X." And I was able to feel my power at any given moment, limited as it was, but in relation to them, not to being a girl. And since I define lesbianism, not merely by the fact that I sleep with women, but as a sense of a really deeply ingrained self; that I have a right to deal my power, whatever it is, however I can manage to do it. The word lesbian for me has a connotation that's far beyond sexual. And in that sense, my father had something to do with it. I learned a lot from both my parents, not the least of which was how to survive them both.

Many of the emotional aspects of lesbianism have to do with my mother, although the life-death struggle I felt for my father was also a factor. That was translated to other male relationships. When men threatened me, I'd really want to kill them. And more importantly, I felt able to. But it was a part of myself that I didn't want to deal with for a long time.

ES: How did he react to your writing?

AL: Well, first of all, let me say that I started writing as a child because it was the only outlet I had for the emotions I felt. My poetry was a lifeline; I think I'd be insane if I hadn't fallen upon it. It was, in the truest sense, a totally subversive activity. I think I became so good so quickly because whatever I had to get off, it could not be very obvious.

My mother, however, had an unconscious that was like a velvet/steel trap. She knew instantaneously what it was all about without having to understand. She could smell rebellion a mile away. That was the level on which we fought. My father, on the other hand, didn't key into it on that level, but said, "Oh, this is something educational and different and interesting. Very good, you're excelling and doing something." He didn't understand it; he didn't become involved with it. My mother recognized it as a threat to her authority, even though she didn't understand it. My father underlined it as an achievement, but he didn't key into it.

ES: What were your earliest poems about him like?
AL: I didn't write about my father when I was very young. The first poem I wrote was shortly after he died. I guess I was too afraid to deal with the problems involved. Somehow I thought, if he really recognized me, he might gain the power to destroy me. Even though he was the one who supported so much of what I did, I felt he did it without dealing with what I was saying. The terror was so deep, and I was locked into battle for my life, with people who were supposedly my only protectors in an even more hostile world.

I was the enemy in some way. In a very real sense, even though he had a part in creating me, I felt that if he really saw me, he might recognize me as the enemy, and we still had that world outside to survive in.

ES: How are you trying to prevent your son from becoming like his father?
AL: I must allow him enough space so he can deal with his emotions and I have to create it artificially because the society certainly doesn't want him to have it. But if he knows he has a right to that space, and if he can become comfortable enough in using it emotionally, I know that once it gets good to him, he'll never let it go. Once he has that consciousness of self, neither the world nor I, in my lesser moments, can take it away from him. He may have to pay for it (nobody likes being crossed), but he will have it. I guess I want Jonathan to know that when he bleeds, it hurts. Do whatever you need to do to make that hurt better, but at least recognize you're hurting.

I try to teach my son that I do not exist to feel for him, that he must do that for himself in order to survive as a human being. And that is not always easy, for him nor for me. Because it's hard to see someone you love feel hurt, and to know that there are some pains you cannot, must not, protect your children from, if they are to grow up tough and whole. It's so much easier to teach them by order or example not to feel at all. ("Don't feel that way! It makes me feel uncomfortable . . . or, if it hurts you too much . . .") But in that direction lies the premature ghost of my father.

I really thank God that one of my children is a boy. Not for all the old reasons, but because it's so easy to forget; to take the easier path. And I always say that Jonathan helps to keep me honest; to deal with those really knotty problems. And he's there, and I love him. And I'd rather kill him than have him grow up to be some of the men I know.

ES: If your father were sitting beside you now, what would you say to him?
AL: I would say, "Hey look. You really ought to be proud of me, "cause I'm doing it. I really *am*." That's hard to say, but it's honest. I would also say, "Why didn't you do this, you bastard, and why didn't you make it easier for me? Why couldn't you love who I was?" I'd say, "Hey, look. You see what I've done? You helped me to be able to learn how, so why the hell didn't you learn, too?" But that's pointless. I think everyone says the same things to their parents once they've gone, no matter what the words are. When we become parents ourselves, symbolically or otherwise, I think we say "Hey, look. You see what *I've* done."

ES: And what would he think of you?
AL: I don't think my father could deal with my lesbianism, so he'd probably do the same thing my mother does: ignore it. In one way, I'm glad he's dead. I think we would probably have the kind of pain that occurred in the last lucid moment I had with him before he died. I had left home; he would rather die than ask me back. On the other hand, he was very disapproving. He was interested in what I was doing, but he wouldn't let me see that. It would probably be very much like that.

I've cried about him since, and for the ways in which he hurt me. I feel free of him in a way. I cannot thank him for what he has given me, and put to rest what he hadn't given me because I've found out how to give it to myself. And I'm just glad that I wasn't destroyed.

Audre Lorde: Interview

Karla M. Hammond / 1978

From *Denver Quarterly* 16.1 (1981), 10–27. The interview was conducted in
October 1978. Reprinted by permission.

Karla Hammond: "It's going to take a new generation of young Black and
White critics to assess the thrust of American writing of the last twenty years"
(Ishmael Reed, *Interviews With Black Writers*). Who are some of these
younger critics?
Audre Lorde: God, I'm sorry that he was the one who said it [laughs]. Yes,
that's probably true. I'd say . . . Lorraine Bethel, Barbara Smith, Susan Cavin,
Gloria Hull. The work these women are doing is exciting and excellent.

KH: How do you respond to the belief (on the part of some critics) that the
Black poet has not so much created new themes as retold older ones, giving a
new view and dimension to the human situation where identity was the central issue?
AL: It's been my experience that white critics are so busy trying to disprove
the reality of the Black experience that they get *totally* outside of themselves.
As soon as most white critics start talking about Black poetry, they become
bizarre. I can't get anything from them. I feel they believe they need to
disprove or somehow level something of which they're not a part. That's so
wasteful. All poets are human, and we come out of certain human feelings
particularized by our experience. The Black experience in this country is something that's duplicated nowhere else. But then my experience is not duplicated
completely anywhere else either. So this can be said about all poets. We try
to focus on those things out of our experience that tell somewhere a deeper
truth—that speak to many people with different experiences. With any
oppressed people—and this is true of women, although it started with the
Black poets—the ability to speak out of your experience and see it as valid, to
deal with your definition of self and recognize that we must identify ourselves
(because if we don't, someone else will to our detriment) is a human problem. But when you're a member of an oppressed group you'd better learn it
early or you're not going to learn anything because you won't survive, except

as a cipher. When I was at the Women's Meeting at MLA [in 1977] I spoke of women teaching women's literature courses who said that they could not teach Black women's poetry because it was so totally outside of their experience. That's bullshit because you teach Shakespeare and, God knows, that's outside of your experience. But you have to have learned to enter the work. You must delve into it and see what it tells you about yourself.

KH: It's an evasion that culture and educational systems foster.
AL: I had to learn your language, and it was difficult. That's part of what I was saying. Most poetry didn't have any meaning to me.

KH: Have you ever used African languages as an integral part of a poem?
AL: No, I've used some of the rhythms, but I don't know any African languages except for some certain words and names like Ocucudwiadwia. My knowledge of African languages is slight. They're highly complex languages. Judith Gleason has worked with the Yoruba language, and she has some interesting material on Yoruba divination and some of the gods.

KH: I would think that this would make for choral poems: expression in several dimensions.
AL: Kofi Awoonor, a Ghanian poet, has done a lot of work with that. There's an interesting book that I picked up dealing with Yoruba poetry. There are basically three kinds of poetry: first, poetry which is divine (inspired); secondly, poetry which is crafted; and thirdly, poetry which is inherited. It reminds me of Gerard Manley Hopkins. He has a letter to a friend of his in which he speaks of writing and how there are three voices of the poet: the Olympian (inspired); the Parnassian (when you're really a good poet, you don't write bad poetry but sometimes you write so-so poetry), and finally, there's jargon. In Yoruba and Dahomean poetry, the poet, the linguist, is the speaker of tradition's deepest truths. Poetry is an art, like any other art, and has a function. The function is to make each one of us more who we are—to empower us. So when Kofi Awoonor talks about the three different kinds of poets, he's speaking of something akin to the druidic sense of the teacher, the poet, the artist. There is the poet who speaks a poetry divine—who has the connection with gods and goddesses. This poet is possessed, in a sense. Next there is the poet who has studied and learned. Then there is the secret of the poet for whom there is no explanation. There are words for these three different kinds of poets and he gives some

examples in his text. It's a fascinating book. It makes me feel not so crazy. The function of much of what I read about Africa and about Black women, that is meaningful to me, is frequently to keep me from feeling crazy. That's one of the horrors of being locked into the mouth of the dragon: not only do you not have any role models, but there's no resonance for your experience. That's what made me begin to think about writing what I've been writing. We (Black lesbian feminists) have been around a long time. There haven't been many of us but we've been there and for every one of us that speaks there are a number more down your street, who survive through silence. Yes, we do need role models. I wish I'd had some. It would have saved a lot of time.

KH: That's the benefit of women's magazines, especially a magazine such as *Conditions.*
AL: Yes. We need the archives. We need to have access to Alicia Johnson . . . to these Black women who wrote forty, fifty years ago. That's not a lifetime. I never knew Anne Spencer. I never knew these women's writings even when I read about the Harlem Renaissance because their experience wasn't underlined, as Barbara Smith so aptly says in her marvelous bibliography, *"All the Blacks were men and all the women were white, but some of us were brave?"* [laughs].

KH: "It is possible that white writers are more conscious of their own evil (which, after all, has been documented for several centuries—in words and in the ruin of the land, the earth) than black male writers, who, along with black and white women, have seen themselves as the recipients of that evil, and therefore on the side of Christ, of the oppressed, of the innocent" (Alice Walker, *Interviews with Black Writers*). Would you add anything to her statement?
AL: Alice's statement is true; however, we must remember that Black males have been the recipient of that evil to the extent that they have internalized it. What is terrible about oppression is that it becomes a part of your consciousness, and you become not only your own oppressor but the oppressor of the people with whom you once shared a common goal. Of course, this divide and conquer situation, very prevalent in the Black community, is very evident. As Black people—male and female—we have to realize that it is not our destiny to repeat white America's mistakes. To the extent that Black men realize that, then they move out of the danger of that seductive trap. To the extent that they don't, they begin to ape the oppressiveness of the white American male.

KH: I've encountered a great deal of hostility toward Ishmael Reed.

AL: Ishmael is violently sexist. He's extremely homophobic and sexist because he has found that he receives goodies (rewards) for assuming these positions in the white male media. It's been his stick. It's unfortunate because the man is rather talented, but he's lowered himself to a level of viciousness which really makes me question where his real art lies.

KH: His statements seem very glib.

AL: Much too glib. They feel bought. Ishmael isn't my real enemy, but if he chooses to ape the positions and words of those who are, he becomes indistinguishable from those enemies, and must be dealt with as such. It's another case of a Black man allowing himself to be used by . . .

KH: A white culture?

AL: Yes.

KH: Can you think of any male poets whose work and life are integrated to the point at which they are not using or abusing women in their poetry?

AL: I can't think of any offhand. I can think of poems by white men that have been very meaningful to me.

KH: I was thinking of an article Kenneth Pitchford had written in *Ms.* several months back. He seems to have a genuine understanding or appreciation of what women are trying to do.

AL: Good for him. I don't know how real his understanding is, but I do know that he has been supportive of Robin [Morgan]. For a while he had a magazine called the *Effeminist*. If there are men who have that kind of understanding, I can say to them (what I have said to white people in the sixties) "that's very fine, and you have a lot of work to do in your communities."

KH: "Minority women poets are in some ways a separate strand in the tradition's development, because theirs is a triple bind involving race *and* sex oppression. From their overwhelming awareness of race oppression comes the model for political poetry, in which the poet is no longer a writer who 'happens' to be Black (or happens to be a woman, to translate into feminist terms), but a Black poet who writes of, to, for, her or his people—in the language of that people" (Suzanne Juhasz, *Naked and Fiery Forms*). Do you agree?

AL: That comes out of a feeling that Black women are freer, and we're not. It's just that we've had to fight harder. It's been a question of survival. To the extent that Black women no longer see it as survival, we buy this line of propaganda.

KH: The term "easy blackness" seems to be a term focal to the meaning of "Between Ourselves." Could you elaborate on this?
AL: Easy anything. I mean those easy identities that we pull over ourselves, like water blankets, that usually wind up smothering us. To be what is fashionable, what is easiest to be, is always dangerous.

KH: [quotes from Lorde] ("Who Said It Was Simple," *From A Land Where Other People Live*). [quotes from Lorde] ("A Litany for Survival," *The Black Unicorn*). In what ways has poetry been a means of survival for you?
AL: It has always been survival for me and continues to be . . . but survival in a different way because survival and teaching are two inseparable works.

KH: What are some of the ways that we, as women, can reclaim language so that it will cease to work against us? Shouldn't it be the responsibility of the poet to "humanize" language?
AL: We can reclaim it by using it, getting into the process I referred to before. Remember I told you [prior to the interview] when I was a kid I'd take words apart and fragment them like colors? I would look at light and it would break down. Lights were surrounded by haloes of color because my eyes were so bad. There's a technical word for it.

KH: Prism.
AL: Yes. Every light was a prism. Words were like that. Every word would pop out and it would have all of this energy and color. It can be a painful process, too, because words hurt when they're used too loosely. In my pre-adolescence and in my adolescence, it was a constant state of hypersensitivity in which I remember existing. The responsibility of the poet is to speak truth as she sees it.

KH: [quotes from Lorde] ("Outside," *The Black Unicorn*). The theme of "multiple selves," implicit in *Between Ourselves*, finds expression in your essays and articles. Could you explain the relevance of this conviction in your own life?

AL: The knowledge of and the constant living with those selves is what keeps us honest, is what holds us to the honesty that taps the power within us. When you go into that chaos (of what you know, what you feel before what you've been trained to understand), you sometimes discover very contradictory situations. It's not easy to come to terms with or integrate those warring pieces; but it's necessary to allow them to live and flourish, to move you where you need to go. This is what teaches us a kind of power or strength, gives us a vision. What makes us most vulnerable, makes us most strong.

KH: The reason I asked was for those who might not be familiar with what you've said on this subject elsewhere.

AL: Karla, one of the problems is that I forget what I've said elsewhere [laughs]. Sometimes I have the feeling that I just keep repeating myself over and over again. Maybe to a certain degree this is true. I might say, by next week, "Who was I then?" "Who was I that year? What did we believe that year, Frances?"

There's always someone asking you to underline one piece of yourself— whether it's *Black, woman, mother, dyke, teacher*, etc.—because that's the piece that they need to key in to. They want you to dismiss everything else. But once you do that, then you've lost because then you become acquired or bought by that particular essence of yourself, and you've denied yourself all of the energy that it takes to keep all those others in jail. Only by learning to live in harmony with your contradictions can you keep it all afloat. You know how fighting fish do it? They blow bubbles and in each one of those bubbles is an egg and they float the egg up to the surface. They keep this whole heavy nest of eggs floating, and they're constantly repairing it. It's as if they live in both elements. That's something that we have to do, too, in our own lives—keep it all afloat. It's possible to take that as a personal metaphor and then multiply it to a people, a race, a sex, a time. If we can keep this thing going long enough, if we can survive and teach what we know, we'll make it. But the question is a matter of the survival and the teaching. That's what our work comes down to. No matter where we key into it, it's the same work, just different pieces of ourselves doing it. Finding those different pieces is like fishing.

Frances and I went fishing two summers ago in Minnesota. It was a totally new experience: cold, cold lakes. It gave me a whole new insight on the Protestant Ethic [laughs] in this country. For me, fishing (even in New York) has always been . . . you go out and there's the hot sun and the sea. In Minnesota, you go out and it's dark and it's cold. It's forty degrees and that's when the fish run. As soon as the sun comes up you don't catch anything. If I had to go through that to catch fresh fish . . . no wonder the people began to believe in an angry God.

KH: In speaking of these "selves" warring (immobilizing you) and harmonizing (enriching you), did you mean that equanimity was necessary in order for you to create or write?
AL: Let me preface my answer with some background . . . one of the people who influenced me—to talk about contradictions [laughs]—was an old white, Anglo-Saxon man, Hoxie Fairchild. Bless his heart, he's dead now. He was a teacher, a British scholar, and he came to Hunter one term where he taught a course in the Romantics. This was in the fifties. Just fascinating! I did a great deal of work on connections between the Beat poets and the Romantics—how they were moving out of essentially the same tradition altered by the size of our world (in particular as we are now in an Atomic Age, an age of Enlightenment). It was really a good piece of work. Hoxie Fairchild really turned me on [laughs] to Byron, Keats, Shelley, Wordsworth. When we were in high school we used to raise the poets. Well, Wordsworth said "the child is father to the man" and that poetry is "emotion recalled in tranquility." I must say that he had something there although I wouldn't exactly put it in those same words. But poetry begins with the ability to recognize that you are feeling and to be able to re-create that feeling, to get in touch with it again. It isn't lost. To emote is not poetry. To emote is absolutely necessary, but that is not poetry. It's vital to recall the emotion that moved you and to see through it to the thrill out of which that emotion grew. Then you begin to make connections. It's the seeing through that enables you to begin making the images that connect with an experience different from yours. The magic that occurs with poetry is the ability to see through emotion.

KH: That's the validity of revision, too, as opposed to simply emoting.
AL: Yes, I revise a great deal. Every once in a while we are fortunate enough to be given a poem. But it's not very often. Revision involves bringing into alignment with the world of that poem what that poem needs to be. Simultaneously, it's necessary to know where revision has to stop. Sometimes I find myself saying, "What I want to do is write another poem." The ability to recognize that this is another poem is absolutely essential; otherwise, you treat a

poem like Play-do, trying to get it to do everything, and one poem will never do that. If it could, we wouldn't have books and books. So I do believe in revision—bringing the poem into alignment with itself. When I can't do that—I have some poems that are years old—it is usually because I have not yet salted down or integrated within myself whatever the truth or complexity of truths are out of which that poem comes. And it's a high sign to me.

KH: What are some of the ways in which we can constructively learn to use "the difference between poetry and rhetoric"? ("Power," *Between Ourselves*). AL: That's something that I can't answer for anyone else except myself because that's part of our work: to scrutinize that question very carefully and to realize what it means for each of us. I think that your work, Karla, is different from mine. It's necessary for us to be able to recognize what that work is and move into it, that none of us has three hundred years. To see that work and move into it, on a real level is what that difference between poetry and rhetoric is about.

KH: Are there any women now whom you show your work to? AL: Yes. Without my support group I would not have the energy and the guts to say much of what I've said and been attacked for.

KH: Are they all poets? Who are some of these women? AL: No. Adrienne Rich and Joan Larkin are. Frances Clayton (my lover), a psychotherapist, without whom I really would be a different person . . . Michelle Cliff (a writer and art historian), Blanche Cook (historian), Claire Cos (playwright, poet), Bernice Goodman (psychotherapist), Deanna Fleisher (craftswoman).

KH: It's marvelous to have integration in the arts and professions. AL: There are many women who have been incredibly meaningful to me. Barbara Smith, a Black feminist. Yvonne Flowers. Yolanda Rias-Butts. These are women without whom I could not survive. Their energy was vital to me after my recent operation. I just would not be who I am right now, sitting here talking to you, if it weren't for an incredible infusion of love and good feeling. I have been so lucky in the people whom I have loved and who have loved me. I've valued the friendship of women since high school and now I wouldn't be alive without it. That's why I said before "woman" and "poet" are synonymous. Once you touch your own feelings, you can recognize other people's feelings and they become real.

KH: And their poetry becomes real for you, even if they're writing out of a different consciousness?
AL: Yes.

KH: Diane di Prima in the introduction to *The First Cities* speaks of your reading poems to each other in homeroom at Hunter High. Was Diane one of the first poets with whom you shared your work?
AL: I went to Hunter College High School when it was an all-girls school and we were all poets. When I say that I grew up in a largely female society, I didn't mean that my father was absent from my house, but that there were my mother, her sisters, and my two sisters, and we had a very insular home life. I went to a Catholic school where boys and girls were separated from sixth through eighth grade, and then I went to Hunter High School which was marvelous. I really hit my stride in high school: made self-discoveries and discovered connections. I grew up in high school. And we were all poets . . . Diane and a number of people whose names aren't around anymore. We were all very, very intense and full of ourselves and our beauty and duty [laughs]. It was my earliest support group. This was before the first stage of the chrysalis changed, and the importance of that place and time really does seem a bond. It's a connection, too, in that we often later see our girl children in that light; ourselves and our lovers—in the light offered from those differences as well as the things that we shared.

KH: Did you show each other your work?
AL: Oh, yes. We had a group and we worked very hard, mostly in private. Sometimes we'd call up the poets and burn candles. I always felt myself on the outside as an institutionalized position. It's a position that I've often had in my life, not always unintentionally. I am writing about this in the book I'm working on now—that first prose piece that I've mentioned elsewhere. Those things that we, the girls at Hunter High, didn't share were as strong as those things that we did. I was a Black girl in a society that was basically white. Therefore, it was hostile to me in my Blackness even though, at the same time, it was supportive in my femaleness. So our relationships existed in school only. There were about four Black girls in my class when I went to high school— six at most. That was in 1947.

It's crucial to have a support group when you're starting out. I say this to women poets all the time: you've got to have some kind of workshop experience. I also had the Harlem Writers' Guild while I was still in high school. I remember Ricardo Weeks, Jeanne Morehead, Rosa Guy, and others. John Henrik Clarke started the Guild around 1948.

KH: Are there any poets with whom you've studied who have been influential in your consciousness of a poetics?
AL: I've never studied with any poets, per se, although there have been poets whom I've loved and whose work has been important to me. For many, many years there were poets with whom I moved but whom I'd never met. Yet, I felt I knew them because I'd lived so intimately with their work.

KH: Would Margaret Walker be one of those people?
AL: Yes, but later. I did not read her work until later. Later Gwen [Brooks]. Elinor Wylie. Edna Millay. But also T. S. Eliot. It can be determined by the old books that I've never thrown away. I have a number of books from high school—some of which you never hear anymore. Helene Margaret is an example. She was a beautiful poet. I learned a great deal from her. Someone borrowed the book and I don't have it now. She later went into a nunnery and that's probably why she was lost. Her first book of poetry (*Change of Season*) I've never forgotten. She helped me not to be afraid of my unacceptable feelings.

KH: Was she more traditional in terms of structure—using sonnet forms, the villanelle, etc.?
AL: She'd written some sonnets. She had some ballads. *Change of Season* was a collected work. She used a number of different forms. As I said, Wylie and Millay were standard in high school—women whom I really loved. Eliot. That man used to put me on fire with his words. I can remember being in cold sweats. I had a very emotional relationship with poetry when I was young because I was very inarticulate. I didn't speak, probably because I was left handed and had been taught to write with my right hand. I couldn't stutter because I got hit if I stuttered. So writing was the next best thing. The ability to read poetry—the music that sang in my head—was an incredible high for me. I used to get stoned on poetry when I was a kid. When life got just too difficult for me, I could always retreat into those words. If they didn't exist I made them up myself. I mean I was well on my way to becoming a

schizophrenic [laughs] because I lived in a totally separate world of words. So poetry is very important to me in terms of survival, in terms of living. But my early exposure to it was undisciplined. If I picked up a poem and it didn't turn me loose, that was it [laughs]. To some extent it still is. I didn't care by whom it had been written. I thought of most modern poetry as dead, and in terms of: this is the other people's poetry. You know the title of my book, *This Is a Land Where Other People Live?* Well, it is those "Other People" who write that kind of poetry because [laughs] obviously it didn't have any relationship to me. T. S. Eliot, Millay, Helene Margaret, I read and connected with because they made me feel what they were feeling, or wanted to feel.

KH: It's difficult to speak of the sensibilities that attract you to someone else's work, isn't it?
AL: Yes.

KH: If someone says, "What do you look for in a poem?"—it's difficult to answer them.
AL: It's very distressing in some ways to have to invent the wheel every time that you have to go to the store for bread. But there's something very, very refreshing about it, too. In those days what struck me, what really grabbed me, was the kind of emotional complexity . . . intensity that answered—not just the feeling that I was having but, the depths and implications of the feeling that I was having. I spent so much of my life in high emotion—pain, terror, fear, love, fury, whatever. From my mother I learned that you live passionately inside and secret, but you have to be careful of what you do because the world's waiting to really knock you down. That's the constructive paranoia all Black women teach their children. At the same time, you had to feel because if you didn't feel you were lost. Essentially, she was saying, "Be careful of your safety, by washing your face and brushing your teeth, combing your hair and not answering back." Meanwhile, she is this fury, this uncontrolled woman [laughs] who, when she doesn't get what she wants, arranges the world into a new framework to help her get what she wants. She's totally manipulative and powerful in a restricted sphere, and imposes her order upon that world. There's that disparity and conflict.

KH: Would you say that a line such as "rocking dark windows into their whens" ("Rooming Houses Are Old Women," *Coal*) bears the influence of e. e. cummings?

AL: Might be, Karla [laughs]. I really can't say. Perhaps cummings and I were coming out of the same place—a kind of intoxication with words. I can't place enough emphasis on this. In the place that, perhaps, I was disturbed, words were live entities. I had a vocabulary of words which I had never, never used or heard spoken. I only wrote. I didn't know how they were pronounced. They would alter in my head in cadences; you know, *legend* and *frigate* and *monster*. But I'd never spoken them, never heard them. I read them because I would read omnivorously. Words had an energy and power and I came to respect that power early. Pronouns, nouns, and verbs were citizens of different countries, who really got together to make a new world. Some of it has to do, too, with the richness of a West Indian vocabulary. We do speak of before-time, meaning a particular period of time, before the current time which also extends from past to future. It's similar to a pluperfect sense. Words that you use for time, and words that you use for basic human emotions, become very fluid in the same way that pronouns do in West Indian. My parents were both West Indian. They frequently spoke Patois between themselves. So much of what my sisters and I heard at home was West Indian, and we grew up in a West Indian section of Harlem. We were made fun of at school because of our West Indian accents.

Now, cummings was doing the same thing: getting into words, rolling around in them. As a child, I used to charm myself with words. I used to lie awake RIVEN with nightmares. I would wake up and I would have this long conversation with my Guardian Angel; when that didn't work, then I would pick words of which I was most terrified: *monster*, etc., and I would say them until I stripped them of anything but the sound—and put myself to sleep with the rhythms of them [laughs]. I had a very intimate relationship with these silent words—words that went on in my head. When I was still too afraid to deal with my feelings I wrote poetry about them. Today looking at that earlier writing I think "How incredible!—what this child knew." That child didn't understand anything at all, but she knew a great deal. It was a form of automatic writing reflecting some of the cadences and some of my feelings. In those days when I could not afford to know what I was feeling, I wrote a great deal. In that way I could write down what I was feeling and it stood me in good stead.

KH: Your "Poem for a Poet" is a very moving poem for me. Would you consider Jarrell an influence?
AL: Is it really? Tell me about it.

KH: I had a feeling of a scenario—getting into the place you were describing—which became so much more alive for me and then I had a sense of Jarrell. I loved the way it ended.

AL: [laughs] [quotes the poem] I don't know whether Jarrell was an influence or not. He was a lovable person. He was a very pleasant experience . . . the weekend that I was at Women's College; but I couldn't exactly call him an influence. It was a very, very intense four days during which I learned much about myself . . . less so about him. But there's a great deal about him that I respect and much for which I felt sorry. He had the flavor of someone who had retreated, who had performed a final action. Two or three years later he died. He was walking on a road (in Greensboro, North Carolina) one dusk and a car hit him—never knew whether it was intentional or not. They just knocked him down. It felt to me like it had been written in a rising star when I had known him. Randall Jarrell, may he rest in peace. He was a good experience of my trip South.

KH: What is the greatest impotence a poet can suffer—paralysis of feeling or paralysis of action? Or is it impossible to separate these?

AL: I can't separate the two. My personal history is such that movement and feeling have had to be connected because they've been part of my survival. You don't grow up on the streets of New York or as a Black lesbian—an outsider (and I've always been the outsider because I defined it as survival)—without being aware of this. I *didn't* want to be inside what I saw. So it's a position that gives you some power and a great deal of vulnerability. That's a consciousness which is basic to realizing that what makes us most vulnerable also makes us most strong. Being the outsider makes you terribly vulnerable, but it also frees you from certain expectations. You know that some people are never going to love you anyway, so you don't have to meet their expectations or demands. It's not going to buy you anything, right? I mean if you're ugly you don't have to go through all this business of wearing eye make-up, etc., because they're still going to call you fat four-eyes. But you can be your own woman. If you're their woman, they're never going to want you anyway. What makes sense of this is who I want to be and what anyone else wants of me is secondary. You may start selfness for the wrong reasons; but once you get a taste of it, it's very seductive. That's what growing up in a female society does for you.

KH: Even in a white society?

AL: Yes. Except at home, I grew up in a largely white society. I was the outsider there; but, at least, we were all women. That high school experience was crucial for me.

KH: Do you have a particular procedure for writing—certain tools or other materials?

AL: If you ever saw my desk [laughs]. I usually try to clear off a space. When I don't have any more space in my office, I start—as you can see—with all these little piles on the table [the interview is being conducted in the dining room].

KH: Is there a certain kind of paper you use?

AL: I use different color papers. I love papers and I love pens. Now, unlined paper was a big step for me [laughs]. When things are in a certain stage they're on green, then yellow, then pink, and finally on white [mimeo paper]. I kept blue out—blue is for prose. I've just started teaching myself to write prose (English is a second language). The other colors are for poetry. White is what I send poems out on because people don't like to xerox on colors. Because I live in such chaos upstairs, I have to be able to put my hands on things. If I forget things that I jotted down, when I pick them up, the color paper will indicate what stage of writing I'm in. I usually write with brown pens or I type if I'm up at my desk.

KH: Are there certain places where you've done your best writing?

AL: I have a study upstairs, and I pull it around me like a blanket. There's a force field around it. I deliberately kept it small because I'm forever gathering bright shiny objects and the more room I had, the more objects I would have collected. The force field around the room really operated even when the children were younger. This is a big house and we gave them the third floor. Frances has her study on the second, I have my study, we have our bedroom and the guest room. If I'm working in my study, the children come to the door and they stand there and they talk [laughs]. The force field keeps everyone out unless they're invited in. I love it. I do a lot of good writing and good revising there. But lately I've been writing prose here because it's difficult to hold myself in those solid blocks—in that space.

KH: Is this prose piece that you're presently working on different from the articles that you've been writing?

AL: They're all pieces of it. I'm putting it all together. A piece will be out in the Black Women's Condition Issue called "Tar Beach." Perhaps that will give you more of an idea of the flow of a Black woman's consciousness. It's a history. After all, we've been around for a long time. It's a mythic history. I've been trying to decide whether it's historical myth or mythic history. I finally decided that it's the latter.

KH: "I heard a man say recently a very profound thing: 'the dream of every poem is to become a myth'" (Michael Harper, *Interviews with Black Writers*). [quotes from "Dear Toni Instead of a Letter of Congratulations Upon Your Book and Your Daughter Whom You Say You Are Raising to Be a Correct Little Sister"]. Do you feel that what Michael Harper is saying is in any way reflective of what you're saying in this poem?

AL: I like what he said, but I don't really see the connection.

KH: In your own work, do you see in the period between *The First Cities* and *Between Ourselves* a movement away from a more traditional use of poetic forms to a more lyrical structure, thematically and stylistically?

AL: Those two books aren't diametrically opposed but what has happened is that I am less afraid or that I reckoned less with my fear. Poetry is an encoded language, of necessity. I wrote poetry sometimes to be able to deal with those feelings that I was not allowed to openly own or to voice. As I became less afraid, I voiced them more. That made me less popular. I had a poem published when I was seventeen years old and I didn't print again for another ten years. Those are the poems of *Coal.* Some of the poems from *The First Cities* are in *Coal* and in *Cables to Rage*. I can see a very real movement away. You want background . . . I remember standing on a hill in Cuernavaca, in Mexico in 1953. I was on my way down to the square to catch a turismo [a taxi] to go to Mexico City because I was teaching a class there and I was taking classes at the University. I was nineteen at the time, and I found in Mexico an affirmation. It was the first time that I began to speak in full sentences. First of all, being surrounded by people of color was such an incredible high. It was warm and it was beautiful and there was the light. The color was affirmation for me in different ways. It was probably the first time in my life that I had been surrounded with the kind of beauty that used to exist inside my head—when I used to pick, as I say in one of my poems, the grasses between the pavement blocks. And here in Mexico there were flowers.

On this morning, just before dawn, the sun caught the first shimmer of snow on the summit of Ixtacihuatl, Sleeping Woman—the highest mountain in Mexico. The sun before it broke the horizon would catch the white and the crest would be seen just there—hanging in the sky—for miles. Then as I watched, the sun would crest the horizon, but I couldn't see it because of all the trees. But I heard the birds in a crescendo. Watching dawn break on the Sleeping Woman and then the birds started. I stood on this hill, halfway down to the market, and for the first time in that one instant I felt that I could make a connection—that there could be a real connection between the things that I felt most deeply and those gorgeous words that I needed to spin in order to live. That was the first time it became possible for me to deal with the incredibly multi-leveled emotions that I was experiencing never wanting to leave this beauty. And for one minute I thought "I can write a poem that feels like this. I want to get that down in words."

KH: Do you ever have that feeling when you're giving a poetry reading?
AL: I have had that feeling more and more with my later poetry.

KH: What determines the shape of a poem for you?
AL: I don't know. The poem. Its truth.

KH: Helen Vendler (in a *New York Times Book Review*) has spoken of your "photographs" of city life. In writing poetry does the image of photography ever come to mind?
AL: I have an image of imaging all the time. Sight is very important to me. As I told you, I was born almost blind. It was a very critical factor in my growing up. I couldn't wear glasses until I was three years old so my first perceptions of the world were highly visually distorted.

KH: Did this give you a sense of the surreal?
AL: I suppose. "Miss Lorde, are you a nature poet?" asked someone fifteen years ago, and I thought, "What are you talking about?" I remember the first time that I saw the leaves of a tree with my glasses. I was so astonished. I'll never forget it. I was with my mother and we were walking along Lenox Avenue. I saw this plane tree in the park and it had individual leaves. It's still a vivid image. Prior to that, trees to me had been a green cloud formation

with a trunk. It never occurred to me to question it. Suddenly the leaves were individual and particular. It's like that when you speak of the surreal. I mean here are these green clouds down on earth and these white clouds up in the sky. Some are trees and some are clouds. Suddenly it all becomes very different. When I speak about the craft of writing and when I try to teach that loosening of self (the only thing that you can teach when you teach people about their own poetry), a number of the exercises that I encourage people to do are exercises of imaging, visualization. It's learning how you build images, where they come from, and what does it feel like to express that feeling. That's very precious and rich experience. It's something you fall into in the same way that you count sheep to go to sleep. You image when you're waiting for a bus or when you're having a conversation and someone's boring you. Here's something that I love to image—the inside of people's heads or the insides of their mouths, the way the tongue moves [laughs]. It's a very visual process for me.

KH: [quotes] ("Change of Season"). Can you explain why summer is a central season for you? Does it have anything to do with the fact that fire and the sun are important images ("Summer Oracle," *Coal*) to you? i.e., [quotes] ("Chorus," *The Black Unicorn*)?

AL: Summer is very important to me because the concept of sun as a female image is one that is very real. It always has been, even before I gave words to it—finding a correlation for it in African mythology where Mawu-Lisa (the Sun-Moon Principle) are inseparable. The sun and the earth are generative. They're two sides of the same principle. They are always seen as separate in Western cosmology because there's less sun [laughs]. The sun fertilized the earth and so on. In Africa the sun, moon, earth are all together and the same. I find it interesting that the Celts (who are just about as Black as you get in Western European civilization) did not gear their sense of time to days. They reckoned time by nights. I suspect it's because they were originally matriarchal—moon people.

But, yes, fire, sun, warmth . . . I'm an Afro-American woman and my traditions are those of heat.

KH: Can you tell me how you came to write "Solstice"?

AL: I don't remember how I came to write "Solstice." It just came. It was a given poem. A very deep poem.

KH: In saying [quotes] ("Scar"), did you mean the marriage name or females seeking male approval?

AL: I dealt out all of those levels. It's a removal of self (as I speak of in "Between Ourselves") to give those faces which we hate to someone else, those faces we can't deal with inside of ourselves. It's about how we use corrupted power to create pain.

KH: Can you tell me how you came to organize *The Black Unicorn* as you did? When did you first begin writing the poems that constitute the first part of this book?

AL: I organized *The Black Unicorn* because I like the poems that are together and because they seemed to spark a particular dialectic in that order. It wasn't chronological. All those poems are from '75—so it's three, nearly four years. Very productive years.

KH: For those who have not yet read *The Black Unicorn*, could you say something about the title—its personal relevance to you?

AL: I've been very interested in the mythic unicorn. The Western concept of the unicorn reminds me so much of a shadow image or a negative of the many African cave paintings . . . the outlines of the Chi-Wara (the African antelope).

KH: Would you elaborate on what you meant in saying [quotes] ("A Woman Speaks," *The Black Unicorn*)?

AL: That has to state itself [laughs]. I don't believe in talking about what I mean—rather how it feels to me. But that's a long business, too—power, strength, what is old and what is new being very much the same.

KH: Do you teach African study courses on the college level and has this been instrumental in your writing *The Black Unicorn*? Or was this knowledge gathered from reading and intuition?

AL: No, I don't teach African study courses. It's all been knowledge I've felt moved to gather and explore in my trips to Africa and through my reading.

KH: Can you tell me something about the West African Market Women Associations—their organization, function, goals, etc.?

AL: I can mention some books on the West African Market Women Associations. You can find references to them in Herskovits, *Women of Tropical*

Africa, African Women in Urban Societies—Their Changing Roles. They deal with the Yoruba Riots and the rise of the African Women's Market Associations. These Associations function in nearly all the Western African countries—certainly in Ghana, Togo, Dahomey, Nigeria. At Festac . . . you could look up in the bleachers . . . this huge arena was packed with people . . . and there across the stands—this swath of blue and white. The Market women were all in the same color and it stood out like a pattern. They'd dyed their cloth all the same color and they always appear together as a show of force. In other words, "we" are here—as a group, as a force. They've been very instrumental, for instance, in their role in Ghana.

KH: William Demby (*Interviews with Black Writers*) feels that an artist has the responsibility to make some connection with the past: "That is, to illustrate how much of the past is living in the present and how much of the present is only the future and the past."

AL: We have to deal with the strengths, the powers, and the weaknesses that come from the past and the intimations of that for a future. Once we stop seeing ourselves as the apex of a triangle and open it into a triad (that we are part of a whole line) it unburdens us of a great responsibility; yet, simultaneously, it makes us even more responsible in a positive sense.

An Interview with Audre Lorde

Adrienne Rich / 1979

From *Signs: Journal of Women in Culture and Society*, 6.4 (Summer 1981), 713–36. The interview was conducted 30 August 1979. © 1981 by The University of Chicago. Reprinted by permission.

Audre Lorde has published seven books of poetry, most recently *Coal* (1976) and *The Black Unicorn* (1978), both published by W. W. Norton. Her *Cancer Journals,* a collection of prose, was published by Spinsters Ink in 1980. She was born in New York City, attended Hunter High School and Hunter College, received her degree as a librarian, and is a professor of English at the John Jay College of Criminal Justice in the City University of New York. She is now at work on a novel. This interview, held on 30 August 1979, was edited from three hours of tapes we made together. It was commissioned by Marilyn Hacker, the guest editor of *Woman Poet: The Northeast* (general editor, Elaine Dallman), where portions of it appear.

(Montague, Massachusetts)

Adrienne Rich: What do you mean when you say that those two essays—"Poems Are Not Luxuries" and "Uses of the Erotic"—are really progressions?
Audre Lorde: They're part of something that's not finished yet. I don't know what the rest of it is, but they're very clear progressions to me, in feeling out something that is connected also with the first piece of prose I ever wrote. The one thread I feel coming through over and over in my life is the battle to preserve my perceptions, the battle to win through and to keep them—pleasant or unpleasant, painful or whatever—

AR: And however much they were denied.
AL: And however much they were denied. And however painful some of them were. When I think of the way in which I courted punishment, the way in which I just swam into it: "If this is the only way you're going to deal with me, you're gonna have to deal with me this way."

AR: You're talking about as a young child?
AL: I'm talking about as an infant, as a very young child, over and over again throughout my life. I kept myself through feeling. I lived through it. And at

such a subterranean level, I think, that I didn't know *how* to talk. I was really busy feeling out other ways of getting and giving information and whatever else I could, because talking wasn't where it was at. People were talking all around me all the time—and not either getting or giving much that was useful to them or to me, or that made sense to me at the time.

AR: And not listening to what you tried to say, if you did speak.
AL: When you asked how I began writing, I told you how poetry functioned specifically for me from the time I was very young, from nursery rhymes. When someone said to me. "How do you feel?" or "What do you think?" or asked another direct question. I would recite a poem, and somewhere in that poem would be the feeling, somewhere in it would be the piece of information. It might be a line. It might be an image. The poem was my response.

AR: Like a translation into this poem that already existed, of something you knew in a preverbal way. So the poem became your language?
AL: Yes. I remember reading in the children's room of the library. I couldn't have been past the second or third grade, but I remember the book. It was illustrated by Arthur Rackham, a book of poems. These were old books, the library in Harlem used to get the oldest books, in the worst condition. Walter de la Mare's "The Listeners"—I will never forget that poem.

AR: Where the traveler rides up to the door of the empty house?
AL: That's right. He knocks at the door and nobody answers. " 'Is there anybody there?' he said." That poem imprinted itself on me. And finally, he's beating down the door and nobody answers, and he has a feeling that there really is somebody in there. And then he turns his horse and he says, " 'Tell them I came, and nobody answered. That I kept my word,' he said." I used to recite that poem to myself all the time. It was one of my favorites. And if you'd asked me, what is it about, I don't think I could have told you. But this was the first cause of my own writing, my need to say things I couldn't say otherwise, when I couldn't find other poems to serve.

AR: You had to make your own.
AL: There were so many complex emotions, it seemed, for which poems did not exist. I had to find a secret way to express my feelings. I used to memorize my poems. I would say them out. I didn't use to write them down. I had this

long fund of poetry in my head. And I remember trying when I was in high
school not to think in poems. I saw the way other people thought, and it was
an amazement to me—step by step, not in bubbles up from chaos that you had
to anchor with words. . . . I really do believe I learned this from my mother.

AR: Learned what from your mother?
AL: The important value of nonverbal communication, beneath language.
My life depended on it. At the same time living in the world and using language. And I didn't want to have anything to do with the way she was using
language. My mother had a strange way with words; if one didn't serve her or
wasn't strong enough, she'd just make up another word, and then that word
would enter our family language forever, and woe betide any of us who for-
got it. But I think I got another message from her. . . . that there was a whole
powerful world of nonverbal communication and contact between people
that was absolutely essential and that was what you had to learn to decipher
and use. One of the reasons I had so much trouble growing up was that my
parents, my mother in particular, always expected me to know what she was
feeling and what she expected me to do without telling me. And I thought
this was natural. But my mother would expect me to know things, whether or
not she spoke them—

AR: Ignorance of the law was no excuse.
AL: That's right. It's very confusing. And eventually I learned how to acquire
vital and protective information without words. My mother used to say to
me, "Don't just listen like a ninny to what people say in their mouth." But
then she'd proceed to say something that didn't feel right to me. You always
learned from observing. You have to pick things up nonverbally because people will never tell you what you're supposed to know. You have to get it for
yourself: whatever it is that you need in order to survive. And if you make a
mistake you get punished for it, but that's no big thing. You become strong by
doing the things you need to be strong for. This is the way genuine learning
takes place. That's a very difficult way to live, but it also has served me. It's
been an asset as well as a liability. When I went to high school, I found out
that people really thought in different ways, perceived, puzzled out, acquired
information, verbally. I had such a hard time; I never studied, I literally intu-
ited all my teachers. That's why it was so important to get a teacher who I
liked or could deal with, because I never studied, I never read my assignment,

and I would get all of this stuff, what they felt, what they knew, but I missed a lot of other stuff, a lot of my own original workings.

AR: When you said you never read, you meant you never read the assignments, but you *were* reading?
AL: Yes, I was constantly reading, but not things that were assigned. And if I read things that were assigned I didn't read them the way we were supposed to. Everything was like a poem, with different curves, different levels. So I always felt that the ways I took things in were different from the ways other people took them in. I used to practice trying to think.

AR: That thing those other people presumably did. Do you remember what that was like?
AL: Yes. I had an image of trying to reach something around a corner, that it was just eluding me. The image was constantly vanishing around the corner. There was an experience I had in Mexico, when I moved to Cuernavaca . . .

AR: This was when you were about how old?
AL: I was nineteen. When I went to Mexico I felt myself just opening up, walking on the street, seeing all these dark people and the sunlight and the heat. I was in total ecstasy. And I was also terrified. I had never lived that far from New York before. I had gone to Stamford to work in the electronics factory, but that was a little trip. From Mexico City, I moved to Cuernavaca and I met Eudora and I was commuting to Mexico City for classes. In order to get to my early class I would catch a six o'clock *turismo* in the village plaza. I would come out of my house before dawn. You know, there are two volcanoes, Popocatepetl and Ixtacihuatl. I thought they were clouds, the first time I saw them through my windows. It would be dark, and I would see the snow on top of the mountains, and the sun coming up. And when the sun crested, at a certain point, the birds would start. But because we were in the valley it would still look like night. But there would be the light of the snow. And then this incredible crescendo of birds. One morning I came over the hill and the green, wet smells came up. And then the birds, the sound of them I'd never really noticed, never *heard* birds before. I was walking down the hill and I was transfixed. It was very beautiful. I hadn't been writing all the time I was in Mexico. And the poetry was the thing I had with words, that was so important. . . . And on that hill, I had the first intimation that I could bring those two together. I could infuse words

directly with what I was feeling. I didn't have to create the world I wrote about. I realized that words could tell. That there was such a thing as an emotional sentence. Until then, I would make these constructs and somewhere in there would be a nugget, like a Chinese bun, there would be a piece of nourishment, the thing I really needed, which I had to create. There on that hill, I was filled with the smell and feeling and the way it looked, filled with such beauty that I could not believe—I had always fantasized it before. I used to fantasize trees and dream forest. Until I got spectacles when I was four I thought trees were green clouds. When I read Shakespeare in high school I would get off on his gardens and Spanish moss and roses and trellises with beautiful women at rest and sun on red brick. When I was in Mexico I found out this could be a reality. And I learned that day on the mountain, that words can match that, *re*-create it.

AR: Do you think that in Mexico you were seeing a reality as extraordinary and vivid and sensual as you had been fantasizing it could be?
AL: I think so. I had always thought I had to do it in my head, make it up. I learned in Mexico that you can't even make it up unless it happens, or can happen. Where it happened first for me I don't know; I do remember stories my mother would tell us about Grenada in the West Indies, where she was born. . . . But that morning in Mexico I realized I did not have to make beauty up for the rest of my life. I remember trying to tell Eudora about this epiphany, and I didn't have the words for it. And I remember her saying, "Write a poem." When I tried to write a poem about the way I felt that morning, I could not do it, and all I had therefore was the memory that there must be a way. And that was incredibly important. I know that I came back from Mexico very very different, and much of it had to do with what I learned from Eudora and the ways in which I loved her, but more than that, it was a kind of releasing of my work, a real releasing of myself, a connection. I think probably also that I'd passed a very crucial adolescent point.

AR: Then you went back to the Lower East Side, right?
AL: Yes, I went back to living with my friend Ruth, and I began trying to get a job. I had had a year of college, but I could not function in those people's world. So I thought I could be a nurse. And I was having such a hard time getting any kind of work, I felt, well, a practical nursing license, and then I'll go back to Mexico—

AR: With my trade.

AL: Yes. But that wasn't possible either. I didn't have any money, and black women were not given practical nursing fellowships. I didn't realize it at the time, because what they said was that my eyes were too bad. But the first thing I did when I came back was to write a piece of prose about Mexico, called "La Llorona." La Llorona is a legend in that part of Mexico, around Cuernavaca. You know Cuernavaca? You know the big *barrancas?* When the rains come to the mountains, the boulders rush through the big ravines. The sound, the first rush, would start one or two days before the rains came. All the rocks tumbling down from the mountains made a voice, and the echoes would resound and it would be a sound of weeping, with the waters behind it. Modesta, a woman who lived in the house, told me the legend of La Llorona. A woman had three sons and found her husband lying in another woman's bed—it's the Medea story— and drowned her sons in the *barrancas,* drowned her children. And every year around this time she comes back to mourn the deaths. I took this story and out of a combination of ways I was feeling I wrote a story called "La Llorona." It's a story essentially of my mother and me, it was as if I had picked my mother up and put her in that place, here is this woman who kills, who wants something, the woman who consumes her children, who wants too much, but wants not because she's evil but because she wants her own life, but by now it is so dis- torted. . . . It was a very strange unfinished story, but the dynamic—

AR: It sounds like you were trying to pull those two pieces of your life together, your mother and what you'd learned in Mexico.

AL: Yes. You see, I didn't deal at all with how strong my mother was inside of me, but she was—nor with how involved I was. But this story is beautiful. Pieces of it are in my head where the poetry pool is—phrases and so on. I had never written prose before and I've never written any since until just now. I published it under the name "Rey Domini" in a magazine. . . .

AR: Why did you use a pseudonym?

AL: Because . . . I don't write stories. I write poetry. So I had to put it under another name.

AR: Because it was a different piece of you?

AL: That's right. I only write poetry and here is this story. But I used the name "Rey Domini," which is "Audre Lorde" in Latin.

AR: Did you really not write prose from the time of that story until a couple of years ago, when you wrote "Poems Are Not Luxuries"?

AL: I couldn't. For some reason, the more poetry I wrote, the less I felt I could write prose. Someone would ask for a book review, or, when I worked at the library, for a précis about books—it wasn't that I didn't have the skills. I knew about sentences by that time. I knew how to construct a paragraph. But communicating deep feeling in linear, solid blocks of print felt arcane, a method beyond me.

AR: But you'd been writing letters like wildfire, hadn't you?

AL: Well, I didn't write letters as such. I wrote stream of consciousness and for people who were close enough to me this would serve. My friends gave me back the letters I wrote them from Mexico—strange, those are the most formed. I remember feeling I could not focus on a thought long enough to have it from start to finish, but I could ponder a poem for days, camp out in its world.

AR: Do you think that was because you still had this idea that thinking was a mysterious process that other people did and that you had to sort of practice? That it wasn't something you just did?

AL: It was a very mysterious process for me. And it was one I had come to suspect, because I had seen so many errors committed in its name, and I had come not to respect it. On the other hand, I was also afraid of it, because there were inescapable conclusions or convictions I had come to about my own life, my own feelings that defied thought. And I wasn't going to let them go. I wasn't going to give them up. They were too precious to me. They were life to me. But I couldn't analyze or understand them, because they didn't make the kind of sense I had been taught to expect through understanding. There were things I knew and couldn't say, I couldn't talk about them, but I knew. And I couldn't understand them.

AR: In the sense of being able to take them out, analyze them, defend them?

AL: . . . write prose about them. Right. I wrote a lot of those poems you first knew me by, those poems in *The First Cities*, way back in high school. If you had asked me to talk about one of those poems, I'd have talked in the most banal ways. All I had was the sense that I had to hold on to these things and that I had to air them in some way.

AR: But they were also being transformed into language.

AL: That's right. When I wrote something that finally had it, I would say it aloud and it would come alive, become real. It would start repeating itself and I'd know, that's struck, that's true. Like a bell. Something struck true. And there the words would be.

AR: How do you feel writing connected for you with teaching?

AL: Adrienne, I know teaching is a survival technique. It is for me, and I think it is in general; and that's the only way real teaching, real learning, happens. Because I myself was learning something I needed, to continue living. And I was examining it and teaching it at the same time I was learning it. I was teaching it to myself *aloud*. And it started out at Tougaloo in a poetry workshop.

AR: You were ill when you were called to go down to Tougaloo?

AL: Yes, I felt—I had almost died.

AR: What was going on?

AL: Diane di Prima—that was 1967—she had started the Poets Press; and she said, "You know, it's time you had a book." And I said, "Well, who's going to print it?" I was going to put those poems away, because I had found I was revising too much instead of writing new poems, and that's how I found out, again through experience, that poetry is not Play-Doh. You can't take a poem and keep re-forming it. It is itself, and you have to know how to cut it, and if there's something else you want to say, that's fine. But I was repolishing and repolishing, and Diane said, "You have to print these. Put 'em out." And the Poets Press published *The First Cities*. Well, I worked on that book, getting it together, and it was going into press. . . . I had gotten the proofs back and I started repolishing again and realized, "This is going to be a book!" Putting myself on the line. People I don't even know are going to read these poems. What's going to happen? It felt very critical, and I was in an absolute blaze of activity, because things financially were so bad at home. And I went out and got a job, I was with the two kids in the daytime and worked at the library at night. Jonathan used to cry every night when I left, and I would hear his shrieks going down this long hall to the elevator. I was working nights, and I'd apprenticed myself to a stained-glass-window maker, and I was working in my mother's office, and making Christmas for my friends, and I became very ill—I had overdone it. I was too sick to get up, and Ed answered the phone. It was Galen Williams from the Poetry Center asking if I'd like to go as poet in residence to Tougaloo, a black college in Mississippi. I'd been recommended for a grant. It was Ed who said, "You have to do this." My energy was at such a low ebb that I couldn't see how—first of all, it was very frightening to me, the idea of someone responding to me as a poet. This book, by the way, hadn't even come out yet, you understand?

AR: And suddenly you were already being taken seriously by unseen people out there.
AL: That's right. In particular, I was asked to be public; to speak *as*, rather than *to*. But I felt as if I'd come back from the dead at that point, and so everything was up for grabs. I thought, hey, very good, let's see—not because I felt I could do it, I just knew it was new and different. I was terrified to go south. Then there were echoes of an old dream: I had wanted to go to Tougaloo years before. My friend Elaine and I were going to join the Freedom Riders in Jackson when we left California in 1961 to return to New York, and Elaine's mother got down on her knees in San Francisco and begged us please not to do this, that they would kill us, and we didn't do it. So going to Tougaloo in Jackson was part of the mythic—

AR: But it sounds as if earlier you had been more romantic about what going south would mean, and six years later, with two kids *and* everything that had happened in between in the south—
AL: I was scared. I thought: "I'm going." Really, it was the first thing that countered the fury and pain I felt at leaving that little boy screaming every night. It was like—all right, if I can walk out and hear that child screaming in order to go down to the library and work every night, then I'm gonna be able at least to do something that I want to find out about. So I went.

AR: Were you scared at Tougaloo, in terms of teaching, meeting your first workshop?
AL: Yes, but it was a nurturing atmosphere. I'd lived there for two weeks. I went around really gathering people, and there were eight students who were already writing poetry. The ways in which I was on the line in Tougaloo. . . . I began to learn about courage, I began to learn to talk. But this was a small group and there was a dynamic between us. We became very close. I learned so much from listening to people. And all I knew was, the only thing I had

was honesty and openness. And it was absolutely necessary for me to declare, as terrified as I was, from the very get-go as soon as we were opening to each other, to say, "The father of my children is white." And what that meant in Tougaloo to those young black people then, and to deal with it, to talk about myself openly, to deal with their hostility, their sense of disillusionment, to come past that, was very hard.

AR: It must have been particularly hard since you knew by then that the marriage was going nowhere. It's like having to defend something that was not in itself defensible.

AL: What I was defending was something that needs defense. And this almost moved it out of "I'm defending Ed because I want to live with him." It was "I'm defending this relationship because we have a right to examine it and try it." So there's Audre as the northern black poet, making contact with these young southern black people who are *not* saying, "This is what we need you for," but were telling me by who they were what they needed from me. In the poem "Black Studies" a lot of that starts coming through. Tougaloo laid the foundation for that poem, that knowledge born five years later. My students needed my perception, yet my perception of their need was different from what they were saying. What they were saying aloud was, "We need strong black people"—but what they were also saying was that their ideas of what strong was had come from our oppressors and didn't jibe with their feelings at all.

It was through poetry that we began to deal with these things—formally, I knew nothing. Adrienne, I had never read a book *about* poetry! Never read a book about poetry. I picked up one day a book by Karl Shapiro—a little thin white book. I opened it and something he said made sense. It was, "Poetry doesn't make Cadillacs." That was a symbol for all the things I was—yes. So I would talk to the students, and I was learning. It was the first time I'd ever talked about writing, because always before I'd listened—part of my being inarticulate, inscrutable, because I didn't understand in terms of verbalization, and if I did I was too terrified to speak anyway. But at Tougaloo *we* talked about poetry. And I got the first copies of my book there at Tougaloo. I had never been in this relationship with black people before. Never, There had been a very uneasy dialogue between me and the Harlem Writers' Guild, where I felt I was tolerated but never really accepted—that I was both crazy and queer but would grow out of it all. Johnny Clarke adopted me because he really loved me, and he's a kind man, you know? And he taught me wonderful things about Africa. And he said to me, "You are a poet. You *are* a poet. I don't understand your poetry but you are a poet, you are." So I would get this underlining of me. "You're not doing what you're supposed to do, but, yes, you can do it and we totally expect you to. You are a bright and shining light. You're off on a lot of wrong turns, women, the Village, white people, all of this, but you're young yet. You'll find your way." So I would get these double messages. This kind of underlining and rejection at the same time—it reduplicated my family, you see. In my family it was: "You're a Lorde, so that makes you special and particular above anybody else in the world. But you're not our kind of Lorde, so when are you going to straighten up and act right?"

AR: And did you feel, there in the Harlem Writers' Guild, the same kind of unwritten laws that you had to figure out in order to do right?
AL: Yes, I would bring poems to read at the meetings. And hoping, well, they're gonna tell me actually what it is they want, but they never could, never did.

AR: Were there women in that group, older women?
AL: Rosa Guy was older than I, but she was still very young. I remember only one other woman, Gertrude McBride. But she came in and out of the workshop so quickly I never knew her. For the most part the men were the core. My friend Jeannie and I were members but in a slightly different position, we were in high school, you see.

AR: And so Tougaloo was an entirely different experience of working with other black writers.
AL: When I went to Tougaloo, I didn't know what to give or where it was going to come from. I knew I couldn't give what regular teachers of poetry give, nor did I want to, because they'd never served me. I couldn't give what English teachers give. The only thing I had to give was me. And I was so involved with these young people—I really loved them. I knew the emotional life of each of those students because we would have conferences, and that became inseparable from their poetry. And I would talk to them in the group about their poetry in terms of what I knew about their lives, and that there was a real connection between the two that was inseparable no matter what they'd been taught to the contrary.

I knew by the time I left Tougaloo that teaching was the work I needed to be doing, that library work—by this time I was head librarian at the Town

School—being a librarian was not enough. It had been very satisfying to me. And I had a kind of stature I hadn't had before in terms of working. But from the time I went to Tougaloo and did that workshop, I knew: not only, yes, I am a poet, but also, this is the kind of work I'm going to do.

Practically all the poems in *Cables to Rage* I wrote in Tougaloo. I was there for six weeks. I came back knowing that my relationship with Ed was not enough: either we were going to change it or end it. I didn't know how to end it, because there had never been any endings for me. But I had met Frances at Tougaloo, and I knew she was going to be a permanent person in my life. However, I didn't know how we were going to work it out. I'd left a piece of my heart in Tougaloo not just because of Frances but because of what my students there had taught me.

And I came back, and my students called me and said—they were all of them also in the Tougaloo choir—they were coming to New York to sing in Carnegie Hall with Duke Ellington on April 4, and I covered it for the *Clarion-Ledger*, in Jackson, so I was there, and while we were there Martin Luther King was killed.

AR: On that night?
AL: I was with the Tougaloo choir at Carnegie Hall when he was killed. They were singing "What the World Needs Now Is Love." And they interrupted it to tell us that Martin Luther King had been killed.

AR: What did people do?
AL: Duke Ellington started to cry. Honeywell, the head of the choir, said, "The only thing we can do here is finish this as a memorial." And they sang again, "What the World Needs Now Is Love." The kids were crying. The audience was crying. And then the choir stopped. They cut the rest of it short. But they sang that song and it kept reverberating. It was more than pain. The horror, the enormity of what was happening. Not just the death of King, but what it meant. I have always had the sense of Armageddon and it was much stronger in those days, the sense of living on the edge of chaos. Not just personally, but on the world level. That we were dying, that we were killing our world—that sense had always been with me. That whatever I was doing, whatever we were doing that was creative and right, functioned to hold us from going over the edge. That this was the most we could do, while we constructed some saner

future. But that we were in that kind of peril. And here it was reality, in fact. Some of the poems—"Equinox" is one of them—come from then. I knew then that I had to leave the library. And it was just about this time that Yolanda took my book, *The First Cities*, to Mina Shaughnessy, who had been her teacher, and I think she said to Mina, "Why don't you have her teach?"— because that's the way, you know, Yolanda is.

AR: But also, Mina would have listened to that.

AL: So Yolanda came home and said, "Hey, the head of the SEEK* English program wants to meet you. Maybe you can get a job there." And I thought, I have to lay myself on the line. It's not going back south and being shot at, but when Mina said to me, "Teach," it was as threatening as that was. I felt at the time, I don't know how I'm gonna do it, but that's the front line for me. And I talked to Frances about this, because we'd had the Tougaloo experience, and I said, "If I could go to war, if I could pick up a gun to defend the things I believe, yes— but what am I gonna do in a classroom?" And Frances said, "You'll do just what you did at Tougaloo." And the first thing that I said to my SEEK students was, "I'm scared too."

AR: I know *I* went in there in terror. But I went in white terror: you know: now you're on the line, all your racism is going to show . . .

AL: I went in in Audre terror, black terror. I thought, I have responsibility to these students. How am I going to speak to them? How am I going to tell them what I want from them—literally, that kind of terror. I did not know how to open my mouth and be understood. And my *commadre*, Yolanda, who was also a student in the SEEK program, said, "I guess you're just going to have to talk to them the same way you talk to me because I'm one of them and you've gotten across to me." I learned every single thing in every classroom. Every single class I ever walked into was like doing it anew. Every day, every week; but that was the exciting thing.

AR: Did you teach English I—that back-to-back course where you could be a poet—a writing teacher—and not teach grammar, and they had an English

---

* "Search for Education, Elevation, and Knowledge": A prebaccalaureate program in compensatory education in the City University of New York in which a number of writer-teachers participated in the 1960s and early 1970s.

instructor to teach the grammar? That was the only way I could have started doing it either.

AL: I learned to teach grammar. And then I realized that we can't separate these two things. We have to do them together because they're integral. That's when I learned how important grammar is, that part of the understanding process is grammatical. That's how I taught myself to write prose. I kept learning and learning. I'd come into my class and say, "Guess what I found out last night. Tenses are a way of ordering the chaos around time." About grammar I learned that it was arbitrary, that it served a purpose, that it helped to form the ways we thought, that it could be freeing as well as restrictive. And I sensed again how as children we learn this, and why; it's like driving a car, once we know it we can choose to discard it or use it, but you can't know if it has useful or destructive power until you have a handle on it. It's like fear, once you put your hand on it you can use it or push it away. I was saying these things in class and dealing with what was happening with Frances and me, what was going on with this insane man I lived with who wanted to continue pretending life could be looked at one way and lived another. All this, every bit of it funneling into that class. My children were just learning to read in school, and that was important too, because I could watch their processes. Then it got even heavier when I went up to Lehman College and was teaching a class on racism in education, teaching these white students how it was, the connections between their lives and the fury. . . .

AR: You taught a course on racism for white students at Lehman?
AL: They were inaugurating a program in the education department, for these white kids going into teaching in the New York City schools. Lehman used to be 99 percent white, and it was these students coming out of the education department who were going to teach black children in the city schools. So the course was called "Race and the Urban Situation." I had all these white students, wanting to know, "What are we doing? Why are our kids hating us in the classroom?" I could not believe that they did not know the most elementary level of interactions. I would say, "When a white kid says $2 + 2 = 4$, you say 'right.' In the same class, when a black kid stands up and says $2 + 2 = 4$, you pat him on the back, you say, 'Hey, that's wonderful.' But what message are you really giving? Or what happens when you walk down the street on your way to teach? When you walk into class? Let's playact a little."

And all the fear and loathing of these young white college students would come pouring out; it had never been addressed.

AR: They must have been mostly women, weren't they? In the education department?
AL: Yes, mostly women, and they felt like unwilling sacrifices. But I began to feel by the end of two terms that there ought to be somebody white doing this. It was terribly costly emotionally. I didn't have more than one or two black students in my class. One of them dropped out saying this wasn't right for him, and I thought, wait a minute, racism doesn't just distort white people—what about us? What about the effects of white racism upon the ways black people view each other? Racism internalized? What about black teachers going into ghetto schools? And I saw there were different problems, that were just as severe, for a black teacher going into New York City schools after a racist, sexist education.

AR: You mean in terms of expectations?
AL: Not just in terms of expectations, but of self-image, in terms of confusion about loyalties. In terms of identifying with the oppressor. And I thought, who is going to start to deal with that? What do you do about it, Audre? This was where I wanted to use my energies. Meanwhile, this is 1969, and I'm thinking, what is my place in all this? There were two black women in the class, and I tried to talk to them about us, as black women, having to get together. The black organizations on the campuses were revving up for the spring actions. And the women said, you are insane, our men need us. It was a total rejection. "No, we can't come together as women. We're black." But I had to keep trying to straighten out the threads, because I knew the minute I stopped trying to straighten this shit out it was going to engulf me. So the only hope I had was to work at it, work on all the threads. My love with Frances, Ed, the children, teaching black students, the women.

And in '69 came the black and Puerto Rican occupation at City College. I was dealing with the black students outside of class on the barricades, Yolanda and I would bring over soup and blankets, and see black women getting fucked on tables and under desks—see what went down in those occupied buildings. And meanwhile we'd be trying to speak to them as women, and all we'd hear is, "The revolution is here, right?" Seeing how black women were being used and abused was painful—putting those things together. I said, I want to teach black students again. I went to John Jay College and discussed a course with the dean on racism and the urban situation, and he said, Come teach it. I taught two courses, that one and another new course I introduced to the English department, remedial writing through creative writing. It was confrontation teaching.

AR: John Jay was largely a police college, right?
AL: It had been a police college, but I began in 1970, after open admissions started, and John Jay was now a four-year senior college with a regular enrollment as well as an enrollment of City uniformed personnel. There were no black teachers in English or history. Most of our incoming freshmen were black or Puerto Rican. And my demeanor was very unthreatening.

AR: —I've seen your demeanor at John Jay and it was not unthreatening, but that was a bit later—
AL: —and also, I was a black *woman*. So then I came in and started this course and really meant business. And it was very heavily attended. A lot of black and white policemen registered for it. And literally, I used to be terrified about the guns.

AR: They were wearing guns?
AL: Yes. And since open admissions made college accessible to all high school graduates, we had cops and kids off the block in the same class. In 1970, the Black Panthers were being murdered in Chicago. Here we had black and white cops, and black and white kids off the block. Most of the women were young, black, together women who had come to college now because they'd not been able to get in before. Some of them were SEEK students, but not all, and this was the one chance for them. A lot of them were older; they were very street wise but they had done very little work with themselves as black women, as black people. They'd done it only in relation to, against, whitey. The enemy was always outside. I did that course in the same way I did all the others, which was learning as I went along, asking the hard questions, not knowing what was coming next. Very good things happened in the classes. I wish I had recorded some of it. Like the young white cop in the class saying, "Yeah, but everybody needs someone to look down on, don't they?" By then I'd learned how to talk. In my own fashion. Things weren't all concise or refined, but enough of it got through to them, their own processes would start. I came to realize that in one term that is the most you can do. There are

people who can give chunks of information, perhaps, but that was not what I was about. The learning process is something you can incite, literally incite, like a riot. And then, just possibly, hopefully, it goes home, or on.

By that time the battle over the Black Studies Department had started at John Jay. And again I saw the use and abuse of women, of black people, saw how black studies was being used by the university in a really cynical fashion. A year later, I returned to the English department. I had made a number of enemies. One of the attempts to discredit me among black students was to say I was a lesbian. Now by this time, I would have considered myself uncloseted, but I had never discussed my own poetry at John Jay, nor my sexuality. I knew, as I had always known, that the only way you can head people off from using who you are against you is to be honest and open first, to talk about yourself before they talk about you. It wasn't even courage. Speaking up was a protective mechanism for myself—like publishing "Love Poem" in *MS. Magazine* in 1971 and bringing it in and putting it up on the wall of the English department.

AR: I remember hearing you read "Love Poem" on the Upper West Side, a coffeehouse at 72d Street. It was the first time I'd heard you read it. And I think it was about that time, the early seventies. You read it. It was incredible. Like defiance. It was glorious.
AL: That's how I was feeling. I was always feeling my back against the wall, because, as bad as it is now, the idea of open lesbianism in the black community was—I mean, we've moved miles in a very short time. But in the early seventies it was totally horrible. My publisher called and literally said he didn't understand the words of "Love Poem." He said, "Now what is this all about, are you supposed to be a man?" And he was a poet! And I said, "No, I'm loving a woman."

AR: Well, don't tell me that your publisher had never heard of lesbians.
AL: I'm sure he had, but the idea that *I'd* write a poem—

AR: —That one of his poets in the Broadside Series—
AL: That's right. And he was a sensitive man. He was a poet.

AR: But he did print your work.
AL: Yes, he did. But he didn't print that poem, the first time around. "Love Poem" was supposed to have been in *From a Land Where Other People Live*.

AR: And it wasn't published in that book? You took it out?

AL: Yes. He didn't want it. There was another—was it "American Cancer Society"?—that belonged in *From a Land*. But when you heard me read "Love Poem," I had already made up my mind that I wasn't going to be worrying any more over who knows and who doesn't know that I have always loved women. One thing has always kept me going—and it's not really courage or bravery, unless that's what courage or bravery is made up of—is a sense that there are so many ways in which I'm vulnerable and cannot help but be vulnerable. I'm not going to be vulnerable by putting weapons of silence in my enemies' hands. Being a lesbian in the black community, or even being woman-identified, is difficult and dangerous.

When a people share a common oppression, certain kinds of skills and joint defenses are developed. And if you survive you survive because those skills and defenses have worked. When you come into conflict over other existing differences, there already is an additional vulnerability to each other which is desperate and very deep. And that is, for example, what happens between black men and women, because we have certain weapons we have perfected together that white women and men have not shared. I said this to someone, and she said, very rightly, the same thing exists within the Jewish community between Jewish men and Jewish women. I think the oppression is different, therefore the need for connection is on a different level, but the same mechanism of vulnerability exists. When you share a common oppression you have certain additional weapons against each other, because you've forged them in secret together against a common enemy. It's a fear that I'm still not free of and that I remember all the time when I deal with other black women: the fear of the excomrade.

AR: In "Poems Are Not Luxuries," you wrote: "The white fathers told us, 'I think therefore I am,' and the black mothers in each of us—the poets—whisper in our dreams, 'I feel therefore I can be free.'" I've heard it remarked that here you are simply restating the old stereotype of the rational white male and the emotional dark female. I believe you were saying something very different, but could you talk a little about that?

AL: There are a couple of things. I have heard that accusation, that I'm contributing to the stereotype, that I'm saying the province of intelligence and rationality belongs to the white male. But that is like—if you're traveling a road that begins nowhere and ends nowhere, the ownership of that road is meaningless. If you have no land out of which the road comes, no place that road goes to, geographically, no goal, then the existence of that road is totally meaningless. So leaving rationality to the white man is like leaving to him a piece of that road that begins nowhere and ends nowhere. When I talk about the black mothers in each of us, the poets, I don't mean the black mothers in each of us who are called poets, I mean the black mother—

AR: Who *is* the poet?
AL: The black mother who is the poet in every one of us. Now when males, or patriarchal thinking whether it's male or female, reject that combination then we're truncated. Rationality is not unnecessary. It serves the chaos of knowledge. It serves feeling. It serves to get from some place to some place. If you don't honor those places then the road is meaningless. Too often, that's what happens with intellect and rationality and that circular, academic, analytic thinking. But ultimately, I don't see feel/think as a dichotomy. I see them as a choice of ways and combinations.

AR: Which we are constantly making. We don't make it once and for all. We constantly have to be making it, depending on where we are, over and over.
AL: But I do think that we have been taught to think, to codify information in certain old ways, to learn, to understand in certain ways. The possible shapes of what has not been before exist only in that back place, where we keep those unnamed, untamed longings for something different and beyond what is now called possible, to which our analysis and our understanding can only build roads. But we have been taught to deny those fruitful areas of ourselves which exist in every human being. I personally believe that those black mothers exist more in women; yet that is the name for a humanity that men are not without. But they have taken a position against that piece of themselves, and it is a world position, a position throughout time. And I've said this to you before, Adrienne, I feel that we're evolving. In terms of a species—

AR: That women are evolving—
AL: Yes, that the human race is evolving through women. That it's not by accident that there are more and more women, the—this sounds crazy, doesn't it—the production of women, women being born, women surviving. . . . And we've got to take that promise of new power seriously, or we'll make the same mistakes all over again. Unless we learn the lessons of the black mothers

in each of us, whether we are black or not—I believe this exists in men also but they choose to eschew it, not to deal with it. Which is, as I learned, their right of choice. Hopefully this choice can be affected, but I don't know. I don't believe this shift from conquering problems to experiencing life is a one-generational shot or a single investment. I believe it's a whole signature which you try to set in motion and have some input into. But I'm not saying that women don't think or analyze. Or that white does not feel. I'm saying that we must amalgamate the two, never close our eyes to the terror, the chaos which is black which is creative which is female which is dark which is rejected which is messy which is—

AR: Sinister—
AL: Sinister, smelly, erotic, confused, upsetting—

AR: I think we have to keep using and affirming a vocabulary that has been used negatively and pejoratively. And I assume that's the statement you're making in that sentence, that you make over and over in your poetry. And it's nothing as simplistic as saying "black is beautiful," either.
AL: There's nothing beautiful about a black machine. You know, Adrienne, when I was in high school, I was trying to get a poem about love published in the school magazine. The editor of the magazine was named Reneé—she was very intelligent, very grown-up, very beautiful. And Renée said to me, softening her rejection of my poem, "After all, Audre, you don't want to be a sensualist poet." That, obviously, was something you're not supposed to be.

AR: I was told, as a poet, you're not supposed to be angry, you're not supposed to be personal.
AL: After I published "Uses of the Erotic," a number of women who read it said that this is antifeminist, that the use of the erotic as a guide is—

AR: Antifeminist?
AL: Is reducing us once again to the unseen, the unusable. That in writing it I am returning us to a place of total intuition without insight.

AR: And yet, in that essay you're talking about work and power—about two of the most political things that exist.
AL: Yes, but what they see is—and I address this at the very beginning: I try to say that the erotic has been used against us, even the word itself, so often, that

we have been taught to suspect what is deepest in ourselves, and that is the way we learn to testify against ourselves, against our feelings. When we talk about racism or nationalism we can see it. When we're talking in terms of our lives and survival as women, we don't. The way you get people to testify against themselves is not constantly to have police tactics and oppressive techniques. What you do is to build it in, so people learn to distrust everything in themselves that has not been sanctioned, to reject what is most creative in themselves—to have *them* reject it to begin with, so you don't even need to stamp it out. A black woman devaluating another black woman's work. The black women buying that hot comb and putting it in my locker at the library. It wasn't even black men, it was black women testifying against ourselves.

I have never forgotten the impatience in your voice that time on the telephone—when you said, "It's not enough to say to me that you intuit it." Do you remember? I will never forget that. Even at the same time that I understood what you meant, I felt a total wipeout of my modus, my way of perceiving and formulating.

AR: Yes, but it's not a wipeout of your modus. Because I don't think my modus is unintuitive, right? And one of the crosses I've borne all my life is being told that I'm rational, logical, cool—I am not cool, and I'm not rational and logical in that icy sense. But there's a way in which, trying to translate from your experience to mine, I do need to hear chapter and verse from time to time. I'm afraid of it all slipping away into: "Ah, yes, I understand you." You remember, that telephone conversation was in connection with the essay I was writing on feminism and racism. I was trying to say to you, don't let's let this evolve into "You don't understand me" or "I can't understand you" or "Yes, of course we understand each other because we love each other." That's bullshit. So if I ask for documentation, it's because I take seriously the spaces between us that difference has created, that racism has created. There are times when I simply cannot assume that I know what you know, unless you show me what you mean.
AL: But I'm used to associating a *request* for documentation as a questioning of my perceptions, an attempt to devalue what I'm in the process of discovering.

AR: It's not. Help me to perceive what you perceive. That's what I'm trying to say to you.
AL: But documentation does not help one perceive, at best it only analyzes the perception. At worst, it provides a screen by which to avoid concentrating

on the core revelation, following it down to how it feels. Again, knowledge and understanding. They can function in concert, but they don't replace each other. But I'm not rejecting your need for documentation.

AR: And in fact, I feel you've been giving it to me, in your poems always, and most recently in the long prose piece you've been writing, and in talks we've been having. I don't feel the absence of it now.

AL: Don't forget I'm a librarian. I became a librarian because I really believed I would gain tools for ordering and analyzing information. I couldn't know everything in the world, but I thought I would gain tools for learning it. But that was of limited value. I can document the road to Abomey for you, and true, you might not get there without that information. I can respect what you're saying. But once you get there, only you know why, what you came for, as you search for it and perhaps find it.

So at certain stages that request for documentation is a blinder, a questioning of my perceptions. Someone once said to me that I hadn't documented the goddess in Africa, the woman bond that moves throughout *The Black Unicorn*. I had to laugh. I told her, "I'm a poet, not a historian. I've shared my knowledge, I hope. Now you go document it, if you wish."

I don't know about you, Adrienne, but I have a difficult enough time making my perceptions verbal, tapping that deep place, forming that handle, and documentation at that point is often useless. Perceptions precede analysis just as visions precede action or accomplishments. It's like getting a poem—

That's the only thing I have to fight with, my whole life, preserving my perceptions of how things are, and later, learning to accept and correct both at the same time, and doing this in the face of tremendous opposition and cruel judgment. And I spent a long period of time questioning my perceptions and my first interior knowledge, not dealing with them, being tripped by them.

AR: Well, I think that there's another element in all this between us. Certainly in that particular conversation on the telephone where I said, you have to tell me chapter and verse. I've had great resistance to some of your perceptions. They can be very painful to me. Perceptions about what goes on between us, what goes on between black and white people, what goes on between black and white women. So, it's not that I can just accept your perceptions unblinkingly.

Some of them are very hard for me. But I don't want to deny them. I know I
can't afford to. I may have to take a long hard look and say, Is this something
I can use? What do I do with this?—try to stand back and not become
immersed in what you so forcefully are pronouncing. So there's a piece of me
that wants to resist wholly, and a piece that wants to accept wholly, and there's
some place in between where I have to find my own ground. What I can't
afford is either to wipe out your perceptions, or to pretend I understand you
when I don't. And then, if it's a question of racism—and I don't mean just the
overt violence out there but also all the differences in our ways of seeing—
there's always the question: How do I use this? What do I do about it?

AL: [quotes from her poem "Need"] What holds us all back is being unable
to ask that crucial question, that essential step deflected. You know the piece
I wrote for *The Black Scholar*? The piece was useful, but limitedly so because
I didn't ask some essential question. And not having asked myself that question, not having realized that it *was* a question, I was deflecting a lot of energy
in that piece. I kept reading it over, thinking, this isn't quite what it should be.
I thought at the time I was holding back because it would be totally unacceptable in *The Black Scholar*. That wasn't it really. I was holding back because
I had not asked *myself* the question: Why is women loving women so threatening to black men, unless they want to assume the white male position? It
was a question of how much I could bear, and of not realizing I could bear
more than I thought I could at the time. It was also a question of how could
I use that perception other than just in rage or destruction.

AR: Speaking of rage and destruction, what do you really mean by the first
five lines of "Power"?

AL: [quotes the poem] What was I feeling? I was very involved in a case—

AR: The white policeman who shot the black child and was acquitted. We had
lunch around the time you were writing that poem and you were full of it.

AL: I was driving in the car, and heard the news on the radio—that the cop had
been acquitted. I was really sickening with fury, and I decided to pull over and
just jot some things down in my notebook to enable me to cross town without
an accident, to continue functioning because I felt so sick and so enraged. And
I wrote those lines down—I was just writing, and that poem came out without
craft, that's probably why I was talking to you about it, because I didn't feel it
was really a poem. I was thinking that the killer had been a student at John Jay

and that I might have seen him in the hall, that I might see him again. What was retribution? What could have been done? There was one black woman on the jury. It could have been me. Now I am here teaching in John Jay College. Do I kill him? What is my effective role? Would I kill her in the same way—the black woman on the jury. What kind of strength did she, would I, have at the point of deciding to take a position—

AR: Against eleven white men . . .
AL: . . . That archaic fear of the total reality of a power that is not on your terms. There is the jury, white male power, white male structures, how do you take a position against them? How do you reach down into threatening difference without being killed or killing? How do you deal with things you believe, live them not as theory, not even as emotion, but right on the line of action and effect and change? All of those things were riding in on that poem. But I had no sense, no understanding at the time, of the connections, just that I *was* that woman. And that to put myself on the line to do what had to be done at any place and time was so difficult, yet absolutely crucial, and not to do so was the most awful death. And putting yourself on the line is like killing a piece of yourself, in the sense that you have to kill, end, destroy something familiar and dependable, so that something new can come, in ourselves, in our world. And that sense of writing at the edge, out of urgency, not because you choose it but because you have to, that sense of survival— that's what the poem is out of, as well as the pain of my son's death over and over. Once you live any piece of your vision it opens you to a constant onslaught. Of necessities, of horrors, but of wonders too, of possibilities.

AR: I was going to say, tell it on the other side.
AL: Of wonders, absolute wonders, possibilities, like meteor showers all the time, bombardment, constant connections. And then, trying to separate what is useful for survival from what is distorted, destructive to self.

AR: There's so much with which that has to be done—rejecting the distortions, keeping what we can use. Even in work created by people we admire intensely.
AL: Yes, a commitment to being selectively open. I had to do that with my physical survival. How am I going to live with cancer and not succumb to it in the many ways that I could? What do I have to do? And coming up against:

There's no one to tell you even possibilities. In the hospital I kept thinking, let's see, there's got to be someone somewhere, a black lesbian feminist with cancer, how'd she handle it? Then I realized, hey, honey, you are *it*, for now. I read all of those books and then I realized, no one can tell me how to do it. I have to pick and choose, see what feels right. Determination, poetry—well that's all in the work.

AR: I'm thinking about when you had just had the first biopsy, in 1977, and we were both supposed to speak on a panel in Chicago. On "The Transformation of Silence into Language and Action." And you said there was no way you were going to the MLA—remember? That you couldn't do it, you didn't need to do it, that doing it could not mean anything important to you. But in fact you went out there and said what you said, and it was for yourself but not only for yourself.

AL: You said, why don't you tell them about what you've just been through? That's what you said. And I started saying, now that doesn't have anything to do with the panel. And as I said that I felt the words "silence." "Transformation." I hadn't spoken about this experience. . . . This is silence. . . . Can I transform this? Is there any connection? Most of all, how do I share it? And that's how a setting down became clear on paper, as if the connections became clear in the setting down. That paper and "A Litany for Survival" came about at the same time. I had the feeling, probably a body sense, that life was never going to be the same. If not now, eventually, this was something I would have to face, if not cancer, then somehow, I would have to examine the terms and means as well as the whys of my survival—and in the face of alteration. So much of the work I did, I did before I knew consciously that I had cancer. Questions of death and dying, dealing with power and strength, the sense of "What am I paying for?" that I wrote about in that paper, were crucial to me a year later. "Uses of the Erotic" was written four weeks before I found out I had breast cancer, in 1978.

AR: Again, it's like what you were saying before, about making the poems that didn't exist, that you needed to have exist.

AL: The existence of that paper enabled me to pick up and go to Houston and California, it enabled me to start working again. I don't know when I'd have been able to write again, if I hadn't had those words. Do you realize, we've come full circle, because that is where knowing and understanding mesh. What understanding begins to do is to make knowledge available for use, and that's the urgency, that's the push, that's the drive. I don't know how I wrote the long prose piece I have just finished, but I just knew that I had to do it.

AR: That you had to understand what you knew and also make it available to others?

AL: That's right. Inseparable process now. But for me, I had to know I knew it first—I had to feel.

My Words Will Be There

Mari Evans / 1979

From Mari Evans, *Black Women Writers (1950–1980): A Critical Evaluation* (Garden City: Anchor Press/Doubleday, 1984), 261–68. The interview was conducted by questionnaire in 1979 or early 1980. Copyright © 1983 by Mari Evans. Used by permission of Doubleday, a division of Random House, Inc.

I looked around when I was a young woman and there was no one saying what I wanted and needed to hear. I felt totally alienated, disoriented, crazy. I thought that there's got to be somebody else who feels as I do.

I was very inarticulate as a youngster. I couldn't speak. I didn't speak until I was five, in fact, not really, until I started reading and writing poetry. I used to speak in poetry. I would read poems, and I would memorize them. People would say, well what do you think, Audre. What happened to you yesterday? And I would recite a poem and somewhere in that poem there would be a line or a feeling I would be sharing. In other words, I literally communicated through poetry. And when I couldn't find the poems to express the things I was feeling, that's what started me writing poetry, and that was when I was twelve or thirteen.

My critics have always wanted to cast me in a particular role, from the time my first poem was published when I was fifteen years old. My English teachers at Hunter High School said that this particular poem was much too romantic (it was a love poem about my first love affair with a boy), and they didn't want to print it in the school paper, which is why I sent it to *Seventeen* magazine, and, of course, *Seventeen* printed it.

My critics have always wanted to cast me in a particular light. People do. It's easier to deal with a poet, certainly with a Black woman poet, when you categorize her, narrow her so that she can fulfill your expectations. But I have always felt that I cannot be categorized. That has been both my weakness and my strength. It has been my weakness because my independence has cost me a lot of support. But you see, it has also been my strength because it has given me the power to go on. I don't know how I would have lived through the different things I have survived and continued to produce if I had not felt that all of who I am is what fulfills me and what fulfills the vision I have of a world.

I've only had one writer-in-residence position, and that was at Tougaloo College in Mississippi eleven years ago. It was pivotal for me. Pivotal, because in 1968 my first book had just been published; it was my first trip into the deep South; it was the first time I had been away from the children. It was the first time I dealt with young Black students in a workshop situation. I came to realize that this was my work, that teaching and writing were inextricably combined, and it was there that I knew what I wanted to do for the rest of my life.

I had been "the librarian who wrote." After my experience at Tougaloo, I realized that my writing was central to my life and that the library, although I loved books, was not enough. Combined with the circumstances that followed my stay at Tougaloo—King's death, Kennedy's death, Martha's accident—all of these things really made me see that life is very short, and what we have to do must be done in the now.

I have never had another writing-in-residence position. The poem "Touring" from *The Black Unicorn* represents very much how I feel about that. I go to read my poetry occasionally. I drop my little seeds, and then I leave. I hope they spring into something. Sometimes I find out they do; sometimes I never find out. I just have to have faith.

Primarily, I write for those women who do not speak; who do not have verbalization because they, we, are so terrified, because we are taught to respect fear more than ourselves. We've been taught to respect our fears, but we *must* learn to respect ourselves and our needs.

In the forties and fifties my life-style and the rumors about my lesbianism, made me persona non grata in Black literary circles.

I feel not to be open about who I am in all respects places a certain kind of expectation on me I'm just not into meeting anymore. I hope that as many people as possible can deal with my work and with who I am, that they will find something in my work which can be of use to them in their lives. But if they do not, cannot, then we are all the losers. But then, perhaps their children will. But for myself, it has been very necessary and very generative for me to deal with all the aspects of who I am, and I've been saying this for a long time. I am not one piece of myself. I cannot be simply a Black person and not be a woman too, nor can I be a woman without being a lesbian. . . . Of course, there'll always be people, and there have always been people in my life, who will come to me and say, "Well, here, define yourself as such and such," to the exclusion of the other pieces of myself. There is an injustice to self in doing this; it is an injustice to the women for whom I write. In fact, it is an injustice to everyone. What happens when you narrow your definition to what is convenient, or what is fashionable, or what is expected, is dishonesty by silence.

Now, when you have a literary community oppressed by silence from the outside, as Black writers are in America, and you have this kind of tacit insistence upon some unilateral definition of what "Blackness" is or requires, then you are painfully and effectively silencing some of our most dynamic and creative talent, for all change and progress from within comes about from the recognition and use of difference between ourselves.

I consider myself to have been a victim of this silencing in the Black literary community for years, and I am certainly not the only one. For instance, there is no question about the *quality* of my work at this point. Then why do you think my last book, *The Black Unicorn,* has not been reviewed, nor even mentioned, in any Black newspaper or Black magazine within the thirteen months since it appeared?

I feel I have a duty to speak the truth as I see it and to share not just my triumphs, not just the things that felt good, but the pain, the intense, often unmitigating pain.

I never thought I would live to be forty and I'm forty-five! I feel like hey, I really did it! I am very pleased about really confronting the whole issue of breast cancer, of mortality, of dying. It was hard but very strengthening to remember that I could be silent my whole life long and then be dead, flat out, and never have said or done what I wanted to do, what I needed to do, because of pain, fear. . . . If I waited to be right before I spoke, I would be sending little cryptic messages on the Ouija board, complaints from the other side.

I really feel if what I have to say is wrong, then there will be some woman who will stand up and say Audre Lorde was in error. But my words will be there, something for her to bounce off, something to incite thought, activity.

Black male writers tend to cry out in rage as a means of convincing their readers that they too feel, whereas Black women writers tend to dramatize the pain, the love. They don't seem to need to intellectualize this capacity to feel; they focus on describing the feeling itself. And love often is pain. But I think what is really necessary is to see how much of this pain I can feel, how much of this truth I can see and still live unblinded. And finally, it is necessary to determine how much of this pain I can use. That is the essential question that we must all ask ourselves. There is some point where pain becomes an end in itself, and then we must let it go. On the one hand, we must not be afraid of pain, but on the other we must not subject ourselves to pain as an end in itself. We must not celebrate victimization, because there are other ways of being Black.

There is a very thin but very definite line between these two responses to pain. And I would like to see this line more carefully drawn in some of the works by Black women writers. I am particularly aware of the two responses in my own work. And I find I must remember that the pain is not its own reason for being. It is a part of living. And the only kind of pain that is intolerable is pain that is wasteful, pain from which we do not learn. And I think that we must learn to distinguish between the two.

I see protest as a genuine means of encouraging someone to feel the inconsistencies, the horror, of the lives we are living. Social protest is to say that we do not have to live this way. If we feel deeply, as we encourage ourselves and others to feel deeply, we will, within that feeling, once we recognize we can feel deeply, we can love deeply, we can feel joy, then we will demand that all parts of our lives produce that kind of joy. And when they do not, we will ask "Why don't they?" And it is the asking that will lead us inevitably toward change.

So the question of social protest and art is inseparable for me. I can't say it is an either/or proposition. Art for art's sake doesn't really exist for me, but then it never did. What I saw was wrong, and I had to speak up. I loved poetry and I loved words. But what was beautiful had to serve the purpose of changing my life, or I would have died. If I cannot air this pain and alter it, I will surely die of it. That's the beginning of social protest.

So much for pain; what about love? When you've been writing love poems for thirty years, those later poems are the ones that really hit the "nitty-gritty," that walk your boundaries. They witness what you've been through. Those are the real love poems. And I love those later love poems because they say, Hey! We define ourselves as lovers, as people who love each other all over again; we become new again. These poems insist that you can't separate loving from fighting, from dying, from hurting, but love is triumphant. It is powerful and strong, and I feel I grow a great deal in all of my emotions, especially in the capacity to love.

The love expressed between women is particular and powerful, because we have had to love in order to live; love has been our survival.

We're supposed to see "universal love" as heterosexual. And what I insist upon in my work is that there is no such thing as universal love in literature. There is this love, in this poem. The poem happened when I, Audre Lorde, poet, dealt with the particular instead of the "U N I V E R S A L." My power as a person, as a poet, comes from who I am. I am a particular person. The relationships I have had, where people kept me alive, helped sustain me, people whom I've sustained give me my particular identity which is the source of my energy. Not to deal with my life in my art is to cut out the fount of my strength.

I love to write love poems; I love loving. And to put it into another framework, that is other than poetry, I wrote a paper, entitled "The Uses of the Erotic," where I examine the whole question of loving, as a manifestation. Love is very important because it is a source of tremendous power.

Women have not been taught to respect the erotic urge, the place that is uniquely female. So, just as some Black people tend to reject Blackness because it has been termed inferior, we, as women, tend to reject our capacity for feeling, our ability to love, to touch the erotic, because it has been devalued. But it is within this that lies so much of our power, our ability to posit, to vision. Because once we know how deeply we can feel, we begin to demand from all of our life pursuits that they be in accordance with these feelings. And when they don't, we must perforce raise the question why . . . why . . . why do I feel constantly suicidal, for instance? What's wrong? Is it me? Or is it what I am doing? And we begin to need to answer such questions. But we cannot do this when we have no vision of joy, when we have no vision of what we are capable of. When you live always in darkness, when you live without the sunlight, you don't know what it is to relish the bright light or even to have too much of it. Once you have light, then you can measure its degree. So too with joy.

I keep a journal; I write in my journal fairly regularly. I get a lot of my poems out of it. It is the raw material for my poems. Sometimes I'm blessed with a poem that comes in the form of a poem, but sometimes I work for two years on a poem.

For me, there are two very basic and different processes for revising my poetry. One is recognizing that a poem has not yet become itself. In other words, I mean that the feeling, the truth that the poem is anchored in is somehow not clearly clarified inside of me, and as a result the poem lacks something. Then the poem has to be refelt. Then there's the other process, which is easier. The poem is itself, but it has rough edges that need to be refined. That kind of revision involves picking the image that is more potent or tailoring it so that it carries the feeling. That's an easier kind of rewriting than refeeling.

My journal entries focus on things I feel. Feelings that sometimes have no place, no beginning, no end. Phrases I hear in passing. Something that looks good to me, delights me. Sometimes just observations of the world.

I went through a period when I felt like I was dying. It was during 1975. I wasn't writing any poetry, and I felt that if I couldn't write it, I would split. I was recording things in my journal, but no poems came. I know now that this period was a transition in my life and I wasn't dealing with it.

Later the next year, I went back to my journal, and there were these incredible poems that I could almost lift out of the journal; many of them are in *The Black Unicorn.* "Harriet" is one of them; "Sequelae" is another. "The Litany for Survival" is another. These poems were right out of the journal. But I didn't see them as poems prior to that.

"Power" was in the journal too. It is a poem written about Clifford Glover, the ten-year-old Black child shot by a cop who was acquitted by a jury on which a Black woman sat. In fact, the day I heard on the radio that O'Shea had been acquitted, I was going across town on Eighty-eighth Street and I had to pull over. A kind of fury rose up in me; the sky turned red. I felt so sick. I felt as if I would drive this car into a wall, into the next person I saw. So I pulled over. I took out my journal just to air some of my fury, to get it out of my fingertips. Those expressed feelings are that poem. That was just how "Power" was written. There is an incredible gap occurring between the journal and my poetry, however; I write this stuff in my journals, and sometimes I can't even read my journals because there is so much pain, rage, in them. I'll put them away in a drawer, and six months, a year or so later, I'll pick up the journal, and there will be poems. The journal entries somehow have to be assimilated into my living, and only then can I deal with what I have written down.

Art is not living. It is a use of living. The artist has the ability to take that living and use it in a certain way, and produce art.

Afro-American literature is certainly part of an African tradition that deals with life as an experience to be lived. In many respects, it is much like the Eastern philosophies in that we see ourselves as a part of a life force; we are joined, for instance, to the air, to the earth. We are part of the whole life process. We live in accordance with, in a kind of correspondence with, the rest of the world as a whole. And therefore, living becomes an experience, rather than a problem, no matter how bad or how painful it may be. Change will rise endemically from the experience fully lived and responded to.

I feel this very much in African writing. And as a consequence, I have learned a great deal from Achebe, Tutuola, Ekwensi, from Flora Nwapa and Ama Ata Aidoo. Leslie Lacy, a Black American who resides temporarily in Ghana, writes about experiencing this transcendence in his book *The Rise and Fall of a Proper Negro.* It's not a turning away from pain, from error, but seeing these things as part of living and learning from them. This characteristic is particularly African and it is transposed into the best of Afro-American literature.

This transcendence appears in Ellison, a little bit in Baldwin, not as much as I would like. And very, very, much so in Toni Morrison's *Sula,* which is the *most wonderful* piece of fiction I have recently read. And I don't care if she won a prize for *The Song of Solomon. Sula* is a totally incredible book. It made me light up inside like a Christmas tree. I particularly identified with the book because of the outsider idea. Toni laid that book to rest. Laid it to rest. That book is like one long poem. Sula is the ultimate Black female of our time, trapped in her power and her pain.

It's important that we share experiences and insights. *The Cancer Journals* is very important to me. It is a three-part prose monologue. It comes out of my experiences with my mastectomy and the aftermath: the rage, the terror, the fear, and the power that comes with dealing with my mortality. And since so little is being written about mastectomies, except the statistics, how do you do it, or do you pretend that it didn't happen? I thought we needed a new feminist outlook for Black women on the whole process. And that is the origin of *The Cancer Journals.*

Recent writing by many Black women seems to explore human concerns somewhat differently than do the men. These women refuse to blame racism entirely for every negative aspect of Black life. In fact, at times they hold Black men accountable. The men tend to respond defensively by labeling these women writers the darlings of the literary establishment.

It is not the destiny of Black America to repeat white America's mistakes. But we will, if we mistake the trappings of success in a sick society for the signs of a meaningful life. If Black men continue to do so, while defining "femininity" in its archaic European terms, this augurs ill for our survival as a people, let alone our survival as individuals. Freedom and future for Blacks does not mean absorbing the dominant white male disease.

As Black people, we cannot begin our dialogue by denying the oppressive nature of *male privilege.* And if Black males choose to assume that privilege, for whatever reason, raping, brutalizing, and killing women, then we cannot ignore Black male oppression. One oppression does not justify another.

As a people, we should most certainly work together to end our common oppression, and toward a future which is viable for us all. In that context, it is shortsighted to believe that Black men alone are to blame for the above situations, in a society dominated by white male privilege. But the Black male consciousness must be raised so that he realizes that sexism and woman-hating are critically dysfunctional to his liberation as a Black man because they arise out of the same constellation that engenders racism and homophobia, a constellation of intolerance for difference. Until this is done, he will view sexism and the destruction of Black women only as tangential to the cause of Black liberation rather than as central to that struggle, and as long as this occurs, we will never be able to embark upon that dialogue between Black women and Black men that is so essential to our survival as a people. And this continued blindness between us can only serve the oppressive system within which we live.

I write for myself. I write for myself and my children and for as many people as possible who can read me. When I say myself, I mean not only the Audre who inhabits my body but all those *feisty, incorrigible, beautiful Black women* who insist on standing up and saying *I am* and you can't wipe me out, no matter how irritating I am.

I feel a responsibility for myself, for those people who can now read and feel and need what I have to say, and for women and men who come after me. But primarily I think of my responsibility in terms of women because there are many voices for men. There are very few voices for women and particularly very few voices for Black women, speaking from the center of consciousness, for the *I am* out to the *we are.*

What can I share with the younger generation of Black women writers, writers in general? What can they learn from my experience? I can tell them not to be afraid to feel and not to be afraid to write about it. Even if you are afraid, do it anyway. We learn to work when we are tired; so we can learn to work when we are afraid.

Interview: Audre Lorde
Advocates Unity among Women
Shelley Savren and Cheryl Robinson / 1982

From *The Longest Revolution* 6.5 (San Diego), June 1982, 1 and 8.

Shelley Savren: Audre, we're very excited to hear that you are a co-founder of Kitchen Table, Woman of Color Press. Can you tell us what your goals are for this endeavor?

Audre Lorde: Woman of Color Press is committed to producing and distributing the work of Third World women of all racial and cultural heritages, sexual preferences and classes. Traditionally, as women of color, we have never had control over institutions, or over the production of our own work.

In one sense, we feel that this is both the best time and the worst time to begin. But I think that we can do it. I am very excited about the project and really very pleased to be part of the organizing collective.

We are learning a lot of things about ourselves and about working together as women of color, recognizing that we bring different perspectives on feminism from our separate communities.

What we really want to be is a voice for women of color whose voices have been lost; for women whose voices are not honored or recognized by trade publications or, in many respects, by the small press field. Somehow women of color seem to always fall between the slots. So we decided to take the matter into our own hands.

SS: Sounds like important work. You said that this is both the best and the worst time to begin. What do you mean by that?

AL: Well, I don't know how easy the living is down here in San Diego, but I know it's very, very hard on the East coast. It's not a joking matter. I think we need to recognize that individually we are an endangered species and that collectively we are under extreme pressure. The backlash we spoke about almost theoretically in the late '60s and early '70s has become real and has given rise to Ronald Reagan and to the Moral Majority. What the Family Protection Act is threatening to impose upon this country could actually happen.

Personally, I think what we're seeing is the result of not following through on important issues. Take, for instance, the women's community. Our inability to deal with very real issues of homophobia, racism, and ageism has in many respects led to the kinds of fractures which weaken our ability to resist.

When I say this is the worst time, it's because socially we are reaping the results of that backlash. We've gotta back down from the idea that we can only afford to speak of freedom, speak of liberation, when we are in a comfortable position. Just the opposite is true. Now more than ever is the time to form general coalitions.

I am very excited, though, as I travel from place to place around this country, to see the kinds of grassroots work that is coming together. It is in this respect that I think it is the best of times. This is the way that change will happen.

SS: Audre, as an accomplished poet, what elements do you consider essential to creating strong poetry?

AL: I think there are two things that are most important. First is a genuine commitment to living and to feeling. It is not easy. Everything in our lives works against our dealing with our feelings in a creative and constructive way. The same tendency works against our dealing with our differences.

The second thing that I think is important for creating strong poetry is being committed to breaking the silences—not simply speaking of things that have already been said in a more elegant fashion, but speaking of the contradictions in our lives with a language that can fire us. In other words, looking at these contradictions in new ways, since the old ways have not served.

On the other hand, there are no new ideas under the sun, so we need to re-feel those things that we believe in. We need to re-feel them in some way as to make sense out of our living, and to share this with others. We also need to examine the dialectic that operates between our differences—to ask, where do we want to go? The differences I'm talking about are those between people who share a common goal. I'm not interested in exploring the differences between me and Ronald Reagan; but I am interested in exploring the differences between me and you.

Cheryl Robinson: Audre, what subjects do you feel are particularly important to address in your work now?

Audre Lorde: Well, the subjects that I deal with in my work are the subjects that I deal with in my life. I'm very involved, on a personal level, with the question of loss: how do we deal with it in a way that it doesn't destroy us? What does it mean, for example, when our children leave? How do we love them and let them go? I think that's something we don't talk about enough, as women with children. And, as a lesbian, I certainly think that lesbians have not dealt openly enough with the fact of even having had children.

I also think we need to look at the different kinds of oppression present in the women's community, specifically the ways in which anti-semitism and racism overlap and do not overlap. But this is against a larger grid, Cheryl, because I'm interested in survival: in your survival, in my survival, in the survival of our children, in the survival of this earth. I see nothing as really very separate from that.

So over and over again, these are questions that are coming up. But I think the primary issue that is splitting up communities of women (I say "communities" because I don't think there is simply one "women's community") is again this silence—the fact that we do not speak of real angers, of real problems between us. We go along, business as usual. Whereas if we could deal with and learn from our differences, they couldn't be used against us. As it is, they are very effectively used against us.

I think the same thing happens within the black community. The fracture between Black men and women, for instance, seems to be getting worse—not because in fact it is, but because it is being used as a divisive technique. Homophobia within the black community is another oppressive point, and there's a great deal of pain involved because whenever you share a common oppression and then take a position on something that is different, then you have this backlog of defensiveness. It's very painful.

But I think that what is necessary, as a Movement, is to build coalitions between the disparate groups within our sphere, and then between our communities and other communities.

CR: Here's a question that I want to ask you, partly because it's been a big problem to me and I'd like to know how you have handled it. Being black, a lesbian, and a feminist puts you in a position where you have to deal with what, at times, appear to be three mutually exclusive ideologies or priorities. How do you manage to integrate them all . . . or do you?
AL: Well, Cheryl, as I'm sure you know, it has felt, at different points in my life, like every single way in which I would identify myself was in total conflict with every other way. First of all, there's always going to be some group or

some person who wants you to talk from only one particular perspective. That's very destructive. It's like putting all the eggs in one basket. It also reduces you to one component, and it's just such a terrible injustice to all the other pieces of yourself. It cuts me off from the energy that comes from all those different pieces. So integration is absolutely necessary. *I* have to work on integration for myself. *You* have to do it for yourself. What I've learned, and this was indeed a learning process, is that it is absolutely essential not to allow pieces of myself to be at war with each other.

I have a vision of the kind of future I want, of the kind of person I want to be, of the way I wish to live my life. Whether I am living this vision as a teacher, whether I'm doing it as a mother, whether I'm doing it as a poet, whether I'm doing it as a ditch-digger—I have a manner within that helps guide me as to how. And in that way all the parts of me begin to come together.

But as long as you let yourself be baffled, as long as you let one piece of yourself be cancelled out by another, you will always be subject to the kind of turmoil that sucks energy away. It's hard, it's very hard. But it's not harder than the way they want us to live, which is in categories. And, it's far more productive.

SS: Can you talk about your experiences raising children in an openly lesbian household, especially the experience of having a male child?

AL: I wrote about that experience in *Conditions IV*, the experience of raising a male child in an interracial lesbian household. That was three years ago. I'm still pleased with the things I said, because I think they're true, and they become more and more true as I see my son growing. The things I want for my son are the same things I want for my daughter: that they should both learn that they must be warriors—because they are Black in the mouth of a dragon which defines them as nothing; that oppression comes in all shapes, sizes, colors, and classes; that to fight oppression on every level is part of their survival, is part of who they are; and that the only way they can really fight is by being grounded very firmly in who each of them is. They must value themselves, all their different parts, above all. I think the children of lesbian parents are the hope of this earth. Now, of course, that may sound grandiose, but I think that in actual fact it is true.

SS: Have you had to face situations within the women's community where at times your son was excluded from events because he was a boy?

AL: Yes; I have. It must have been the summer that Jonathan was eleven. "Maidenrock" in Minnesota asked Frances and me to come and take part in a feminist thinktank, a visionary group whose purpose was to explore the future. And one of their requirements was no boy children over ten. I was very upset by this. We wrote back trying to explain we couldn't go to Minnesota to participate in planning a future in which we could all live, while abandoning our eleven-year-old son to childcare in New York.

If we give birth to boy children, then we have made a commitment to a world that includes them. If that world is to include them, then we need to ask: What are the kinds of men with whom we want our daughters to occupy the world? It is just as simple as that, because there are always going to be men with women, as well as men with men, and women with women. So who do we want those men to be? We've got to deal with this: it's a simple fact. Otherwise we are being very, very shortsighted.

I get upset at the lack of concern for our young people, lesbian or straight. Any people, any nation, any movement, any group that does not attend to its own propagation, that does not attend to the future, is participating in its own death.

SS: That's right. If we raise our children in our heritage, then they will pass that heritage on.

CR: Audre, you've been a real model to many women in the way you've dealt with having had a mastectomy. Can you talk a little about your experience?

AL: Unfortunately, many of the feelings that can accompany the loss of a breast are simply a measurement of the control that this whole society has over women. We're supposed to be decorations, right?

Any amputation is going to be difficult. Having a life threatening disease, such as cancer, is a very, very difficult experience. But it's not one that necessarily means your life is over. For women with breast cancer, the situation is particularly tough because it reveals how little value we place on the totality of our beings. This is why I think that wearing a false breast is such a crippling thing: because it once again attaches a false importance to that one part of our body and to the way you look, no matter what else is going on with your health.

I'm also very skeptical when women come up to me and say, "How do you find the courage?" That's not the point! The point is, if we looked at the genuine conditions of our *lives* day to day, week to week, month to month, historically, we would recognize what courage it takes simply for us to *live*! It is the everyday courage that women exhibit that I am most concerned with.

SS: Well, whether you call it exceptional courage or everyday courage, it certainly is something you have shown in your own life. I think you've been an inspiration to many women and would like to thank you for that *and* for talking with us today.

Audre Lorde

Claudia Tate / 1982

From *Black Women Writers at Work*, ed. Claudia Tate, foreword by Tillie Olson (New York: Continuum, 1983), 100–16. The interview was conducted in 1982. Reprinted by permission of the Claudia Tate Estate.

Born in New York City in 1934 of West Indian parents, Audre Lorde received her B.A. from Hunter College and an M.L.S. from Columbia University. She left her job as head librarian of the City University of New York in 1968 to become a lecturer on creative writing, and later that same year, accepted the post of poet-in-residence at Tougaloo College in Mississippi and published her first book-length collection of poems, entitled *The First Cities.*

Describing herself as a "black lesbian feminist warrior poet," Lorde derives the impetus of her poetry's force, tone, and vision from her identity as a black woman who is both a radical feminist and an outspoken lesbian, and as a visionary of a better world. In stunning figurative language she outlines the progress of her unyielding struggle for the human rights of all people. *The First Cities* was followed in 1970 by *Cables to Rage* and *From a Land Where Other People Live* (1973); *New York Head Shop and Museum* (1974); *Coal* (1976); *Between Our Selves* (1976); *The Black Unicorn* (1978); *The Cancer Journals* (1980); and *Zami: A New Spelling of My Name* (1982).

Audre Lorde is currently professor of English at Hunter College in New York City, as well as a freelance writer. She lives on Staten Island with her companion and her two children.

Claudia Tate: How does your openness about being a black lesbian feminist direct your work and, more importantly, your life?

Audre Lorde: When you narrow your definition to what is convenient, or what is fashionable, or what is expected, what happens is dishonesty by silence. It is putting all of your eggs into one basket. That's not where all of your energy comes from.

Black writers, of whatever quality, who step outside the pale of what black writers are supposed to write about, or who black writers are supposed to be, are condemned to silences in black literary circles that are as total and as destructive as any imposed by racism. This is particularly true for black women writers who have refused to be delineated by male-establishment models of femininity, and who have dealt with their sexuality as an accepted part of their identity. For instance, where are the women writers of the Harlem Renaissance being taught? Why did it take so long for Zora Neale Hurston to be reprinted?

Now, when you have a literary community oppressed by silence from the outside, as black writers are in America, and you have this kind of tacit insistence upon some unilateral definition of what "blackness" is, then you are painfully and effectively silencing some of our most dynamic and creative talents, for all change and progress from within require the recognition of differences among ourselves.

When you are a member of an out-group, and you challenge others with whom you share this outsider position to examine some aspect of their lives that distorts differences between you, then there can be a great deal of pain. In other words, when people of a group share an oppression, there are certain strengths that they build together. But there are also certain vulnerabilities. For instance, talking about racism to the women's movement results in "Huh, don't bother us with that. Look, we're all sisters, please don't rock the boat." Talking to the black community about sexism results in pretty much the same thing. You get a "Wait, wait . . . wait a minute: we're all black together. Don't rock the boat." In our work and in our living, we must recognize that difference is a reason for celebration and growth, rather than a reason for destruction.

We should see difference as a dialogue, the same way we deal with symbol and image, in literary study. "Imaging" is the process of developing a dialectic, a tension between opposites that illuminates the differences and similarities between things in apparent opposition. It is the same way with people. We need to use these differences in constructive ways, creative ways, rather than in ways to justify our destroying each other.

With respect to myself specifically, I feel that not to be open about any of the different "people" within my identity, particularly the "mes" who are challenged by a status quo, is to invite myself and other women, by my example, to live a lie. In other words, I would be giving in to a myth of sameness which I think can destroy us.

I'm not into living lies, no matter how comfortable they may be. I really feel that I'm too old for both abstractions and games, and I will not shut off any of my essential sources of power, control, and knowledge. I learned to speak the truth by accepting many parts of myself and making them serve one another. This power fuels my life and my work.

CT: Has the social climate of the eighties suppressed the openness of the seventies?

AL: To begin with, all of these things are relative, and when we speak of the openness of the seventies, we are speaking more of an appearance than a reality. But as far as sexuality is concerned, it is true that in the seventies, black lesbians and gay men saw a slowly increasing acknowledgment of their presence within the black community. In large part this came about because of the number of us willing to speak out about our sexual identities. In the 1960s, many black people who spoke from a complex black identity suffered because of it, and were silenced in many ways. In the mistaken belief that unity must mean sameness, differences within the black community of color, sex, sexuality, and vision were sometimes mislabeled, oversimplified, and repressed. We must not romanticize the sixties while we recognize its importance. Lesbians and gay men have always existed in black communities, and in the sixties we played active and important roles on many fronts in that decade's struggle for black liberation. And that has been so throughout the history of black people in america, and continues to be so.

In the 1970s some of those differences which have always existed within the black community began to be articulated and examined, as we came to learn that we, as a people, cannot afford to waste our resources, cannot afford to waste each other. The eighties present yet another challenge. On one hand, there is a certain move towards conservatism and greater repression within american society, and renewed attacks upon lesbians and gay men represent only the cutting edge of that greater repression which is so dangerous to us all as black people. But because of this shift to the right, some voices once willing to examine the role of difference in our communities are falling silent, some once vocal people are heading for cover.

It's very distressing to hear someone say, "I can't really afford to say that or I can't afford to be seen with you." It's scary because we've been through that before. It was called the fifties. Yet more and more these days, "all of our asses are in the sling together," if you'll excuse the expression, and real alliances are beginning to be made. When we talk about "Dykes Against Racism Everywhere," and "Black and White Men Together," which are gay groups who have been doing active antiracist work in a number of communities, when we see the coalition of black community organizations in the Boston area that got together to protest the wholesale murder of black women in 1978 and '79, we are talking about real coalitions. We must recognize that we need each other. Both these trends are operating now. Of course, I'm dedicated to believing that it's through coalitions that we'll win out. There are no more single issues.

CT: Have your critics attempted to stereotype your work?
AL: Critics have always wanted to cast me in a particular role from the time my first poem was published when I was fifteen years old. My English teachers at Hunter High School said that a particular poem was much too romantic. It was a love poem about my first love affair with a boy, and they didn't want to print it in the school paper, which is why I sent it to *Seventeen* magazine.

It's easier to deal with a poet, certainly with a black woman poet, when you categorize her, narrow her down so that she can fulfill your expectations, so she's socially acceptable and not too disturbing, not too discordant. I cannot be categorized. That has been both my weakness and my strength. It has been my weakness because my independence has cost me a lot of support. But you see, it has also been my strength because it has given me a vantage point and the power to go on. I don't know how I would have lived through the difficulties I have survived and continued to produce, if I had not felt that all of who I am is what fulfills me and fulfills the vision I have of the world, and of the future.

CT: For whom do you write? What is your responsibility to your audience?
AL: I write for myself and my children and for as many people as possible who can read me, who need to hear what I have to say—who need to use what I know. When I say myself, I mean not only the Audre who inhabits my body but all those feisty, incorrigible black women who insist on standing up and saying "*I am* and you cannot wipe me out, no matter how irritating I am, how much you fear what I might represent." I write for these women for whom a voice has not yet existed, or whose voices have been silenced. I don't have the only voice or all of their voices, but they are a part of my voice, and I am a part of theirs.

My responsibility is to speak the truth as I feel it, and to attempt to speak it with as much precision and beauty as possible. I think of my responsibility in

terms of women because there are many voices for men. There are very few
voices for women and particularly very few voices for black women, speaking
from the center of consciousness, from the *I am* out to the *we are* and then out
to the *we can.*

My mother used to say: "Island women make good wives; whatever happens they've seen worse." Well, I feel that as black women we have been
through all kinds of catastrophe. We've survived, and with style.

I feel I have a duty to speak the truth as I see it and to share not just my
triumphs, not just the things that felt good, but the pain, the intense, often
unmitigating pain. It is important to share how I know survival is survival
and not just a walk through the rain. For example, I have a duty to share what
it feels like at three o'clock in the morning when you know "they" could cut
you down emotionally in the street and grin in your face. And "they" are your
own people. To share what it means to look into another sister's eyes and have
her look away and choose someone you know she hates because it's expedient.
To know that I, at times, have been a coward, or less than myself, or oppressive to other women, and to know that I can change. All of that anxiety, pain,
defeat must be shared. We tend to talk about what feels good. We talk about
what we think is settled. We never seem to talk about the ongoing problems.
We need to share our mistakes in the same way we share our victories because
that's the only way learning occurs. In other words, we have survived the pain,
the problems, the failures, so what we need to do is use this suffering and learn
from it. We must remember and comfort ourselves with that fact that survival
is, in itself, a victory.

I never thought I would live to be forty, and I feel, "Hey, I really did it!"
I am stronger for confronting the hard issue of breast cancer, of mortality,
dying. It is hard, extremely hard, but very strengthening to remember I could
be silent my whole life long and then be dead, flat out, and never have said or
done what I wanted to do, what I needed to do because of pain or fear. . . . If
I wait to be assured I'm right before I speak, I would be sending little cryptic
messages on the Ouiji board, complaints from the other side.

I really feel if what I have to say is wrong, then there will be some woman
who will stand up and say Audre Lorde was in error. But my words will be
there, something for her to bounce off of, something to incite thought, activity.

I write not only for my peers but for those who will come after me, to say I
was there, and I passed on, and you will pass on, too. But you're here now, so
do it. I believe very strongly in survival and teaching. I feel that is my work.

This is so important that it bears repeating. I write for those women who do not speak, for those who do not have a voice because they/we were so terrified, because we are taught to respect fear more than ourselves. We've been taught that silence would save us, but it won't. We *must* learn to respect ourselves and our needs more than the fear of our differences, and we must learn to share ourselves with each other.

CT: Is writing a way of growing, understanding?
AL: Yes. I think writing and teaching, child-rearing, digging rocks (which is one of my favorite pastimes), all of the things I do are very much a part of my work. They flow in and out of each other, help to nourish each other. That's what the whole question of survival and teaching means. That we keep our experience afloat long enough, that we share what we know, so that other people can build upon our experience. There are many ways of doing that in all aspects of our lives. So teaching for me is in many respects identical to writing. Both become ways of exploring what I need for survival. They are survival techniques. Because as I write, as I teach, I am answering those questions that are primary for my own survival, and I am exploring the response to these questions with other people; this is what teaching is. I think that this is the only way that real learning occurs. Learning does not happen in some detached way of dealing with a text alone, but from becoming so involved in the process that you can see how it might illuminate your life, and then how you can share that illumination.

CT: When did you start to write?
AL: I looked around when I was a young woman and there was no one saying what I wanted and needed to hear. I felt totally alienated, disoriented, crazy. I thought that there's got to be somebody else who feels as I do.

I was very inarticulate as a youngster. I couldn't speak. I didn't speak until I was five, in fact, not really until I started reading and writing poetry. I used to speak in poetry. I would read poems, and I would memorize them. People would say, "Well, what do you think, Audre? What happened to you yesterday?" And I would recite a poem and somewhere in that poem there would be a line or a feeling I was sharing. In other words, I literally communicated through poetry. And when I couldn't find the poems to express the things I was feeling, that's when I started writing poetry. That was when I was twelve or thirteen.

CT: Do black male and female writers dramatize characters and themes in distinctly different ways? Gayl Jones replied to this question by saying she thought one distinction has to do with the kinds of events men and women select to depict in literature. She thinks black women writers tend to select particular and personal events rather than those which are generally considered to be representative.

AL: I think that's true. This reflects a difference between men and women in general. Black men have come to believe to their detriment that you have no validity unless you're "global," as opposed to personal. Yet, our *real power* comes from the personal; our real insights about living come from that deep knowledge within us that arises from our feelings. Our thoughts are shaped by our tutoring. As black people, we have not been tutored for our benefit, but more often than not, for our detriment. We were tutored to function in a structure that already existed but that does not function for our good. Our feelings are our most genuine paths to knowledge. They are chaotic, sometimes painful, sometimes contradictory, but they come from deep within us. And we must key into those feelings and begin to extrapolate from them, examine them for new ways of understanding our experiences. This is how new visions begin, how we begin to posit a future nourished by the past. This is what I mean by matter following energy, and energy following feeling. Our visions begin with our desires.

Men have been taught to deal only with what they understand. This is what they respect. They know that somewhere feeling and knowledge are important, so they keep women around to do their feeling for them, like ants do aphids.

I don't think these differences between men and women are rigidly defined with respect to gender, though the Western input has been to divide these differences into male and female *characteristics*. We all have the ability to feel deeply and to move upon our feelings and see where they lead us. Men in general have suppressed that capacity, so they keep women around to do that for them. Until men begin to develop that capacity within themselves, they will always be at a loss and will always need to victimize women.

The message I have for black men is that it is to their detriment to follow this pattern. Too many black men do precisely that, which results in violence along sexual lines. This violence terrifies me. It is a painful truth which is almost unbearable. As I say in a new poem, it is "a pain almost beyond bearing" because it gives birth to the kind of hostility that will destroy us.

CT: To change the focus, though ever so slightly. Writing by black Americans has traditionally dramatized black people's humanity. Black male writers tend to cry out in rage in order to convince their readers that they too feel, whereas black women writers tend to dramatize the pain, the love. They don't seem to need to intellectualize this capacity to feel, but focus on describing the feeling itself.

AL: It's one thing to talk about feeling. It's another to feel. Yes, love is often pain. But I think what is really necessary is to see how much of this pain I can use, how much of this truth I can see and still live unblinded. That is an essential question that we must all ask ourselves. There is some point at which pain becomes an end in itself, and we must let it go. On the other hand, we must not be afraid of pain, and we must not subject ourselves to pain as an end in itself. We must not celebrate victimization because there are other ways of being black.

There is a very thin but a very definite line between these two responses to pain. And I would like to see this line more carefully drawn in some of the works by black women writers. I am particularly aware of the two responses in my own work. And I find I must remember that the pain is not its own reason for being. It is a part of living. And the only kind of pain that is intolerable is pain that is wasteful, pain from which we do not learn. And I think that we must learn to distinguish between the two.

CT: How do you integrate social protest and art in your work?
AL: I see protest as a genuine means of encouraging someone to feel the inconsistencies, the horror of the lives we are living. Social protest is saying that we do not have to live this way. If we feel deeply, and we encourage ourselves and others to feel deeply, we will find the germ of our answers to bring about change. Because once we recognize what it is we are feeling, once we recognize we can feel deeply, love deeply, can feel joy, then we will demand that all parts of our lives produce that kind of joy. And when they do not, we will ask, "Why don't they?" And it is the asking that will lead us inevitably toward change.

So the question of social protest and art is inseparable for me. I can't say it is an either-or proposition. Art for art's sake doesn't really exist for me. What I saw was wrong, and I had to speak up. I loved poetry, and I loved words. But what was beautiful had to serve the purpose of changing my life, or I would have died. If I cannot air this pain and alter it, I will surely die of it. That's the beginning of social protest.

CT: How has your work evolved in terms of interest and craft? Let's look at the love poetry, for instance, which dominated your early work [*The First Cities* and *New York Head Shop*] and which appears in *The Black Unicorn.*
AL: Everyone has a first-love poem that comes out of that first love. Everybody has it, and it's so wonderful and new and great. But when you've been writing love poems after thirty years, the later poems are the ones that really hit the nitty gritty, that meet your boundaries. They witness what you've been through. Those are the real love poems. And I love them because they say, "Hey! We define ourselves as lovers, as people who love each other all over again; we become new again." These poems insist that you can't separate loving from fighting, from dying, from hurting, but love is triumphant. It is powerful and strong, and I feel I grow a great deal in all of my emotions, especially in the capacity to love.

CT: Your love poetry seems not only to celebrate the personal experience of love but also love as a human concept, a theme embracing all of life, a theme which appears more and more emphatically in your later work. Particularly interesting, for instance, are the lesbian love poems ["Letter for Jan" and "Walking Our Boundaries"]. It didn't seem to make much difference whether the poems depicted a relationship between two women, two men, or a man and a woman. . . . The poems do not celebrate the people but the love.
AL: When you love, you love. It only depends on how you do it, how committed you are, how many mistakes you make. . . . But I do believe that the love expressed between women is particular and powerful because we have had to love ourselves in order to live; love has been our means of survival. And having been in love with both men and women, I want to resist the temptation to gloss over the differences.

CT: I am frequently jarred by my sometimes unconscious attempt to identify the sex of the person addressed in the poem. Since I associate the speaker's voice with you, and since I'm not always conscious that you are a lesbian, the jarring occurs when I realize the object of affection is likewise a woman. I'm certain this disturbance originates in how society defines love in terms of heterosexuality. So if we are to see love as a "universal" concept, society pressures us to see it as heterosexual.
AL: Yes, we're supposed to see "universal" love as heterosexual. What I insist upon in my work is that there is no such thing as universal love in literature. There is *this* love in *this* poem. The poem happens when I, Audre Lorde, poet,

deal with the particular instead of the "UNIVERSAL." My power as a person, as a poet, comes from who I am. I am a particular person. The relationships I have had, in which people kept me alive, helped sustain me, were sustained by me, were particular relationships. They help give me my particular identity, which is the source of my energy. Not to deal with my life in my art is to cut out the fount of my strength.

I love to write love poems. I love loving. And to put it into another framework, that is, other than poetry, I wrote a paper entitled "The Uses of the Erotic," where I examine the whole question of loving as a manifestation, love as a source of tremendous power. Women have been taught to suspect the erotic urge, the place that is uniquely female. So, just as we tend to reject our blackness because it has been termed inferior, as women we tend to reject our capacity for feeling, our ability to love, to touch the erotic, because it has been devalued. But it is within this that lies so much of our power, our ability to posit, our vision. Because once we know how deeply we can feel, we begin to demand from all of our life pursuits that they be in accordance with these feelings. And when they don't we must raise the question why do I feel constantly suicidal, for instance? What's wrong? Is it me, or is it what I am doing? We begin to need to answer such questions. But we cannot when we have no image of joy, no vision of what we are capable of. After the killing is over. When you live without the sunlight, you don't know what it is to relish the bright light or even to have too much of it. Once you have light, then you can measure its intensity. So too with joy.

CT: Universities seem to be one major source of income for many writers, that is in terms of writer-in-residence positions. Have you had such appointments? What has been their effect?
AL: I've only had one writer-in-residence position, and that was at Tougaloo College in Mississippi fourteen years ago. It was pivotal for me. Pivotal. In 1968 my first book had just been published; it was my first trip into the Deep South; it was the first time I had been away from the children; the first time I worked with young black students in a workshop situation. I came to realize that this was my work. That teaching and writing were inextricably combined, and it was there that I knew what I wanted to do for the rest of my life.

I had been "the librarian who wrote." After my experience at Tougaloo, I realized that writing was central to my life and that the library, although I loved books, was not enough. Combined with the circumstances that followed my stay at Tougaloo: King's death, Kennedy's death, Martha's accident,* all of these things really made me see that life is very short, and what we have to do must be done now.

I have never had another writer-in-residence position. The poem "Touring" from *The Black Unicorn* represents another aspect of being a travelling cultural worker. I go and read my poetry. I drop my little seeds and then I leave. I hope they spring into something. Sometimes I find out they do; sometimes I never find out. I just have to have faith, and fun along the way.

CT: Would you describe your writing process?

AL: I keep a journal and write in it fairly regularly. I get a lot of my poems out of it. It's like the raw material for my poems. Sometimes I'm blessed with a poem that comes in the form of a poem, but other times I've worked for two years on a poem.

For me, there are two very basic and different processes for revising my poetry. One is recognizing that a poem has not yet become itself. In other words, I mean that the feeling, the truth that the poem is anchored in is somehow not clearly clarified inside of me, and as a result it lacks something. Then it has to be re-felt. Then there's the other process which is easier. The poem is itself, but it has rough edges that need to be refined. That kind of revision involves picking the image that is more potent or tailoring it so that it carries the feeling. That's an easier kind of rewriting and re-feeling.

My journal entries focus on things I feel: feelings that sometimes have no place, no beginning, no end; phrases I hear in passing; something that looks good to me; sometimes just observations of the world.

I went through a period once when I felt like I was dying. I wasn't writing any poetry, and I felt that if I couldn't write I would split. I was recording in my journal, but no poems came. I know now that this period was a transition in my life.

The next year, I went back to my journal, and here were these incredible poems that I could almost lift out of it. Many of them are in *The Black Unicorn*. "Harriet" is one of them; "Sequelae" and "The Litany for Survival" are others. These poems came right out of the journal. But I didn't see them as poems then.

---

* Lorde's close personal friend.

"Power" was in the journal too. It is a poem written about Clifford Glover, the ten-year-old black boy shot by a cop who was acquitted by a jury on which a black woman sat. In fact, the day I heard on the radio that O'Shea had been acquitted, I was going across town on 88th Street [New York City] and I had to pull over. A kind of fury rose up in me—the sky turned red. I felt so sick. I felt as if I would drive the car into a wall, into the next person I saw. So I pulled over. I took out my journal just to air some of my fury, to get it out of my fingertips. Those expressed feelings are that poem. That was just how "Power" was written.

CT: A transition has to occur before you can make poetry out of your journal entries.

AL: There is a gap between the journal and my poetry. I write this stuff in my journal, and sometimes I cannot even read my journals because there is so much pain and rage in them. I'll put it away in a drawer, and six months, a year or so later, I'll pick up the journal, and there will be the seeds of poems. The journal entries somehow have to be assimilated into my living; only then can I deal with what I have written down.

Art is not living. It is the use of living. The artist has the ability to take the living and use it in a certain way and produce art.

CT: Does Afro-American literature possess particular characteristics?

AL: Afro-American literature is certainly part of an African tradition. African tradition deals with life as an experience to be lived. In many respects, it is much like the Eastern philosophies in that we see ourselves as a part of a life force; we are joined, for instance, to the air, to the earth. We are part of the whole-life process. We live in accordance with, in a kind of correspondence with the rest of the world as a whole. And therefore living becomes an experience, rather than a problem, no matter how bad or how painful it may be. Change will rise endemically from the experience fully lived and responded to.

I feel this very much in African writing. And as a consequence, I have learned a great deal from Achebe, Tutuola, Ekwensi, from Flora Nwapa and Ama Ata Aido. Leslie Lacy, a black American who lived temporarily in Ghana, writes about experiencing this transcendence in his book *The Rise and Fall of a Proper Negro.*

It's not a turning away from pain, error, but seeing these things as part of living, and learning from them. This characteristic is particularly African, and it is transposed into the best of Afro-American literature. In addition, we have the legends of our struggle and survival in the New World.

This transcendence appears in Ellison, a little bit in Baldwin. And it is present very much so in Toni Morrison's *Sula*, which is a most wonderful piece of fiction. And I don't care if she won a prize for *The Song of Solomon*. *Sula* is a totally incredible book. It made me light up inside like a Christmas tree. I particularly identified with the book because of the female-outsider idea. That book is one long poem. Sula is the ultimate black female of our time, trapped in her power and her pain. Alice Walker uses that quality in *The Color Purple*, another wonderful novel of living as power.

CT: The recent writing by many black women seems to explore human concerns somewhat differently than do the men. These women refuse to blame racism alone for every negative aspect of black life. They are examining the nature of what passes between black women and black men—the power principles. Men tend to respond defensively to the writing of black women by labeling them as the "darklings" of the literary establishment. Goodness knows, the critics, especially black male critics, had a field day with Ntozake Shange's *For Colored Girls Who Have Considered Suicide When the Rainbow Is Enuf*. And they are getting started on Alice Walker's *The Color Purple*. But there are cruel black men, just as there are kind black men. Can't we try to alter that cruelty by focusing on it?

AL: Let me read an excerpt from a piece in *The Black Scholar* for you, which I wrote a while back:

> As I have said elsewhere, it is not the destiny of black America to repeat white America's mistakes. But we will, if we mistake the trappings of success in a sick society for the signs of a meaningful life. If black men continue to do so, defining "femininity" in its archaic European terms, this augurs ill for our survival as a people, let alone our survival as individuals. Freedom and future for blacks do not mean absorbing the dominant white male disease. . . .
>
> As black people, we cannot begin our dialogue by denying the oppressive nature of male privilege. And if black males choose to assume that privilege, for whatever reason, raping, brutalizing and killing women, then we cannot ignore black male oppression. One oppression does not justify another.

It's infuriating. Misguided black men. And meanwhile they are killing us in the streets. Is that the nature of nationhood?

I find this divisiveness to be oppressive and very persistent. It's been going on for a long time. It didn't start with Ntozake. It's been coming more and more to the forefront now. If you ask any of the black women writers over thirty whom you're interviewing, if she's honest, she will tell you. You know there's as much a black literary mafia in this country as there is a white literary mafia. They control who gets exposure. If you don't toe the line, then you're not published; your works are not distributed. At the same time, as black women, of course, we do not want to be used against black men by a system that means both of us ill.

CT: Do you think that had it not been for the women's movement black women would still be struggling to achieve their voice in the literary establishment?

AL: Without a doubt. Black women writers have been around a long time, and they have suffered consistent inattention. Despite this reality, you hear from various sources that black women really have "it." We're getting jobs; we're getting this and that, supposedly. Yet we still constitute the lowest economic group in America. Meanwhile those of us who do not fit into the "establishment" have not been allowed a voice, and it was only with the advent of the women's movement—even though black women are in disagreement with many aspects of the women's movement—that black women began to demand a voice, as women and as blacks. I think any of us who are honest have to say this. As Barbara Smith says, "All the women were white and all the blacks were men, but some of us are still brave." Her book on black women's studies [*Some of Us Are Brave*], which she edited along with Gloria Hull and Patricia Bell Scott, is the first one on the subject.

CT: Are you at a turning point in your career, your life?

AL: I think I have deepened and broadened my understanding of the true difficulty of my work. Twenty years ago when I said we needed to understand each other I had not really perfected a consciousness concerning how important differences are in our lives. But that is a theme which recurs in my life and in my work. I have become more powerful because I have refused to settle for the myth of sorry sameness, that myth of easy sameness. My life's work continues to be survival and teaching. As I said before, teaching is also learning; teach what you need to learn. If we do this deeply, then it is most effective. I have, for example, deepened the questions that I follow, and so I have also deepened the ways I teach and learn.

The work I did on the erotic was very, very important. It opened up for me a whole area of connections in the absence of codified knowledge, or in the absence of some other clear choice. The erotic has been a real guide for me. And learning as a discipline is identical to learning how to reach through feeling the essence of how and where the erotic originates, to posit what it is based upon. This process of feeling and therefore knowing has been very, very constructive for me.

I believe in the erotic and I believe in it as an enlightening force within our lives as women. I have become clearer about the distinctions between the erotic and other apparently similar forces. We tend to think of the erotic as an easy, tantalizing sexual arousal. I speak of the erotic as the deepest life force, a force which moves us toward living in a fundamental way. And when I say living I mean it as that force which moves us toward what will accomplish real positive change.

When I speak of a future that I work for, I speak of a future in which all of us can learn, a future which we want for our children. I posit that future to be led by my visions, my dreams, and my knowledge of life. It is that knowledge which I call the erotic, and I think we must develop it within ourselves. I think so much of our living and our consciousness has been formed by death or by non-living. This is what allows us to tolerate so much of what is vile around us. When I speak of "the good," I speak of living; I speak of the erotic in all forms. They are all one. So in that sense I believe in the erotic as an illuminating principle in our lives.

CT: You've just finished a new work.

AL: Yes. *Zami: A New Spelling of My Name* was just published. It's a biomythography, which is really fiction. It has the elements of biography and history of myth. In other words, it's fiction built from many sources. This is one way of expanding our vision.

I'm very excited about this book. As you know, it's been a long time coming. Now that it's out, it'll do its work. Whatever its faults, whatever its glories, it's there.

You might call *Zami* a novel. I don't like to call it that. Writing *Zami* was a lifeline through the cancer experience. As I said in *The Cancer Journals*,

I couldn't believe that what I was fighting I would fight alone and only for myself. I couldn't believe that there wasn't something there that somebody could use at some other point because I know that I could have used some other woman's words, whatever she had to say. Just to know that someone had been there before me would have been very important, but there was nothing. Writing *The Cancer Journals* gave me the strength and power to examine that experience, to put down into words what I was feeling. It was my belief that if this work were useful to just one woman, it was worth doing.

CT: What can you share with the younger generation of black women writers and writers in general?
AL: Not to be afraid of difference. To be real, tough, loving. And to recognize each other. I can tell them not to be afraid to feel and not to be afraid to write about it. Even if you are afraid, do it anyway because we learn to work when we are tired, so we can learn to work when we are afraid. Silence never brought us anything. Survive and teach; that's what we've got to do and to do it with joy.

An Interview with Audre Lorde

Susan Cavin / 1983

From *Big Apple Dyke News* 3.7 (New York), October–November 1983, 1 and 20–23. Reprinted by permission.

Question: Your August 27 speech at the twentieth anniversary of the 1963 Martin Luther King March on Washington was a historic advance for the Lesbian/Gay Movement. What did that action mean to you, the Black Movement and to the Lesbian Movement?

Audre Lorde: I think that a black lesbian speaking at the march on Washington was very, very important. I think that a black woman stood up and verbalized the outward joining of the lesbian/gay community probably came as a shock to many people, many blacks, out of the hundreds of thousands of people who were there. I think it would be an error for us to romanticize what it is because it took a minute and a half. It was a very short speech. But when I think of all the tremendous amount of work and energy the Washington black lesbian and gay community did to make it happen and all the work done by Gil Gerald and the National Black Coalition of Gays and Lesbians, I can't take credit for it.

Q: Is it true you had a hard time getting to the stage?

AL: Well, yes, it was logistically a very difficult thing because there had been so much controversy about my speaking and because I did not have credentials, it was very difficult to get up there, and I really felt it was a genuine battle. But again I understand how difficult it is for the organizers to put on a march of that magnitude, and things go wrong, and I suppose I should give them the benefit of the doubt.

Q: How did the crowd receive you?

AL: When I first spoke, when I said that I represented the National Coalition of Black Gays and Lesbians, some young people standing on the front row booed me. But they quieted down when I got into my speech, when I described the truth of our situation. What can people do when you tell the truth, but listen?

Q: At the risk of sounding romantic, did you ever dream you'd become the pivot between the Black Civil Rights Movement and the Lesbian Movement before August 1983, or did you just look up one day and find yourself in that position?

AL: You know, I'm not a pivot. A pivot is stationary. All these years I have thought of myself as a lesbian, as a sexual human being for as long as I've thought of myself as a black woman, and certainly I've always known I was born black. These things have always come together for me. I am all these things. I've always known I wasn't the only black lesbian around, although there have been some times I felt I was, I've always known I wasn't. There have always been lesbians in the black community, although they may not have always been recognized. I am not a pivot. A pivot is a stationary point around which other things move. I have always been concerned with these issues in my life and in the life of my children. My life *is* all these issues. I'm not rejecting what you're saying. I'm saying that my internal consciousness of myself is different. It's very difficult for me to think of myself as a pivot. I recognize that it is those of us who refuse to reject any part of our identities, although we stand in an extremely vulnerable position, who understand the positions of all of us.

Q: The lesbian movement is very proud of you that it was a dyke who stood up to make that speech. Is the black movement proud of you as well? Or, do you feel role strain caught between the two movements?

AL: Role strain? (laughter) That sounds like something out of a text book! There has always been some piece of my identity that will offend someone. I am a black lesbian mother, feminist, socialist in an interracial couple with a boy child! Only by keeping all apparently contradictory parts of my identity, at great cost to myself, that I can make all my energy come to life. But I'm speaking personally now. Now in the world of lesbians, *homophobia is a reality* in the black community simply as racism is a reality in the lesbian and gay movement. This has to be dealt with by those of us who work as crucial life issues. I do believe homophobia is a crucial life issue in the black community—not just for black lesbians and gays—the same way that racism is a crucial life issue in the lesbian/gay movement—not just for people of color. These are institutional problems. We will stand or fall based on our ability to recognize each other independently and tolerate and use each other's differences constructively. I can't tell you how many times in the lesbian movement, in the

women's movement, you know, women say "that doesn't really matter—oh,
I never really noticed you were black!" It's the same way in the black community, I mean the black activist community, when people say "oh, you know,
that's right—whatever you do in the privacy of your home is fine—but don't
talk about it." It tires me. I mean, I know I can't win the war against racism in
bed, but it is a fact that whatever I do, whatever lesbians do must be kept
secret—that is not to be trusted.

Q: Now that you've brought that up, I had a question on this. Do you think
that the gay movement is still racist as a whole or in pockets and do you
think that the black movement is still homophobic as a whole or in pockets?
How do you see it? Is it structural throughout or do you think some people
have made some progress in both movements?
AL: Oh, I think there has been some progress in both movements, but there is
still racism in the lesbian/gay movement and still homophobia in the black
movement. But what I want to see happen now is for the lesbian/gay movement as a whole to make racism a *priority* in the same way that Black & White
Men Together have taken racism as a *priority* in their relationships as gay
men. But it is so hard for me to see consistency in their consciousness-raising
groups, in their attention, in their involvement with South Africa, in their
involvement with racism. That is what I want to see happen in the gay community: make racism a priority. I want to see the black community make homophobia a priority problem. That's what I think needs to occur because we live
in a society that is predicated upon institutionalized dehumanization. Both
racism and homophobia are institutionalized into the structure that we live in.
So, as part of those structures, we cannot help but reflect those feelings unless
we take an *active* position against them. It's not enough to just say, "hey, I don't
lynch niggers or burn dykes."

Q: What do you think can be done to forge the coalition between the two
movements?
AL: I think that the kind of grassroots organizing that took place before my
speech at the march, the work within regions, the networking of black lesbians and gays, the work of Dykes Against Racism is important and beginning to happen. The question is: how do we deal with the structure? I mean
the desire now of white men and white women to examine their racism having come out of that structure is crucial, but how do we deal with these

institutions? Coalition building is not romantic; it's very annoying, it is constant, it is very slow. I think that's where the real coalitions are made on the everyday, grassroots level. Bernice Reagon said something about it in *Home Girls*, Barbara Smith's new book published by Kitchen Table Press. She said that people don't build coalitions because they want to, but because we really need it. It's really true. It feels right to me.

Q: Do you think that black lesbians and gays are accepted now in the mainstream Black Civil Rights Movement?
AL: I think that that is going to vary by state, by region. I think in New York and California that changes have been made in the last few years in increasing numbers, and I would have to say it's less than I anticipated, but it's something, you know.

Q: That's fascinating because white faggots claim that they draw more fire than lesbians from white society. That's interesting if the reverse is true in the black community.
AL: Yes, I think there's a much greater tolerance for male homosexuals in the black community. Maybe if you speak to black gay guys, they might say the same thing as white gay men. But when I have talked about this, some black movement activists say, "Oh, but look at so and so, he is gay and nobody says anything about that."

We have been informed to be quiet about our sexual preference and our identity or else we could hurt the black movement. I think that is changing. What we are demanding is that we speak, as I said in my speech, *in our own name*. But, I also recognize that it's a very long struggle, because the East Coast and California are not representative of the rest of this country. I think it's not happening yet in Austin, Texas, for example.

I think for some reason on some levels that black male homosexuals are almost more acceptable to the black community than black lesbians. I'm not sure why. Maybe because men are accepted as just more sexual creatures, or perhaps maybe it is because lesbians politically and ideologically genuinely pose an even greater threat to the social structure as we know it. I suspect that's probably the reason. A sexually free woman has always been seen as a tremendous threat, even if she's a heterosexually free woman. Now a lesbian who has taken the position that she is not bound by either emotional or sexual ties to men, that leaves her a very large question mark. Question marks are dangerous, so she's much, much more dangerous to society.

Q: Do you know what Coretta Scott King's position on lesbianism was during the negotiations that preceded your speech?
AL: No, I don't know what Coretta Scott King's position on lesbianism is. (laughter) She did say to me when I went up to speak, "We're so happy you could be with us today." I feel sure that whatever her personal opinions or feelings are about gay people, I'm sure she recognizes that justice has political implications of our coming together.

Q: Are you for Jesse Jackson for President or who?
AL: I really can't say. One's vote for President is a very personal choice. I think that Jesse Jackson's run for the Presidency is something crucial and very, very important. I totally disagree with those people who say that he's fracturing the black vote. I think that the objections to him have not held water. At this point all of us have to support anything that would galvanize the black community and recognize how disenfranchised they are, to begin to take part in the voting process. Understand the importance of it. On the other hand, to make a man "the leader" creates a real problem: utter dependence on "the leadership." There will come a leader who will lead us out of Babylon. That's very dangerous. I see that political liberation is not possible until each one of us begins to think of ourselves as power principles, as a nest of power relative to other people's power, of course. Until we become self activated, we're never really going to change things. We have to stop waiting for someone, a leader, to come up and tell us what to do. That leader is also at our mercy. What happens when that leader is shot down? What happens when that leader is called an embezzler, a prostitute or a lesbian or gay? It's dangerous.

Q: What do you think is the next step politically for lesbians and gays?
AL: Acting for change, not just talking or thinking about it. Change the structure. Each one of us has to look at the environment of our lives. The places where we are actively involved are the places where we can best effect changes and we have to work for that change. At the same time, we have to look at our goals, if your goals match my goals, whatever our differences may be, we must work together for change.

Q: Do you think poets generally make good political activists or are you an exception?

AL: Well, of course, poets make good political activists! Poetry is not just a poem. Poetry is a way of life. It is a way of stepping through life outwardly aware of our internal consciousness. That self-consciousness is where the change begins to happen, not from the outside, not from someone telling you, not from a leader saying "hey this has to happen." It is a genuine feeling that comes out of the understanding of what is going on. I think we can learn that from poetry. That is one of the first steps that gives us a sense of how we cope because it is our vision, it is our dream, we must lay that groundwork before genuine political action is allowed. In other words, what are we doing with the power? Are we sitting on it? That's why I call poetry the skeletal picture of our lives. That is the first way poetry is political. Once we genuinely see these things, once we have a vision of what can be and is not yet, then our need for change comes out of its powerlessness. We can change. I think that whatever planes of political structures we have, poetry as I define poetry, speaks to people to develop that sense of self conscious living and at the same time the entity of the whole.

Q: Who is your favorite poet?

AL: I can't say right now. I go to poetry for real sustenance. I mean I have poets in my class at Hunter College who when things are really bad, I go through my class and pick out a poem that someone wrote—then I can make it. Then, you know, my mind is very, very clear.

Q: Which do you like doing best: writing, teaching or political activism or the combination?

AL: If I had my druthers, I guess I would write. The realities of my life are such that that is not possible. I do many things. I enjoy writing, I enjoy teaching. They're all very important. I wish I could just write and have a world where I didn't have to be an activist.

Q: What are you working on now as a writer?

AL: I'm editing a collection of essays. My work at Kitchen Table Press is probably the most important political involvement I have right now. Kitchen Table Press is a woman of color press. We are a press which is dedicated to publishing and distributing works of women of color. Our work concerns the future of women. What *is* our future? Taking control of our institutions.

Women of color have not traditionally had control of writing institutions. It is very hard. It is really hard to do a publishing venture now.

Q: Do you have a dream and what is it?
AL: Oh, yes. I dream of a future for my children where they can learn to be self-actualized. For myself, I dream of freedom from rage and despair. Right now, you have to understand this is 9 o'clock on a Thursday morning and I've had a very difficult week. But despair is not just a personal problem. However, it doesn't go away because we want those conditions that encourage it unless we work for another order. I'm speaking about universal changes. I recognize that we must live in the now. There are problems we have to address: we have to deal with the power that is now. Yet, at the same time, we have to constantly keep a vision of how we want it to be. That change requires genuine alterations in the power structure.

Q: Do you ever think there will be a revolution in this country? A political revolution?
AL: I think that a political revolution is something that starts within each of us. Yes, I think there will be a revolution. There *must* be a revolution. I think there *must* be a revolution in this country. But I think that the revolution of institutions cannot really add a new solution or really take unless it is the revolution that begins with the self based on the internal demands of the people. As Che Guevara said shortly before he died, the great revolutions are those revolutions guided by the basic principles of love. And I am not speaking of wishy-washy flowery love, I'm thinking of what I have been saying to you for the last half hour that requires the nitty gritty alterations of institutions into our dreams.

Q: What do you think will happen in 1984? Big Brother?
AL: (laughter) Do you mean in the Orwellian or political sense?

Q: Both.
AL: In 1984, I will be half a century old. I never thought I would live to see that day. I don't know what will happen in 1984—if they'll blow up the world or if we may be able to bring about these changes. There's a piece of me that sees 1984 as part of a continuum. I think that politically and socially we are in a very dangerous, very ambiguous position. I think though when I travel about me, I see such a groundswell of connections, of awareness beginning.

Because people are being forced to recognize where their best interests lie. I trust that power. I trust it. I trust the power of the people. I do not romanticize it. But I trust it.

Q: Is there anything else you'd like to say? About Kitchen Table Press or anything?
AL: I urge you and the people who read *Big Apple Dyke News* to support The Table because it is crucial to support all those institutions that are attempting to break the mold that come out of our community. And The Table is one of them. There are others. There is the Third World Women's Archives. Look around your community. There are a number of them. See what is offering some kind of genuine nourishment to your life, cultural nourishment. Support those institutions. They are vital. We cannot live without our culture. The story of a people, the story of a movement is a story of its culture. The function of culture, the function of art is to nourish us, to make us *more* whoever we want to be. And I really urge you and your readers to support women's culture and the institutions of our dreams.

Q: What is the political destiny of lesbians?
AL: To recognize the power we have and to develop the power and connections of the process of revolutionizing lesbians. We are in a vanguard position to see social change. If we have survived our past, in our identities, we have had to recognize the institutions that oppress us. But there are so many other problems, racism, sectarianism, problems of how we identify with the total. What do I do with lesbians in the KKK and fascist lesbians, for example?

Q: Do you think there are lesbians in the KKK?
AL: Yes. When we say "we are everywhere," we have to deal with the fact that *we really are everywhere!* I just want to thank you for your kind words. It really makes me feel supported. I'm speaking woman-to-woman now. But I don't want to be objectified as a symbol. The system destroys us by either making most lesbians invisible or by making a few too visible, objectified and lonely. I must protect myself against that. I know what it feels to be invisible. I was invisible for many years. It's crushing. But I don't want to be a visible symbol on the backs of all the dead lesbians, the alcoholic lesbians, all the women who have gone insane. I can never forget all the women crushed by invisibility.

Speaking the Unspeakable: Poet Audre Lorde

Karla Jay / 1983

From (Philadelphia) *Gay News*, 15 March 1984. The interview was conducted 5 October 1983; a copy of the tape is in the New York Public Library's Karla Jay Papers. *Gay News* article © 1984 by Karla Jay. Reprinted by permission.

When I caught up with Audre Lorde at Hunter College, she was in between talking to a student and rushing off to teach a writing class, just two of her lesser-known activities. In the past two years, her collected poems, *Chosen Poems Old and New* (Norton) was published, as well as *Zami: A New Spelling of My Name* (The Crossing Press), Lorde's biomythography about growing up in the fifties. Among the topics she discussed:

- the fifties ("America breeds nostalgia like rabbits breed bunnies");
- the collapse of *Zami*'s first publisher, Persephone Press ("Persephone Press has . . . set back feminist publishing . . . a significant amount");
- the role of the poet in today's society ("Poetry is the most subversive kind of art there is");
- lesbian health issues ("While we're busy running around being Superdyke and Superwoman and Supermommy, . . . we have a physical plant");
- the twentieth anniversary of Dr. Martin Luther King, Jr.'s speech ("It was not the coming together of the lion and the lamb").

Karla Jay: Why did you decide to write an autobiography at this point in your life?

Audre Lorde: *Zami* isn't an autobiography. I started to write *Zami* for a number of reasons. There were stories that had to be told, not only my stories but the stories of many black women, black West Indian women raising children, raising daughters, stories of black lesbians on the street in the '50s, stories that just weren't being told. I felt a real connection within my own life and what I had seen. I was getting feedback that there was a big empty space where these stories should be, to mull over, to go on from, to dispute, to laugh about, whatever.

Because there was a gap, *Zami* was written, and so *Zami* is not only an autobiography, but mythology, psychology, all the ways in which I think we can see our environment. And this is what I think good fiction does. And it is fiction. I attempt to create a piece of art, not merely a retelling of things that happened to me and to other women with whom I shared close ties. I define it as biomythography because I've found no other word to really coin what I was trying to do.

KJ: Do you think that women have difficulty perceiving what it is you're try-ing to do as biomythography, and are thinking that you're giving some kind of accurate blow-by-blow account?
AL: But I am giving an accurate account of a time and a place, of a connec-tion between black women with African roots, in terms of how we raise our children, how we maintain strength, how we find ourselves, the question of the Black Goddess, the creator, in all of us, what happens with home life. Home is in fact so important. What does it mean when I say all black women are lesbians? They have to be in order to survive. All of these are threads. It is as accurate as I know it to be, and I think that fiction has got to be, in order to have power. Another part of what *Zami* is, is just a kind of life history. I wanted to put down what the black women were wearing at parties, whether I wore it or not.

KJ: A lot of things have been written now about the 1950s, from Ann Bannon's pulp novels to Joyce Johnson, who wrote a book recently about Jack Kerouac. What do you think the interest in the '50s is?
AL: I think that America breeds nostalgia like rabbits breed bunnies. It's always easier to look back and relish rather than look forward or look at what is happening. We should have passed out of this '50s nostalgia already, and we haven't. The '60s were a really active period, and to embrace the '60s, to look back on the '60s, we have to look back on some of the problems of an incom-plete vision, as well as on the real challenges, some of which have been met, some of which have not.

The '50s, as I said in *Zami*, was straight white America's cooling off period. In the '40s, during the war, there was a lot of privation, there was a lot of anxi-ety. I think the fact that we entered the atomic age was very, very important in the '50s, and I think people were beginning to create a life in the '50s which we inculcated as a sense of all of our destinies. When I say "we" I mean people who were about my age, who were adolescents at that time. That was very formative in terms of the beats and real change in popular culture.

Within gay and lesbian circles specifically, this was one of the really becoming times. Most of the people who are now asking these questions, or are writing, who are lesbians, who are gay, remember or have contact with people who remember what the '50s were. It was very closeted, but also very positive.

KJ: Do you think that a lot of the nostalgia is about the old butch/femme roles?
AL: It was secure, in that this had been laid out already. In the '50s there was a lot of copying in roles and transposing them into gay and lesbian lifestyles, without question. It's very easy to be unconventional in a conventional manner. In bad times, and I think we're in terrible times right now, the tendency is to go back to a time when things appeared to be simpler.

KJ: But that was an appearance, wasn't it? In *Zami* you certainly point up that it was a very complex time.
AL: Extremely. We saw on a small scale many of the same uncertainties that we see now.

KJ: What happened with Persephone Press, which published *Zami*? They've gone out of business. What was the reason for that?
AL: I was one of the authors who was left to pick up the pieces, and one of the authors who I feel was really used by them, the women who ran Persephone Press. More than that, I don't have any idea what happened. But I know that by and large, it was women of color who were left holding the bag, since I never saw any royalties at all from *Zami* and wound up having to pay thousands of dollars to make sure that I have the right to reprint my own book. It's once again a case of exploiting a black woman. It was a terribly unpleasant experience, because I and a number of other women were prepared to support Persephone in whatever way we could, because it certainly took the lead in feminist publishing. And what Persephone Press has done is to set back feminist publishing, hopefully not a great deal, but a significant amount. Whether this was their intention or not, I have no idea. I simply know that is a fact, a result.

KJ: In 1982, Norton also published another anthology of your poems, *Chosen Poems Old and New*. Do you think you primarily define yourself as a poet?
AL: Yes. I will always be a poet. Being a poet is not only a question of what you produce. It's a question of a whole way of seeing oneself moving through

the world and seeing the world through which we move. That's why poets have got to be revolutionaries. Poetry is the most subversive kind of art there is, I think. I'll always be a poet. What I write, what I turn out, what I produce, will be determined I think by what I determine to do with it. That's how I live my life.

KJ: How can poetry be subversive?

AL: Well, I think poetry is the skeleton architecture of our lives. I think it is in our poetry, as it is in our dreams, that we begin our inner vision, that we begin to create visions of what has never been before, that can possibly be. Poetry is not a luxury. Our poems and our dreams extend us, make our knowledge beyond where we can understand, begin to give shape to the chaos in a way that we can then attend to it.

Poetry lays a groundwork. It lays a pathway for action in the present that is not only survival, that is not only meeting the crisis.

In other words, genuine change comes about not just in dealing with the particularities of our oppression and our situation, which is always necessary. In addition to that, and at the same time, we have to be able to posit the kind of future that we are moving towards, so that we are not just moving toward the same, weary scenario.

That positive, what lies beyond, is, I think, made real in our poetry, as it is in our dreams.

KJ: How do you manage to be so prolific?

AL: I'm not prolific at all. What I am impressed with in myself constantly is how much there is to do, that I am not yet doing, that I haven't done. But once I stopped keeping certain artificial barriers between what I did, a lot of energy flowed more easily between these things.

So I began to see that there was less and less of a difference between teaching and writing poems and reading on the road.

Now there are hierarchies within me of things that I prefer to do. If I had my druthers, I would write all day long, with a little foray out once a week into teaching, because I enjoy that particular kind of thing. But then I'd have ten more hours to the day.

As someone said to a friend of mine very recently, I'm not a political activist—I'm not a revolutionary—by choice. I am out of necessity, I can't help but be . . . because it's there to be done.

I would like to live another life, a calmer life. I would like to be able to deal at a more reasonable pace with the truth and the urgencies I feel. But we don't have that much time.

What I think we need to do as creative people is not let that take us to the wall. It's another kind of impotence to allow that urgency to lure us into a kind of superficiality, a kind of rapid, unconsidered action in any given sphere, at any given time.

And it's hard, it's hard.

KJ: Let's talk about the *Cancer Journals* for just a second. You and I know that for women, the primary cause of death in this country is breast cancer.
AL: With breast cancer, it's now down to one in eleven.

KJ: And what do you think about health issues for lesbians in particular? Do you think that this should take more priority in the community?
AL: Well, I think it has great priority in the community, and I think it should be attended even more. I would like to see lesbians more involved with the National Gay Health Network, which had a conference in Denver in June of 1983. I think they're having one in New York next summer.

I think lesbians, as all women, need to focus on the fact that while we're busy running around being Superdyke and Superwoman and Supermommy and all the rest of it, we have a physical plant. The physical institution is not replaceable, and we have to attend to that level also.

Of course, I think we need to involve ourselves more actively with health issues, and lesbians need to deal more directly with even the subject of breast cancer. Basically, this has been thought of until very recently as a straight woman's issue, and that's bullshit.

KJ: Yes, there's a lot of mythology about what lesbians get and what lesbians don't get.
AL: There's a lot of mythology, that's right. Lesbians are women, and are subject to all the diseases, all the problems and all of the stuff that, you know . . .

KJ: During the summer of 1983 you spoke in Washington at the twentieth anniversary of Dr. Martin Luther King, Jr.'s speech. What were the circumstances of your speaking there?

AL: There was a lot of opposition to having me as a speaker for the gay and lesbian community. A lot of work was done behind the scenes, by a lot of very dedicated people.

And as you know, there was still not really a speaker from the gay and lesbian community. It was a symbolic one-and-a-half minute part, which I had in the litany of commitment. It's certainly not what we would have wanted. It's certainly not what I would have wanted, or what we should have had. But I think nonetheless that it was extremely important, I think someone had to do it, and I'm really glad that it was done.

I think it was very, very necessary to have a black woman stand up in front of over 200,000 people and say, "I represent black lesbians and gays, and we're here openly in our own name." Of course lesbians and gays have always been part of the civil rights movement as everyone who has worked in the movement knows. I think it was great to have them openly acknowledged.

In Washington right now, months later, it's important that it happened and that you can't undo history. And it's important that we do not believe that it is something that it was not, i.e., the final coming together of the lion and the lamb. I don't think that's true at all. I think there's a lot of really hard grassroots work that has to be done in terms of holding political people to their promise, holding people to working for gay civil rights in Congress, to pass gay civil rights acts in Congress, and to keep underlining the stuff.

KJ: Do you think that the women's movement, particularly the lesbian movement, is seriously dealing with racism?
AL: What keeps me going is that it varies from place to place. There's some places where there's an abysmal "no" and there's some places where yeah, I think it's starting to happen. It's a little slow and a little late, but I really do believe in progress.

I believe in movement, and so wherever it happens, I've got to recognize it. At the same time it's like Washington, at the same time recognizing that this is not nearly enough. I just don't want it to be too little and too late.

By and large, American society doesn't deal with racism. Women's groups have been notoriously reluctant to deal with it. They have started to deal with it. It's very easy to get sidetracked by guilt and terror and all the rest of it. But if we don't solve it, it will fracture the movement apart, and to a large degree it has.

Poetry, Nature, and Childhood:
An Interview with Audre Lorde

Louise Chawla / 1984

Published for the first time, by permission of Louise Chawla, who transcribed her taped interview for this collection. The full transcript includes additional dialogue in which Chawla develops comparisons with four other New York poets whom she interviewed for her book *In the First Country of Places: Nature, Poetry, and Childhood Memory* (State University of New York Press, 1994). The Audre Lorde interview was conducted over lunch in Greenwich Village on 5 January 1984.

Audre Lorde: I started writing very early.

Louise Chawla: You were already writing when you were in high school?
Audre Lorde: Yes, I wrote my first poem when I was in seventh grade, I remember. They were "I love my country" poems. But I was in the seventh grade.

LC: They were "I love my country" poems?
AL: Yes, yes. It was during the Second World War. And poems for my mother.
   The next step after that, when I was in about the eighth grade and the first years of high school, I really started touching the kind of beauty that I couldn't explain. Where I lived, at 142nd Street and Lenox Avenue, my mother would take us—there were two places where she would take us. She would take us down to the water. You can't see it now because there is the Harlem River Drive, but before there wasn't. So we could go down to the Harlem River at 142nd Street. That was one place. And the other was up Seventh Avenue at 155th Street there was a project. It was called the "new project park." This was one of the first projects in Manhattan, and they had just a little greenery. And it banked on the water. She would take us there and we would play on the swings. *That* place, the green, the trees, and the water, formed—all through high school I would write about it—my forest of Arden. And I would write about beautiful scenes. It was the only green place I ever saw.
   And so, the first time that I gave a reading at Tougaloo, I will never forget, after my first book, some students said, "Miss Lorde, would you call yourself a nature poet?" And I thought, "What? Me?" And then I realized how wedded to

these images I was. And they come from this pocket park. I would fantasize about sun on a red brick roof. It was the shards of sun against the wall, with this new kind of brick that they build with now, but which was totally unlike most New York architecture in the forties. And that became entrenched in my mind as beauty. The sun on a red brick roof. And a rose trellis.

LC: That was in the park?
AL: I never found the rose trellis. I don't know where that came from. I think perhaps there may have been a white structure through which you went into this park. And I fantasized a rose trellis, because I had never seen one.

(The food comes, and as Lorde and Chawla begin eating, Chawla briefly describes the other poets from the city of New York that she is interviewing.)

LC: They are all city people, and yet nature is in there so much. That was one of the surprises.
AL: We have a hunger for it. We have a hunger for it. I think we find it wherever we can. I mean, that is true. I used to go home from school, at 138th Street, to my house, which was at 142nd and Lenox. There were no trees, there was nothing there. You know how blades of grass grow up between the pavement? I had read about flowers, and I used to pick these grasses and tie a little something around them and bring them home to my mother like flowers. Like flowers.

LC: When people have gone around and talked to children in projects—not only here but also in Europe—and asked them what they would like to add, *the* most common answer is trees, green. And it is not advertised on TV.
AL: That's right. I grew up with no concept of the existence of rural poverty. And I mean this is very very late—I was a grown woman, and still I had difficulty. Up to the sixties, when they started to talk about Watts and the fact that Watts was the ghetto. And they were showing some of it, and my first reaction to that was, "That's not a ghetto! They have trees!" I would really rather have trees and still be poor.

(More eating and food talk, while Chawla explains that she has read Lorde's work, as well as her interviews in *American Poetry Review* and with Adrienne Rich in *Signs.*)

LC: I have just a few questions about putting things together that I couldn't do by myself, and I wanted to check up with you how I was doing them, in terms of childhood memories, city memories. I feel you have really got to look at memory in context.

AL: You know the first poem in *New York City Head Shop and Museum*—it's included in *Chosen Poems*. The title of it is "New York City." That whole book, *New York City Head Shop and Museum*, really blackens perceptions of the city. It uses my memories. I wrote the poems in that book at a point where I was ready to leave. I wanted to go West. It was at that point I realized I had to commit myself to the city. And that is what that poem comes out of. And with my children now, I know that I made the right decision. That poem really deals with a kind of loss of innocence on one level, with the city, and also the power of a real commitment to it.

LC: It is quite clear in your work that you are here by commitment and not just by accident.

AL: Mm-hmm. I am trying to leave now, you know. I am trying to arrange my life in such a way that I can move West. My children are grown. My lover and I, we were afraid of moving after the earthquake, plus I really felt that the kids needed the city. But now I am tired of having to greet every day as a warrior. To live in New York, you have to move out into it like *war*. I love the city, but I want another consciousness to illuminate my life now.

LC: To move into more open space?

AL: Moving to more open space, moving to a warmer climate. A part of me longs for it. Moving to the kind of ambiance that I find enlarging. It is a different tenor of living.

LC: So it was essentially your own children that kept you here all that time?

AL: Yes. I felt, you know, in that whole period—late '60s, early '70s—I had to reexamine that because I also wanted to leave. I wanted to go to the green places. I wanted to follow that part of my dream. At that point, when I was ready to leave New York, I had to ask myself, "But if I stay in New York?" My husband and I had separated. I saw the children, and that was what made me want to stay. What happened, very specifically, was that my daughter came home—she was in the second grade—and she was crying. She was crying because they had had a little mock election in her class, and Nixon had won.

She was crying because we talked politics at home all the time. I saw this child, and I thought, how out of touch she was with the world out there. I thought, I had to raise my children armored, and I want their dreams to be strong in a different way from mine. And I knew the city was a very important part. Even now, until we solve the problems of our cities, this country cannot exist in any viable way. That was fourteen years ago. And it is still the same. I felt it in so many ways. When I look at them and I look at their power, I feel vindicated. I know this is so. I see the way my son moves through the city. I feel I have done my work now, right?!

Now, it may be that I am not seeing the fact that I will miss a great deal. I think I will. That has to do with the fact that at this point in my life I travel a lot. So I will always be able to come back.

LC: Will it be easier to leave when you still have that attachment?
AL: Yeah, yeah. [a thoughtful silence for a few moments]

LC: I loved the city enormously as a child.
AL: You had the Village and Chinatown.

LC: It's funny. I have looked at autobiographies, and the first time you begin to see irony regarding the environment is in the 1950s, in people who grew up in the suburbs. The whole excuse for the suburbs was that they were the right place to raise children, but in autobiographies of people who grew up there, you get this tremendous boredom, irony, satire. The adolescents themselves are turning against the suburb. You don't get that in the city. It is a real place.
AL: How would you like to live your life ferrying children back and forth?

LC: There is one thing that does seem to me continuous in all of your work. The city seems to represent a place of oppression that you have to survive.
AL: The city to me represents almost a speeded up version of America, of the problems of America. They are symbolized in very different ways certainly in the South, the Midwest, or even in the West. But New York, Boston, Washington, Detroit—these industrial cities to me seem to be almost symbolic not just of oppression, but of the kinds of pressures. When I have to characterize the pressures that I was submitted to all the time, I image it as a subway. And yet, some of the most powerful poems that I wrote in the '60s and '70s were poems that either used the subway as the primary image or

were born on the subway. "Coal." This poem "New York City"—it started on the subway.

LC: "Coal" started on the subway?
AL: Literally, riding the subway. That's right. And I still think of the subway as a primary symbol of pressure.

What I think, you know—I think that the places of our power are also the places of our biggest strain. I think it is the tension between these two things that generates a kind of creativity, in the same way that building a bridge does. I mean the image is really the bringing together of similarities and differences, with sparks between them. Like lightning. That is true of the city. I think that is true about anything that is both onerous and vital. I see the city as those two polarities. Very much, very much. In my life, and in general.

LC: That is why survival is connected with your whole sense of the city too.
AL: Well, you can't grow up Black in New York, and conscious, without recognizing that survival is not theoretical. It is a day-to-day living decision, and one that you make over and over again. You can't be theoretical about survival. You live it in too many ways.

LC: One of the questions that I have is that Harlem doesn't come across as home for you?
AL: Harlem does not come across as home for me? Well, in some respects, Harlem probably was not home, although it was home to begin with. I found the whole city very early. I found the whole city, first with my mother, because she used to take us downtown. And then very rapidly, in high school my friend Gennie and I, we reclaimed the city. The whole city was our playground. I know Manhattan like . . . to this day—I have lived here fifteen years—and in Manhattan I know the streets that go this way, and I know about 4th Street and 10th Street, and I know the Village. It really was, it was our playground.

But . . . Adrienne Rich, she was here the last few weeks for Michelle Cliff's book party. And we were driving to pick up the meat patties, because Michelle is Jamaican. So we went uptown to the New Home Bakery, which is a place I know, a little place at 146th Street that makes the best meat patties in the world. So we went in, and they weren't ready yet. So I drove Adrienne around. Because we used to teach together at City College. I drove her around, and I took her to places of my childhood. And it was so real. And I remember the streets and how they looked. And she said, "You have such a vivid image of how it was. It is like a painting." I thought, "Well, I guess, it is part of me too."

LC: What comes across as home is Carriacou.
AL: As I have said in *Zami*—you have to understand—I think this is still true of many West Indians, but I know it was true at the time—"we were sojourners in a place that was not ours." And that is both a strength and weakness of my work. Since I have always been the outsider, it is again both an asset and a liability in my life and my work. A source of strength as well as a source of great vulnerability.

When my parents spoke of home, my mother would tell stories of home, it was always Grenada. They would speak of "this place" as the place where we lived.

LC: And they thought they would go back?
AL: Oh yes, always, always. Then my father died.

LC: Your mother is still living?
AL: Yes, my mother is still alive. She lives at 152nd Street. She is blind. She still lives in the apartment I bought in my later years. They came here meaning to work for a few years and then go back home. And then of course the Depression came and they never did.

Someday we would go *home*, to the good place.

LC: But you never saw it as a child, not until much later?
AL: Never, never, never. I never even saw Carriacou on a map until I was in library school. I went to Barbados in 1973 and I went to Grenada in '78. When I was growing up, it was a dream. But it was home.

And it was useful in the sense that this was not all. I think that is why that green and those trees were so magical, because my mother used to tell us stories about the fruit trees, and how she would get up in the morning and there would be dew on the bucket of water that they would haul back and forth. You know, the children would go downhill and get their bucket of water and carry it up and let it sit in the night air, and it would grow cool, and the dew would fall on it. And this is what they would wash with in the morning.

LC: When you went to Mexico, and when you went to Africa, it sounds like that was the next step.

AL: Mexico was wonderful for me. Wonderful in so many ways. It was so beautiful! So *beautiful,* so open, so self-affirming. All of these brown people in the majority was very very wonderful for me. And I was very young. I was eighteen or nineteen.

LC: One of the things I wondered about—you talked about the hill in Mexico. You talked about that quite a bit in your interview with Adrienne Rich. You talked about it as realizing that your words and your world could come together. I wondered, then, when you came back to New York City, when again you were out of that beauty that you had always imagined and then found that it was real, how that still applied?

AL: Well, I was living on 7th Street on the Lower East Side. The consciousness that I had that they could come together came out of the excess of feeling and the beauty of these birds and the mountain that I could see, and that feeling of almost not being able to contain it. But it was not restricted to that alone. So that, when I came back to New York, the first thing that I wrote was a very poetic short story that you have not seen.

LC: I did. With Adrienne, you talked about it.

AL: And it incorporated many beautiful things about Mexico but it was also about this river and I think really my mother. So in a sense I was trying to bring together what I could think about it consciously. Now, in retrospect, the grown-up Audre looks at that story and sees that at that point I just had to write this. But by the same token I began, then not thinking about it, to bring my writing and things I was feeling more strongly together. It was a gradual process.

For instance, I can remember that poem I wrote, "To Girls Who Know What Side Their Bread Is Buttered On"—which in a sense is a fantasy, but it also brings stuff close that I was feeling while I was on the Lower East Side. But it was a very gradual process. I *knew* that that was possible. I knew the way it felt when it happened in a line or a verse or a piece. I didn't know how to do it, but it was like biofeedback. When it happened I knew it had happened, and the more it happened, the more I was able to do it. So, I never studied it. I didn't get degrees in philosophy or go to poetry workshops.

LC: It seems to me that I see a change in your poetry coming, like with "Walking Our Boundaries" and "Coping." You are using what is around you in a different way, by using what is right there, and the poem is right in there. I think it is in "Walking Our Boundaries" you have that line about not needing a symbol when the substance is right here.

AL: "Lies up close at hand, waiting to be held." Mm-hmm.

Well, you know, moving out to Staten Island, it was the first time I have lived very closely with green, and I have been able to grow things, have a garden. I have a little garden. I have a vegetable patch, grass, a tree.

LC: And you are on an island again.

AL: That's right! I think it is a wonderful poem, I love it: "Going Away to San Francisco, I Passed Over You and the Verrazano Bridge." It is a very powerful poem. It was printed in *Contact* 2 this year, an issue where they did a lot of interviewing. I think the last issue. A couple of people interviewed me, and wrote some commentaries about my work, and they had a couple of poems, and that was one of them. It came out this summer.

That ties together more than poems have for me in a long time. A great sense of place. What happened was that I was on my way to San Francisco, and I was really on overload. I had been working too hard, running around, giving talks, teaching. I was looking forward to this trip to the West Coast, and we were held up in a tremendous air jam, and I was in the air circling my house. I could tell, because we live about two minutes from the Verrazano Bridge. And there is the Verrazano Bridge, and the plane is circling. I was inspired by the fact that I was considering *leaving*, you see, so there is another change of place coming up. And all of a sudden, all these thoughts—why I am leaving, New Jersey, Ellis Island, South Africa. All this! But it is very much a place poem, where place connected incredible things, while the plane is circling. And I wrote it down in my journal.

LC: There is a very different feeling toward nature among the three men poets I have been talking with. If I include myself with you and Marie Ponsot, then that is three women with a very different feeling.

AL: I think it is very important. I think men have a very basic difference in their attitude towards the earth, and I think we are about to be destroyed by it.

LC: These are poets. These are not destructive people.

I started by working with the three men, and it was a shock, because I felt as if I was suddenly having to see the world through new eyes. Then I got back to your poetry and Marie Ponsot's, and I felt I was returning back to the world I knew. What I feel and what I see in your writing and Marie Ponsot's writing is essentially, when you come down to the line, there is a connection. The earth isn't Another. It is not something alien. Their sense of death is connected with their sense of nature. Their sense of nature and their sense of earth—it is connected with their sense of death for them.

AL: And they feel a need to conquer the earth in the same way they feel a need to conquer women, I think. I often want to move it beyond the question of maleness to speak of that principle which is in all of us, that is on the line more for men than it is for women. I think women are capable of that alienation too. Although I think the thing that we have built in that guards against it has very essentially to do with the giving of birth, the giving of life, the fact that it was women who first labored in agriculture, the first ones to make the earth bear, historically.

LC: What I am seeing is not at all as if you don't have a consciousness of death or Marie Ponsot does not have a consciousness of death—I mean, that would be ridiculous to suggest, especially in your case. But somehow it is not something destructive. And I feel it is connected with your sense of the earth.

AL: It is connected with a sense of renewal. It has to do with renewal, with a belief in renewal.

LC: I get a sense in your work, when you talk about evolution, it seems to me you are talking about evolution spiritually, and then you are talking about ancestors' voices, their being able to speak through you without constricting you, and then your speaking for children . . . it is that sense of continuity, and somehow it seems connected with your sense of the earth.

AL: There is an early poem that comes to my mind when you are talking about this. Because, so often when I have these conversations, you know, I want to say, "Oh yeah, well, I talk about that in a poem." The name of the poem is "To Marie in Flight." I talk about, "there is something in my body teaches patience is no virtue." The earth renews itself over and over again. None of us lives 300 years is another way of saying it. You can't have one without the other. A renewal requires a going into dust, to rise again.

LC: At the end of your introduction to *The Cancer Journals*, you talk about fishing at dawn in the river and feeling this is yours forever.

AL: Yes, that sense. That I could take this in, and I could own it, and use it wherever else I was for the length of my time that is coming to me, and someone else, my children or my children's children or someone else's children, will stand in that place and see that sweetness also. But the two things—that I must take it in and not hold it away. I take it in, I carry it with me. It is mine forever. I experience it and I will take it to death with me. It will go on forever. Do you understand what I am saying? It is mine forever because it exists. It will exist within me and it will exist outside of me. I could own it in myself by recalling it, remembering it, and taking it in. I could own it because other human beings, other women, will stand there.

LC: Then there is a sense of being part of those other women.
AL: Yes, yes.

LC: I think what you are saying is that you are yourself but you are also fluid.
AL: I am myself and I must define myself, right? But I am connected. I am part of a . . . [she breaks off and begins again] and I get this feeling more and more and more the older I get . . . I am part of a chain, I am part of a continuum. It did not start with me and it will not end with me, but my piece is vital. I feel this so strongly now.

LC: That is the difference. You feel your piece is vital, and that is what I don't get with the men. They feel they are not going to go on living in any sense. It is a very different sense of self.
AL: You know, I don't quite understand this either, because, yes, I do have children, but I think this operates in women who do not have children too. I believe that the raising of children is encultured in the species, beyond whom you open your legs and give birth to.

(Chawla talks briefly about her own daughter's struggle to come to terms with being half Indian—a struggle beginning at the age of three. Lorde responds that a sense of difference is still constantly reinforced in children of color in the United States.)

LC: In that interview with Karla Hammond, she quoted Alice Walker. Do you remember that?
AL: No, I don't!

LC: She quoted Alice Walker in terms of Walker saying that if there is one thing Black poets in this country took as a rule from Africa, it was animism, the feeling that everything is made of spirit. And you said that you absolutely agree.

AL: Not only that everything is made of spirit, but there is a connection before even there is life. I felt this very very strongly in Africa. And it resounded. It hit something deep inside of me. The whole book *The Black Unicorn* comes out of that consciousness. I had just gone to Africa, and when I came back I studied a great deal, and it illuminated so much. It pulled together things that I had felt but I had not been able to articulate. That is another kind of use of place.

The thing that strikes me so much when I go to Carriacou, and to Grenada and Barbados—I am really attracted to those islands. I went to Africa before I went to the islands, and the resonances are incredible. The things that are so familiar. The thing that runs through it is the very African relationship between family members, between mothers and daughters, between the youngest daughter and the father. Which was almost nonexistent, but it is the one place, it is the one place where I identified with my father, which is, you know, the youngest daughter carries the food. There are things that rang true for me, which I would otherwise never have put together. So one of the things that I wanted to do in *Zami* was underline the connections between Africa, the African Caribbean, and Africans in America.

LC: Which you were able to do after you had been to Africa and the West Indies?
AL: Yes, mm-hmm. I went to Africa first and then to the Caribbean.

LC: You weren't ready to write that book until after that?
AL: That's right. Well, I never imagined writing a prose piece. I was a poet!

LC: It is very much poetry too. Especially when you talk about Carriacou, it is poetry put in prose.
AL: Out of my mother's mouth.

LC: When did you connect up with Black American poetry—the Harlem Renaissance, Alice Walker and others?
AL: Well, I connected with Alice Walker in Tougaloo. She wrote me in '68. There was like an underground of Black poets that existed during the '60s, which we all knew.

LC: That is how Langston Hughes picked you up in his *New Negro Poetry* before he died?

AL: That's right. He came after me. At the time, I was not published at all, in '61, '62. I was not a popular Black poet, because some of the things I said ran very counter to a line that was the line in Black poetry at the time. And there was a lot of sexism involved too in those days—not that there isn't now, but it was particularly then. So, my relationship with Black poets was very checkered. Also because I was a lesbian, and most were quite aware of that and rejected it out of hand. So I was suspect. I have always been suspect in different situations.

LC: But he was open to you in spite of that?

AL: Langston? Yes. I wasn't aware of it at the time, but I think it had a lot to do with it, that he was closeted.

LC: When you wrote your poems in high school, you are talking about white models, like Edna St. Vincent Millay.

AL: Yes. When I was in high school, I had never read Black poetry. The one poet of color whom I had read, and loved, was Pablo Neruda. I have to say that Neruda and Millay were the two poets I *loved*. All the others didn't make much sense. Except Eliot. He really got to me. That man really did it for me with language.

LC: That is his great power.

AL: I mean, the intensity was sexual, it was so powerful.

It was Edna St. Vincent Millay, Eliot and Pablo Neruda.

(An interruption to discuss ordering dessert and coffee.)

LC: Then after you finished high school, you went to the Harlem Writers' Guild?

AL: Well, that was my first introduction. I met Langston Hughes when I was quite young, still in high school. John Henrik Clarke was a young man at that time, and I was in high school. He happened to run into me. I used to ask for poetry at the library, and one time, the librarian said, "Oh, well maybe you would like to attend. There is a group of poets that meets here at the library." We were maybe sophomores or juniors in high school when I came. That is how I met John Henrik Clarke and Langston Hughes. Langston Hughes left the workshop soon after that because he was under attack by the House

Un-American Activities Committee. It was a very very painful time for him. So he only came about six months and then he was out. But that was my first connection.

LC: Do you think that changed your sense of poetry?
AL: I think it changed my sense of self. And therefore it changed my sense of poetry also. Now let me see. Johnnie Clarke was the first person who really said to me, "Now, you're a poet. Hang in there." For all the differences that I have had with him over the years, I will always remember him and be thankful to him for that. I was a child. I was only fourteen, fifteen years old. And he said that. He said, "Someday, someday, you're going to win the Yale Series of Younger Poets." Huh? I didn't understand what he was saying. Because writing poetry was something that I did and I had to go and hide it. And that was the kind of communication that I got *nowhere else*. Later, I got it from one teacher in high school. And that was it. That was it. So that was very important.

Now, subsequently, I go on, and I really separated in some ways from my Black community. I used to go up to Harlem to the Writers Guild in the '50s. But then I had a child, and there was that. Then that carried over to the '60s, with the developing interest in Black poetry and its greater visibility. The poems that I wrote remained in some respects not Black enough, you see, but they were Black enough for me, because they came out of who I was and I certainly was Black!

LC: It seems to me there were two things that had to happen for you to be working here in this country in New York City as a poet. One of them we talked about, in terms of Mexico, feeling that words and feeling could come together. Another thing would have to be a feeling that you could be a poet here, yourself, and finding Black poetry must have had a lot to do with it.
AL: But you must understand what that means. That simple, apparently ordinary connection between poetry and feeling was *terribly* threatening, and very very dangerous. I am Black and I am a woman. I took the next step in poetry with the feeling that automatically I was committing myself to exploring a kind of fury that could be totally destructive. How to keep that alive and not be destroyed by it is a tension that runs through all of my work, and I believe the work of every serious Black woman poet, every outsider poet in America. I think that is what lends a kind of power and reality to our work. And I think we have reclaimed poetry as a result.

An Interview with Audre Lorde

Joseph F. Beam / 1984

From *Blacklight Online www.blacklightonline.com/lordeinterview.html*. The interview was conducted in March 1984. © 2000 Blacklightonline.com. Reprinted by permission.

Audre Lorde is like a multi-faceted diamond. She is a mother, poet, novelist, publisher, socialist, feminist, and Lesbian. Sharp. She cuts through the bramble of political correctness and does not hold her tongue. Reflective. She shows not only where we are but where we wish to be. Brilliant. She does not obscure her vision with intellectual jargon but writes simply, yet eloquently. Despite her rigorous schedule, I was able to reach her by phone at her Staten Island, New York, home. What follows is most of our early morning conversation.

Joseph Beam: How do you manage to balance all the aspects of self: poet, Lesbian, mother, feminist, and so on? How do you nurture and attend to all those roles concurrently and still find time to read the newspaper and wash the dishes?

Audre Lorde: Well, lots of times the dishes don't get washed. That's one of the problems. As Frances [her lover] and I always note, ruefully, everything we do nurtures everything else, as well as competes for time. It has to be like that or else I would just collapse under the weight. I think, for most of us, once we soften that categorizing sense that compartmentalizes us with the various lives we live, once we allow all our stuff to flow more freely, once I am who I am, a lot of energy is freed for the questions that arise rather than the roles to be played.

JB: Are you going to continue with your story that you began in *Zami: A New Spelling of My Name*?

AL: Now that *Sister Outsider* is done I want to start on a second piece of fiction but it's not going to be "biomythography." I call *Zami* biomythography because it's made up of myth, history, and biography, all the ways in which we perceive the world around us. I would like to do another piece of fiction dealing with a number of issues: Lesbian parenting, the 1960s, and interracial relationships in the Lesbian and Gay community. I'm being very vague about it because I'm not really sure how I'm going to construct that.

JB: One issue I haven't seen you address in print is the interracial relationship in which you are involved. Interracial relationships seem, at different times, to be more or less of an issue in the Gay and Lesbian community.
AL: It's always an issue! I get really bored with how much of an issue it continues to be. But, on the other hand, I get bored with racism too and recognize that there are still many things to be said about a Black person and a White person loving each other in a racist society. I've spoken about the relationship between Frances and me a little bit in the *Cancer Journals*. More in *Sister Outsider*, in a long article called "Eye to Eye: Black Women, Hatred and Anger." There's a long poem, "Outlines," in my new collection of poetry which looks at the evolution of Black and White women who do not love each other and the relationship between Black and White women who do love each other.

JB: The literary establishment in America has a tendency to select and honor one Black writer per year. A couple of years ago it was Toni Morrison. Last year it was Alice Walker and, to a lesser extent, Gloria Naylor. Do you see this tendency, which has been employed for decades, as problematic?
AL: I think it has been employed for decades and it is problematic. I am very, very happy for Alice Walker. When I saw her picture on the cover of the *New York Times Book Review* I thought, "Well good for you Alice! I wish it had been me. But if it wasn't me, I'm really glad it's you." I really can't see a picture of a Black dyke on the cover of the *New York Times Book Review*. I would start to get real worried, saying the kinds of things I do, and knowing what I'm trying to do, if I did wind up on the cover of the *Times Book Review*. I'd begin to ask myself what that meant as a Black Lesbian feminist committed to radical social change. But the Gay and Lesbian community contributes to this invisibility. What do you think it means when Lambda Rising, Washington D.C.'s Gay bookstore, that says it "celebrates the Gay experience," takes a full page ad in *Blacklight* and does not include one single title by a Black Lesbian? Should Barbara Smith, Pat Parker, Ann Shockley, Cheryl Clarke and others, laugh or cry? It's not only the literary establishment that renders us invisible.

JB: Let's talk about your work with Kitchen Table: Women of Color Press.
AL: I'm very excited about Kitchen Table. I think it's an important manifestation of what has to happen. We need to build our own institutions. When we
create out of our experiences, as feminists of color, women of color, we have to
develop those structures that will present and circulate our culture. We have to
be able to publish those things that would not be published otherwise, or be
available to the different communities of women of color. It's a struggle but
that's why we exist, so that another generation of Lesbians of color will not
have to invent themselves, or their history, all over again.

JB: The difference that I noticed between *Home Girls: A Black Feminist
Anthology* and *This Bridge Called My Back: Writing by Radical Women of
Color* was the material in *Home Girls* seemed so much more accessible while
This Bridge felt very intellectual.
AL: That's interesting because I feel *This Bridge* has that quality of accessibil-
ity, also. Many grassroots organizations and people who have used it seem to
feel that way too. I think they are very different books because they come out
of very different visions. *Home Girls* was originally a third world women's
issue of *Conditions* magazine. Therefore it had, from its inception, a different,
much broader focus than *This Bridge*, which was conceived as a collection
of writing by radical women of color. So they served different kinds of
functions.

JB: In the past couple of years Lesbians of color have formed presses and are
being published by some of the major presses. . .
AL: What Lesbians of color are being published by some of the major
publishers?

JB: Norton has published your work as well as the Crossing Press. Perhaps
they're not huge presses like Harper and Row. . .
AL: Norton is, that's true but that's one! Look at how many Black Lesbian
writers there are whose names are not known. Why isn't Gloria Hull a household name because of the research she's done on women of the Harlem
Renaissance? What about Pat Parker? She's a really powerful poet. Norton is
probably one of the finest poetry publishers in this country but I'm only one
Black dyke and I'm greedy. I want more of us read and seen. Alice Walker is
not a Lesbian. She has made very positive and sympathetic statements of

"solidarity" with Lesbian sisters but she has made it perfectly clear that she is not a Lesbian and I think that's a real factor in her acceptability.

JB: What words of inspiration, or advice, do you have for Gay men of color who have been silent? How do we begin to write about our experience?

Lorde: I'm not sure whether Black Gay men have been silent or whether they just don't have avenues for getting their work heard. That's one of the reasons why I'm really pleased to see the Blackheart Collective in New York and publications like *Blacklight* in Washington. These are important institutions that have to be developed as outlets of Black Gay writing. However, Gay men of color need workshops and discussion groups as well as magazines. Art does not exist in a vacuum. There is the necessity for Gay men of color to examine the truths within their experience which can be shared and, at the same time, develop a vision of some future which those truths can actively help shape because this is the function of any art, to make us more who we wish to be.

Audre Lorde on Her Cancer Illness

Dagmar Schultz / 1984

Orlanda Women's Press editor Dagmar Schultz (DS below), with sociologist Erika Fink (EF): previously unpublished interview, conducted in Germany in May/June 1984. Published by permission of the interviewers.

Dagmar Schultz: What interests us first is the question about the diagnosis and the way medical people were dealing with you, and what options you had left.
Audre Lorde: Well, the first time I was told that I had to have a biopsy, I was told that I had an 80 percent chance of a malignancy. I got the name of another surgeon, a breast cancer surgeon in New York, and was pretty much told the same thing.

DS: But you went both times to a surgeon.
AL: I went both times to a surgeon because I had gone to my regular doctor, my gynecologist, an internist, and a radiologist who did the mammography. From there the choices were breast surgeons—the only people I knew, and who had been recommended to me, who dealt with breast tumors. My gynecologist had done what she could, which was to say: oh, there's something there, go to a radiologist. The radiologist said: u-huh, there is something there. I did not at that point have enough knowledge to do something else. I went to see four doctors, and then both Frances [Clayton, Audre Lorde's partner] and I talked to them. They kept coming up with these incredibly high percentages—almost certain that this was malignant, even without a biopsy.

So I started reading whatever I could about this. Started really thinking about what it meant, how I felt, the terror, the sense that I had to get more information, and more information was difficult to find. And also trying things. And I really made the decision on the doctor, the surgeon I went with, because he was a person who gave me and Frances together the most time, just in terms of explaining some of the stuff, of answering my questions, of going over these questions again. Yeah, that's Peter. And also, he's the doctor who recognized the relationship between Frances and I and treated her as my family, as my closest. And that was also something that we had to have.

The reading that I had done made me think about what I would do if this was malignant, and since it probably was malignant, what then? I knew I had to keep control over the space of time, so I had already decided I would separate the biopsy from any further operation. Did I want an operation? I started reading as much as I could then about alternatives, also about radiation, and I felt this really very strongly, that chemotherapy and radiation were bad, very bad news. Some of the stuff I came across said, well, you know, biopsies aren't even really necessary. If you don't want to cut, you can take radiation. A lot of this came from things I'd read, because I read a lot of medical stuff anyway.

DS: That's what I was thinking, because you're a librarian and . . .
AL: I had access. I had access. But, even so, I would say at the minimum the questions are finding a doctor who will talk to you, who will answer the questions, who will recognize that no, you don't know it all, but yes, you have a right to know because this is your life. And that I felt was really important.

DS: But what if another woman comes to Peter, and she doesn't have the questions that you know? Can we even develop the questions without getting into that kind of reading you got into?
AL: All women now seem to know, for instance, that there's an alternative of lumpectomy and radiation. Somehow that has managed to seep into the grass roots. And it's done it by articles in the *Daily News*, in *Ladies Home Companion*, in *Ms.* Well, on that level, I'm interested in spreading information about alternatives.

In 1978, when I had a mastectomy, the choices were radical and modified radical. Right? Peter mentioned the fact that there is this choice of lumpectomy and radiation, and he mentioned it in the context of: this is being done and you need to know about that, but I do not recommend it. I said, oh? He said, first of all, it is too new; I don't know what the statistics are. I think that there's almost as much disfigurement; I don't see the point of the option, and I think there's no point in playing with fire. I remember asking whether he also felt that radiation is carcinogenic. Of course, he's a doctor. All he said was: well, I can't say that radiation is carcinogenic, but I can say that we know little enough about it, that we really shouldn't expose anyone to it. And I heard a lot of stuff coming from him that I respected at that level. But he was still a doctor. Lumpectomy was not spoken of. That was not common knowledge. Now, this is 1984, and when you have breast cancer the choice that all the doctors give is modified radical or this lumpectomy and radiation, lumpectomy and chemical attack. It still really upsets me. But I know very close friends of mine, women who I love and respect, who've opted for that. It doesn't make sense to me, but . . .

DS: Chemotherapy?
AL: No, the two. A lumpectomy, which means they take out the lump, and then they radiate. Now there's distortion. If the point is to maintain a breast, I mean, you're not maintaining a breast. Then why do it?

EF: It's horrible.
AL: It is to me. I'm sorry, it really is to me, the idea of it. So that's what I mean about alternatives. That piece of information in four years seeped down to the general public, that there are choices. It seeped down through the establishment because the surgeons, or the powers that be, or the Cancer Society wanted it to seep down. So articles came and came and came. It's harder to find out about the genuine alternatives. It really is. It is not impossible—there are articles around that people clipped and sent to me. But they clipped and sent them to me because I made a thing out of needing information and needing information quickly. Those articles should appear in other places. They now appear in *Prevention* magazine. Well, *Prevention* magazine is a grassroots publication, but not that many people read it. More read it than read *Psychology Today*, you know, and it's geared for the *Reader's Digest* level.

There is an emphasis now on health fads of all kinds in the States. In community magazines, articles have to start up. I did see one of them, on the enzyme Wobemogus. That's where I first read about the stuff that was being done here in Germany, by the anthroposophic company Weleda. They had maybe four lines of information in a two-page article. Most of it was: but still, a-ha!, something else—on that level. What I've said to women there, and I guess it would apply to women here in Germany, too, is that you have to be: a) really aggressive about trying to get information and b) also speak to women's institutions, saying that we have a responsibility to get the articles out, to have them around, to try to impress upon women in general that there are alternatives, and to check them out—so that this is knowledge aforehand, this is in our consciousness in the event that a lump occurs.

But we also have to talk about having it be a real concern. Cancer is a woman's concern. Breast cancer is a feminist concern. It's a feminist concern of the twenty-one-year-old feminist who doesn't know it is. We need to reach women on that level, I think, rather than have it be a secret. Look how long menstruation was a secret little thing that we didn't talk about. We thought: we're going to build the future, we have a feminist vision, and we have a lot of work to do. But nobody mentioned that we should make sure there are always Tampax in the bathroom, because we are women and we do menstruate, right? It's like there are certain parts of our lives we were cut off from. Well, what I'm saying is: breast cancer is something we cannot afford to be cut off from, because it is rising. And it's a feminist concern because there is work that can be done as women, informed women.

I know the work that I did finding out about cancer in that period, that year, not only informed me, and made me more able when I finally had to deal with cancer to make some panic decisions—it also made my head really work about what's going on: cancer is a political fact. And it's necessary, as I said, for us to see what some of those implications are. The question of the relation between fat and breast cancer, or the kinds of pollutants that are carcinogenic—these are issues that we need to raise and protest against.

DS: After the operation, did you decide on further therapy, together with your doctor?

AL: No. My nodes were clear. The question of further therapy did not come up with Peter. No. I had decided that, if the nodes weren't clear, I wasn't going to do radiation. But I did not have to make that decision because my nodes were clear. No, Peter at no time suggested anything about the immune system. That is in the stage of experimentation. A doctor I went to after that, an oncologist, spoke about the immune system, but only in terms that this was involved.

Peter, my surgeon, implied that I might want to think about diet, but he didn't tell me what. He implied that I should stay away from fats—and this is the best there is, right?—and I remember his saying: well, some people are thinking about the connection between fat and cancer, so maybe you'd just better watch that too. They haven't done anything on it yet, but I've been hearing a lot of stuff. And it was on that level. Now when I pursued that and started reading myself, there was loads of material. But just not in the *AMA Journal.* On the connection between animal fats and stuff. And yet, as I say, if gold rusts, then what should iron do? Because he's as close to a holistic medical person as I've met. You know you talk about how here there are medical doctors. . . . Peter's about as close as that, and he's so far away.

There are other aspects doctors usually do not talk about: for instance, the effects on the functions of the brain. There are three parts of the brain. The limbic system is the old brain. In other words, the most primitive, the most original. It controls involuntary muscles. But we know that we can affect it. That's what biofeedback is all about, putting yourself in a place to literally affect involuntary responses. Well, you can strengthen the limbic system, for instance, to do extra battle. And in that respect, I think visualizations, visualizing the cancer attacking and so forth, those things are very useful.

DS: Waltraut Ruf, in her afterword to the German translation of your book *The Cancer Journals* (*Auf Leben und Tod: Krebstagebuch*), talks about the difficulties of dealing with fears of people around you and the importance self-help groups have in this context. How did you confront the fear others have of the illness?

AL: People on the outside tend to either ignore the illness or objectify it in some way. I have a lot of respect for someone like Ms. X, a woman I met in Germany, when I said something about cancer. The look on her face was just, yuck, why did you mention it! But she could just come right out and say, Oh, that is one thing I have an absolute terror of. And I mentioned then, of course, my book, *The Cancer Journals*. But she did say that is one thing I have a terrible fear of. More than anything else. And she talked a little bit about it. I thought, well that's good. And I said something about, well, that's why I wrote it, to help get over that fear.

DS: She didn't ask you for a copy?

AL: No, no. Her response to a woman with breast cancer would be to avoid her, you see. And her husband's a medical doctor. He stood there looking totally uncomfortable and unconnected, like all of a sudden he didn't understand the language.

DS: How did you feel about the fact that you were writing the essays rather than poetry after your operation?

AL: Oh! Oh, you mean about the loss of one's creativity. I can talk about it, but I used to say that I'm not certain about this. This is something I'm still feeling out. While I wrote *The Cancer Journals*, I wasn't writing poetry. It just seemed to be impossible to write poetry, and it was such a terrible time for me because of that in addition to the cancer. Now I think that they weren't unconnected. I think that probably there may have been some kind of additional separation of the right/left brain. Because it was really severe. In *The Cancer Journals*, I write some about it. I would like to address this in a more direct way and try to examine some of the real fractures that happened in that three-year period after cancer.

When Michaela Rosenberg, the doctor I have seen in Berlin, talked to me about six years being a very short time in terms of the assault on the immunological system, it was like for the first time someone was dealing with that. Because you know, in the States, you get a month, then hey, you're good, right? Including the women with mastectomies. They say hey, oh that's fine. There's nothing wrong with me, I'm in great shape. You know? I feel better. And I thought, Audre, what is going on? Because I know it literally took me three years. And I kept thinking, was there something I was doing wrong? But I just know that for three years I was in a desperate battle. I knew it all through my system. And I would like to chronicle that in some way. When Dr. Rosenberg said that about the six years, I thought: she's the first person I have ever heard imply that. Even doctors. They test you. They say, you have to keep coming back for testing. They say, five-year period—but nobody talks about how long it takes to recuperate from it.

DS: The five-year period doesn't mean anything about how you feel.
AL: That's right. And . . . hey, you're fine, and uplift, and new prosthesis, and new hairdo, and—I didn't write a word of poetry, you know?

EF: You always have to be a nice guy, huh?
AL: And people got tired—a lot of people got really tired of me in those three years. They really did. It was like, now come on. Enough is enough. And I was saying, no, enough is not enough. This is my life. And sometime I will try to put that down, just because I think it might be useful to some other women, and also because what you said, Dagmar, is really true: I was in a position to do that work, right? I could get a leave of absence from Hunter. Frances could carry me and the kids for half a year. But you know, most of the women who have breast cancer aren't in that position. Certainly most black women who have breast cancer certainly aren't in that position, just economically. So how do they touch the centers of what I'm saying? These are all questions I want to raise.

All of this comes under the fact that how we deal with this is an index of how we've dealt with our whole lives. From the very first, how do you withstand the pressure from the doctor? A lot of it has to do with that kind of strengthening I keep talking about that we have to work at. I know there are things in my life since then I would not have been able to do if I had not done that kind of work. I would not have been able to make the decision I wasn't going to take radiation the year before if I hadn't faced other things, come across other things in my life. In other words, what I'm saying is that we build, become strong by doing the things we need to be strong for. And we do them a little bit at a time. And it builds up. That's why it's important to speak to the cab driver who makes insulting remarks about women. Some days you won't bother because you may be doing something else. And sometimes you don't do it and, hey, you just notice it and think, well, maybe next time I will. That's part of just making yourself strong. One thing comes after another. We meet breast cancer like we meet every other crisis, out of a composite of who we are.

It all comes back to a certain line about a certain way of living one's life. Now, it's not even learning how to move through the world. It's not even that specific. Because god knows, I see women moving through the world all the time in ways I wish I could and know I can't. Or moving through the world in ways I think are *terrible*. But in all those different ways they may be moving through the world, one thing comes across, which is a certain determination to use whatever they have. And I recognize this in them. Well, I am talking about that. I'm talking about a certain kind of development of power, personal power. And I'll deal in another place with what you're using that power for. I really do believe that helping this power be developed is something that is a positive good.

I am talking about why I believe empowered women are important. It's not because I think women cannot embody evil or act incorrectly. It does not mean that I can't envision a time when my enemies are women. What I am saying is, I'll take that chance.

DS: But I think that for some it really is harder than for others, you know? In terms of who they are around, or who's around them. The kind of people they're dealing with. Whether they have five kids and a husband who has no interest in acknowledging the illness, no support from other persons, no knowledge, no practical information.

AL: Yeah. Except I never will forget that woman in the pink nylon. I'll diverge a minute to tell you. There's a certain kind of pink nylon that is for me the epitome of a-humanness, okay? It's very similar to that stuff that an artist wrapped around a whole island. If that is not the ultimate modern nightmare, right? Green island surrounded by pink nylon. Okay. This woman, little, *dyed* red hair, pink nylon robe, with a rose in her hair—it's in the book [*The Cancer Journals*]—extended herself to me. I heard in her voice, what I didn't recognize at the time, but I'll never forget it. I heard in her voice a kind of real change. And I thought, hmm, all right, I would never have met this woman on any other level, except of breast cancer. I mean I might have met her in a supermarket because she's probably a checker, you know, supermarket checker or something. Her life is very different from mine. I don't know what her options are. Now how she deals with it in her life, I don't know. But I recognized it in her.

EF: Another aspect that is important is the effects of a breast operation on the work situation.
AL: Yeah. Well, you know a lot of response to this question of prosthesis versus not prosthesis has been on two levels. One: (Gasp) Oh, you're going to ruin your body. Which, of course, is bullshit. You know that you're going to be unevenly proportioned and therefore do terrible things to your posture. But no one deals with, for instance, women whose breasts are unequal in weight. Most women, and particularly large-breasted women, have great differences in their breast weight. No one ever deals with what it means for a woman, for a lifetime of carrying babies on her hip, one baby after the other. But that's been one level.

And the other level has been from women who say, ah, yes, but there's so much discrimination against me to begin with, I didn't even want to tell them I had breast cancer. I'd say it was plastic surgery. They're terrified that they would lose their jobs, that people's attitudes—. And I can really hear that. Except I know—and the reason why I know this is because I was born black and a woman in the United States of America—I know that the way to fight that stuff is not to pretend it didn't happen. I mean, that really is like saying the way to combat racism is to pretend you're white. Moving against it in some way is the only thing that's going to make it begin to yield. There are women who cannot; they cannot. But there will always be women who can. There are women who are in positions, who can do this, who are unassailable. I'm talking to them.

DS: What did you feel your position was? Did you feel it was unassailable?

AL: I think it was pretty unassailable. I mean I can't really see the University of the City of New York firing me because I had breast cancer or because I didn't wear a prosthesis. My students were a little upset; some people left my class. I think they were people who thought I was very bizarre. But there are people who think I'm bizarre anyway. I feel, rightly or wrongly, I often go through life feeling I'm unassailable. I feel both things at once. I feel totally vulnerable and totally unassailable. So it's like the two extremes. The reality is somewhere in the middle, but meanwhile I'm operating like both. And usually I manage to bungle my way through. (Laughter.)

So I felt I was unassailable. But when you ask what made you able to feel unassailable, I have to say, the same way when people say, how could you live in Berlin for three months, it's so white. And I keep saying, you only ask that question because you don't know what it feels like to live in the United States of America as a black woman. So if I feel unassailable and vulnerable and support the two at the same time, it's because I move through my life with a knowledge of the immensity of the contradictions all the time. Contradictions in myself, personally, contradictions on the street outside.

DS: After your operation, you designed clothes and jewelry for one-breasted women who do not wear a prosthesis. I think everyone would agree that this was a remarkable, positive response. Can you say something about the reactions?

AL: I think, by the way, a change in fashion has already started, and no one's even saying anything. Just the same way that elasticized pants, women's pants, started long before people really focused on the fact that maternity clothes were necessary. I think it shows in the emphasis that's come out in the last couple of years with diagonals, like the thing I'm wearing now, which is *perfect* for me. I think that is a beginning response.

DS: Unconscious or conscious? Is it planned?

AL: No, I don't think it's been planned. I think it is a response because they have become very popular, but not only among women who have one breast.

DS: When did it become known that you design clothes and jewelry?

AL: In '79 it was published in *Ms.*

DS: Don't you think that you were the first one?

AL: Oh, I know I was the first one.

DS: Don't you think some fashion designers might have said, Did you see *Ms.* last week, what about this? That somebody keeps track of the statistics of one-breasted women?

AL: Oh, it might be. Yes. It could be like that. 'Cause I know I do. I'm constantly on the lookout for certain patterns, I mean; diagonals are a factor in what I buy. I think it's true for other women too. Even women who wear prostheses, interestingly enough. I now meet women who don't wear prostheses. There's a growing group of women on the West Coast, and they are very, very physically oriented. I think I told you this, Erika. There's this wonderful poster of Dina Metzger. She's jumping up, and she has a rose tattooed over her scar. Those women sometimes wear prostheses and sometimes don't. Now that is probably what most women would take as a position, right? Sometimes I do, sometimes I don't. In other words, there's a freedom. It's like black women saying, well, sometimes I'll have a permanent, sometimes I won't. But in the '60s it was very different.

DS: How important has the ability to withstand pressure been for you? How did you deal with doctors who put pressure on you?

AL: I want to say that, the doctors who insisted on treating me like the little lady, I didn't go back to. Okay? I found a doctor who I felt respected me.

DS: And he was the main person you had to deal with.

AL: He was the main person I had to deal with. That's right. This question of withstanding pressure has got to be addressed because in the event that a woman makes a decision for anything different than what her doctor suggests, there is an enormous amount of pressure that's brought to bear. I don't care who the doctor is, I think that this would be true. I have had to deal with doctors who laid the most enormous and bone-crunching pressures upon me, for instance, to have other biopsies. And it is just terrible. It is terrible, because they do. They threaten you with not only that you are going to die, not only that you are stupid and emotional, they also threaten you with withdrawing their support. You know, I won't be responsible for this. And it's frightening. It is really terrifying.

The only thing that I think we can answer that with is having built up a process of learning how to withstand pressures in our lives. Recognizing the kinds of pressures that we are always under. And this is why I said that how we deal with breast cancer, how we deal with doctors, how we deal with physical crises is made up in the whole way in which we deal with our lives.
I think, for instance, all the way from when you teach kids how to deal with peer pressure, and that's a vital part in keeping them away from dope, keeping them away from hard drugs, just teaching them how to, and then they're freer to make their own decisions—the process of encouraging women to become more able to make decisions, more able to say we have a right to make these decisions is an ongoing one. It's not something that happens when they say, Oh, Mrs. X, a lump. Or even if it starts then, you can work very, very fast, but you gotta work very, very fast.

I just don't know how else to put it. But I do say very, very urgently that, for women who don't have breast cancer, the point is less breast cancer than that we develop a warrior stance to our bodies in all the areas of our lives. That we learn how to say no, I do not believe that is in my best interest. And that is very hard to do. It's very hard to do when you go into KaDeWe [large department store in Berlin], and you know that you want a size 14 and there's a size 16, and the saleswoman says, Oh, it looks very nice on you, dear. Look! Get it! It's fine!, and be able to smile and say, Thank you, but no. On that level! And it goes all the way up to being able to say, No, I don't want reconstructive surgery. That's a message a lot of women don't get.

I have to tell you, in terms of self-help groups, I think that they do a very good job, very good work in the community. I think more attention has got to be paid to see self-help in a broader sense. To see that a health self-help center for women has got to involve itself in how do you develop the ability to make decisions. It has got to involve itself in how do you acquire information about your health that we may not have here at the center. Involve itself in the fact that women ultimately are going to have to go out into a what you call school-medicine place for any number of things, if only that they really need X-rays. So how do you develop an informed women's public, who is going to have to go out of the health self-help center to institutions of regular medicine. And help develop a posture for dealing with that. And it does start with things like decision-making. With resisting pressure. With peer-group opposition.

The Law Is Male and White: Meeting with the Black Author, Audre Lorde

Dorothee Nolte / 1986

From *Der Tagesspiegel*, 10 August 1986, Women's Life section. The interview was conducted in June 1986 in Berlin. Reprinted by permission of *Der Tagesspiegel*, Berlin. Trans. Francis J. Devlin.

"Something about me troubles everyone," says Audre Lorde and laughs disarmingly, "be it that I am black, that I am lesbian, poet, feminist, mother, warrior—I have always been an outsider." But just these problematic traits in our personalities, she hastens to add, are also those from which we have drawn our greatest strength—and, when in her tranquil, positive way she pronounces the word "strength," she knows what she is talking about. "For us who have grown up as black women in a society such as the U.S.A., the law is defined as male and white; survival, not a theoretical question but a part of our daily life." What's it like to grow up in the New York of the thirties and forties, the author of nine volumes of poems and three prose works—who was born in Harlem in 1934—has described in her book *Zami,* which has just appeared in German.

Audre Lorde designates her work as a "biomythography"; that is, she combines elements of myth, history, and autobiography in her book. "In African cultures, the ritual bestowing of a name is of great significance," she comments on the title of her book. "A child receives its first name eight days after birth, but it receives new names at decisive events its whole life long." "Zami" is one such "new name" for herself. The word derives from the Caribbean island, Carriacou, the island of her mother's birth, probably a derivative of the French "les amies," and it represents friendship and love between women.

And thus, in a captivating way, and in often poetic language, Audre Lorde recounts her experiences as the youngest, "fat, and almost blind" daughter of a West-Indian household in New York. She was one of the few black pupils in a Catholic girls' school, later an employee of an x-ray factory, and later still a drop-out in Mexico. In the late fifties, she was a member of the New York milieu. She gathers all of that under the perspective of her relationships with women. For the book *Zami*, she had to learn how to write prose—"just like a second language." For her "first love" and primary mode of self-expression is poetry, she says emphatically. One readily believes her after hearing her at her readings: the uniquely singing tone which makes her presentation almost a conjuring, if not, at least, a real experience, reverberates even when she reads her prose.

It has always been women who have helped her over crises, she says; even over the crisis she experienced eight years ago when one of her breasts had to be removed—a sad experience about which she has written a moving book, *Auf Leben und Tod—Krebstagebuch* [*The Cancer Journals*]. The networking and system of reciprocal aid among women, which can be observed in all cultures of African origin, has strengthened her from early on. "We need that for survival," she says straightforwardly.

She has traveled throughout the Caribbean islands and Africa as well, and she describes this with enthusiasm. In West-African Dahomey, she encountered a history and a mythology to which she felt particularly attracted. "Normally in African myths there is a split between the women, on the one hand, who give life and till the soil and men, on the other hand, who take lives, that is, wage war," she says. "In Dahomey, however, there is a tradition of warlike women, amazons who figure as especially dangerous warriors. I like that a lot since we black women in the United States are also both: life-givers and warriors."

Warriors against oppression by black men and, at the same time, against all-pervasive racism, against the fact that differences between people are constantly being used to oppress certain groups. "We must use our differences creatively," Audre Lorde says insistently in response; "So we need even now to form alliances with other groups where the situation for women and minorities in the U.S.A. is getting worse and worse." She welcomes the fact that the white women's movement in the U.S.A. has finally begun to tear down the barriers between white and black women. Yet she warns against erasing the differences between groups that are discriminated against. "We cannot and may not deny that we have a very different background and, to some extent, different goals."

"Differences" is one of her favorite words; "language" is another. In *Zami*, she writes that her parents never spoke with their children about the racism that surrounded them. If a white person spat at the children, they acted as if it were a completely random insult which could just as easily have happened to a white child.

They treated racism as "private suffering," and it's no surprise that she reacted inarticulately when a waitress in Washington refused to serve her family because they were black: "I had no words for racism." Now she has them and she constantly emphasizes how important it is to verbalize problems, to share them with others, and to give a voice to people who never had one before. One approach to that is the publishing house Kitchen Table Women of Color Press, whose founding she was involved in, and which specifically publishes works by women of color.

The Berlin visit in June was not the first one for Audre Lorde; in 1984, she served as visiting professor at the John F. Kennedy Institute, and she taught African American literature and creative writing there, as she does today at Hunter College in New York. Even here, she says, she has occasionally encountered racism. Her impression is that the people in the Federal Republic do not intend to be racist, but they are not working hard enough at overcoming the remnants of racism. For example, she felt it demeaning to see billboards with advertisements for "Nigger Kisses" or "Moors' Heads"—"of course, people say that that means nothing. But that is exactly the insidious aspect of racism: one accepts it without even noticing it. Only victims of racism notice it—but when they react against it, people consider them hypersensitive."

The Creative Use of Difference

Marion Kraft / 1986

From *EAST. Englisch Amerikanische Studien. Zeitschrift für Unterricht, Wissenschaft & Politik*, issues 3/4 (December 1986), 549–56. Reprinted by permission.

Marion Kraft: Audre, you are an Afro-American woman of Caribbean descent, a mother and a lesbian, feminist, essayist, professor of English, and a poet. Is poetry the most important part of all these various aspects of your life?

Audre Lorde: Poetry is not the most important part of my life. Poetry is the strongest expression I have of certain ways of making, identifying, and using my own power. Because poetry is not a presentation, is not a product. Poetry—for me—is a way of living. It's the way I look at myself, it's the way I move through myselves, my world, and it's the way I metabolize what happens and present it out again. So, it is an inseparable part of who I am. All the other aspects of me, when I say, "I am a Black lesbian feminist warrior poet mother," I am plucking out certain arbitrary pieces of me. I could pluck out different ones, if I wanted to, but I find that those that are most problematic are usually also the sources of our strongest power, and so, for that reason, it is a ritual, it has always served me to underline for myself and for other people the sources of my power.

MK: In *Poetry is not a Luxury* you wrote that it could be something like an allusion to the architecture of our lives.

AL: Yes, poetry is, in fact, the skeleton architecture of our lives; because it helps to form the dreams for a future that has not yet been, and toward which we must work, when we speak of change. Then, to speak of change in the absence of vision is to court chaos for ever.

MK: I've read in an essay by one of your critics that Audre Lorde is not per se a *Black* poet, she is a woman poet who also happens to be Black . . .

AL: There are some phrases that absolutely *tick me off,* and they usually start with "who happens to be." As a matter of fact, I have a brand new poem—in my brand new book—the title of which is "To the Poet who happens to be Black and the Black Poet who happens to be a Woman." Very seriously, the reason I

146

think this is so dangerous is because those of us who are committed to survival and to teaching—no, we don't *happen* to be anything. We are here, as Bernice Reagon says, over and over again, because somebody before us did something to bring us here. We are not ashored in our existence. So I didn't happen to be anything.

Being Black is very important, and being a woman is very important. I have paid a great deal to be both, consciously.

MK: In one of your poems, that I like very much, there is that image of your mother as a woman with two faces who actually is *two* women borne on the poet's back, "one dark and rich . . . the other pale as a witch. . . ." And then, there is this outcry, "Mother . . ."

AL: That's from *From the House of Yemanjá*. Yemanjá is the mother of us all. She is the aura of goddess, of rivers, of love, and of war. And that poem really deals not only with the split consciousness that so many light skinned Black women from the islands have, but also how it is necessary for each one of us to claim all of the parts of our ancestry, and at the same time to recognise the great nourishment and the great power of our Blackness. The Black mother being the source of nourishment, the source of power for us all—black, white, male, and female.

MK: In some of your essays you have also used this image of the Black mother in opposition to the "white father."

AL: Yes, the white fathers are the ones who have said "I think, therefore I am," having the concept that it is only through our thoughts, through our intellectual, rational processes that we gain freedom. This is not true. I speak of the Black mother as that part of us which is chaotic, messy, deep, dark, ancient, old, and freeing. And, the struggle is constantly one to harness the left brain with the rational parts to do the service of what is original and deep, which is the right brain, the emotions.

We think with tools that have been given to us. If we are to create a new order, we must go back, back, back to what is primary, and those are our feelings; and take those feelings and bring them forward enough, so we can cobble a new way out of them. In other words, a *screeaam* is just a feeling—but it is not a poem, it's not a piece of art. We must take the emotion behind that scream and make something out of it that is articulate and powerful and communicative.

MK: So, it is not that old stereotype, women are emotional, and men do the thinking?

AL: No, not at all. That is, I believe, a real distortion of reality. I think that patriarchy has elevated the whole question of rationality to a point where it no longer has a context; and let me say this: rationality is a tool, it is a bridge, a road. Like any road it must lead from somewhere to somewhere, or else it is just an exercise in futility. If we cannot anchor that rationality in our feelings and, on the other hand, have it lead toward a future where we can in fact survive, then rationality has no meaning; and we are now trapped in the age of rationality that has no vision at one end and has no acknowledgement of the true sources of self on the other. It would be ridiculous to believe that we can exist cut off from any part of ourselves. But there has been a false emphasis in Western European thought upon what is rational and a total rejection of what is emotional.

MK: Is that what you mean when you focus on the difference between poetry and rhetoric?

AL: Yes. That is exactly the difference. When I say that the difference between poetry and rhetoric is being ready to *kill ourselves instead of our children,* I mean, if we are really ready to put ourselves behind what we believe, then we can bring about change. Other than that, it is only empty rhetoric, and it is our children who will have to live out our destinies.

MK: In *Uses of the Erotic: The Erotic as Power* you described the erotic as one of the sources of power and knowledge in our lives.

AL: The Power of the Erotic, the Uses of Anger, we must not run from these parts as women. We have been encouraged to reject the power of the erotic, because the erotic has been used so cruelly against us, but we must be able to acknowledge all of the parts of ourselves and see how they contribute to the work we have to do in this world.

MK: You described this power of the erotic in your book *Zami* where it is also based on old African and Caribbean legends, but could you explain why you called it a biomythography?

AL: I called it a biomythography because it is not only autobiography. It also partakes of myths and history and a lot of other ways we use knowledge; and I used those myths in *Zami*, the myth of MawuLisa and her youngest daughter, Afrekete who is changed into Eshu, the prankster because I believe that there are some very, very definite ways in which African women, women of African descent, raise their children that hold true in many different places, and that does in fact reflect the sources of our power. For example, it is the West African women of Dahomey who have the legend, who have the belief and who demonstrate this, that there is not a contradiction between the taking of lives and the giving of life, and the making of war, so that you have your Dahomeyan amazons who were the fiercest warriors of the king. It is very important to have that, because, in fact, in the lives of so many Afro-American women, my mother, my mother's generation, I saw that these women were nurturing, they were cherishing, they were loving, but they were also really tough warriors, you know. So, we need to know that that is part of our tradition. This is why I think it is so necessary, I think, to weave myths into our world.

MK: Why did you choose the title *Zami: A New Spelling of My Name*?
AL: Well, in West African systems, the question of naming is a vital one. So, their children are born, and they are not named for eight days, because this is the time that a child spends deciding whether it wants to stay in this world. Once a child decides that it is going to stay, then a name is given. And many names are given. There are some secret names, there are names of times, names of family; and throughout your life, in Yoruba traditions, when something important happens, you gain another name, or you are given another name. The American Indians have this also. So, the process of naming is a way of rebirth, of underlining rebirth. And it is something that is happening in the book. Now, *Zami* is a word that is used in Carriacou, meaning *women who work and live together*, and it is a very beautiful word. I remember my mother using this word when I was a child, meaning just friends. I didn't know what it meant, I didn't know that it meant women-identified women, women who love each other, but when I came across it, I really wanted to claim it as my own, as a Black lesbian. And, originally, it probably came from Patois, which is a combination of French and Spanish, probably from "les amies," the friends.

MK: But in *Zami* you not only described the love between women, but also the isolation of Black lesbians in the fifties; and this reminded me of Gloria Naylor's *The Women of Brewster Place*, where in one story she delineated the homophobia in the Black community in the late sixties or early seventies. Has this climate changed in the eighties?

AL: Well, the homophobia in the Black community was a real reality; and yes, it is changing slowly. It is changing slowly because of the work of a number of very, very brave women, and also because Black lesbians, and Black gay men also, have assumed much more of a presence. We have come out of our isolation, and in mending together have had a presence about which we have been able to say, "We are Black, we have always been Black, we are involved, have always been involved in our communities," and this, of course, is true.

Along with that terrible homophobia has always gone a sort of silent acknowledgment of the maiden aunt or the unmarried people in our community. Within the Black community, difference has been used so cruelly against us, that we tend to trigger on it and believe that Black can be defined in some kind of homogeneous way. Well, this is not true. And to the extent that the Black community begins to recognize that, the Black community is also touching its strength in difference; we are Black, we are different.

MK: In your essay *The Uses of Anger*, you pointed out that each of us had a right to her own name, a right that often is ignored, even among white academic feminists. Do you see any development of the awareness about the importance of differences within the white feminist movement?

AL: Well, the feminist movement, the white feminist movement, has been notoriously slow to recognize that racism is a feminist concern, not one that is altruistic, but one that is part and parcel of feminist consciousness. If it is not, then the white feminist movement cannot really exist, and to a certain degree it almost floundered on this point. I think, in fact, though, that things are slowly changing, and that there are white women now who recognize that in the interest of genuine coalition they *must* see that we are not the same. Black feminism is not white feminism in Black face. It is an intricate movement coming out of the lives, aspirations, and realities of Black women. We share some things with white women, and there are other things we do not share. We must be able to come together around those things we share.

MK: Would you say that there is also a difference in the writings of Black and white women—for example, as far as the use of language is concerned?

AL: I think that there is. Because Black English feeds into a lot, even in the writings of those of us who don't use it. I think that the roots of Black poetry, coming from way back, were certainly articulated in the sixties, and still exist in much of our work where there is an emphasis upon music and rhythm, and Black speech. Now, this shows through in a lot of Black women's work. There is also a difference, I believe, because those of us who are Black women poets are intimately involved in a kind of survival that very often white women poets do not recognize for a long time. They are also intimately involved in survival, but they have different stakes. It is easier for them not to recognize that. So, I think that there is a tradition of struggle as well as music in Black women's poetry, that shows through over and over again.

MK: Is there a similar difference in the writings of Black women and Black men?
AL: There are certain similarities. Yes, I think that there are similarities in the work of Black men and women. I think, though, that there are again real differences in the poetry of Black women and Black men—and Black men are not really doing that much in poetry. I think that Black women on all the creative fronts are really exploding right now. As we examine our identities, as we reach for our power, we are developing and forming an art and a literature that speaks to our needs. So, it is very, very exciting. Very exciting.

MK: And that includes a different use of language?
AL: I think that we are reclaiming the language. I think we are, in fact, making the language new. And that's a difference. That's a difference, yes, and we have to do that, we have to make the language our own and use it in the ways that we need to use it. In the same way that we reclaim the word "Black."

MK: In "The Master's Tools Will Never Dismantle the Master's House," a paper you gave at a women's conference in the United States, you made it clear that all women need these different tools, not only in fiction and poetry, but also in academic discourse—if we want to bring about change.
AL: It means different tools in language, different tools in the exchange of information, it means different tools in learning. It means that we use the tools of rationality, but we do not elevate it to the point that it is no longer connected to our lives. It means that we do not require from each other the kinds of narrow and restricted interpretations of learning and the exchange of knowledge that we suffered in the universities or that we suffered in the narrow academic structures. It means that we recognise that, while we are functioning in

the old power, because we must know those tools, we cannot be ignorant of them, we are also in the process of redefining a new power, which is the power of the future.

MK: When you call teaching "a survival technique," do you mean teaching how to use these different tools?
AL: I think that we teach best those things we need to learn for our own survival. So, as we learn them, we then reach back and teach, and it becomes a joint process. I think that this is what keeps us new, that we do not learn from what goes on in a book. We learn from that interaction that takes place in the spaces between what is in the book and ourselves.

MK: And that is what people could learn from your poetry and from your writing as a whole?
AL: Well, as I've said, the poetry and fiction, *Zami,* and the nonfiction, the theory, are really three different ways of presenting—Audre Lorde, of presenting what I know to be so.

MK: So, who is your audience then?
AL: My audience is *every* single person who can use the work I do. Anybody who can use what I do is who I'm writing for. Now, I write out of who I am, all of the ways in which I describe myself, and so, all those people who share those aspects of me, who are Black, who are warrior women poets, lesbians [. . .] may find themselves closer to what I'm doing, but I write out of who I am for everyone who can use what I'm saying. And, I got letters from the strangest people saying, "You know, this really was important," or, "you know, I'm very different from you, but [. . .]," or "You know, I'm a white woman, and I'm not a lesbian, but [. . .]," or "I am a teacher, a white male teacher, but [. . .]," and I thought, "well, all right, that's good, I take my hat off, fine."

MK: Audre, let me ask you one more question—You have not only raised your voice for Black women in America, but also for Third World women, women of color, you are a member of SISA (Sisters in Support of Sisters in South Africa), and you had the initial idea for a book about the history of Black women in Germany . . .
AL: I think it is so exciting, Marion, that we are now beginning to make these kinds of contacts, set up those kinds of networks, because I think, whether

we describe Black, meaning of African descent, part of the African diaspora, or whether we use *Black* as it is used in New Zealand, in Australia, to mean those of us who stand outside who are people of color, who are outside the structures, and who are reclaiming our land and our lives, in other words, people who use Black, women who use Black as a symbol of resistance,—we have intimate connections, our oppressions are rooted in the very same systems that have stolen our land, our heirs, our children, our men, our lives. We need to identify those oppressors and to begin to see how we can move against them. What is it then, that we can learn from each other? Now, what we must learn from each other is how we are *different*, and be able to stand up and look at those differences—without sentimentality and without insecurity. Because if we can recognize how we are different, and how we are the same, that is to say, the similarities of our goals and the differences of the particulars of our lives, we can add to each other different ways of battling.

And it is a way in which the creative use of difference will help us really move toward change, toward that future we can share.

MK: And are you hopeful as well?

AL: Yes, I'm very hopeful, I have to tell you, I'm really very hopeful. It is a hope, however, grounded in a very realistic estimation of the enormity of the forces aligned against us. Because that is the only real hope there can be, if we are honest about how much it is that we have to do; and I believe we can do it, and not only that, I believe we can do it with *joy*!

Poetry and Day-by-Day Experience: Excerpts from a Conversation on 12 June 1986 in Berlin

Karen Nölle-Fischer / 1986

From *Virginia* (Germany), no. 3 (October 1987), 4–5. Reprinted by permission of the interviewer. Trans. Francis J. Devlin.

Karen Nölle Fischer, translator of the biomythography Zami, *published by the Orlanda Press in 1986, is a professor of literature in the field of English studies and American studies and taught from 1976 to 1984 at the Rhine-Westphalian Technical Institute Aachen. She is an independent translator and publicist and is currently working on Utopian impulses in contemporary women's literature (fiction and nonfiction).*

Karen Nölle-Fischer: While translating *Zami*, I realized that it was not easy to write this book, that it is the product of a painful process. What motivated you to write this book?

Audre Lorde: You know it wasn't simple to write the book *Zami*, but painful process is not really the right phrase. It was a very instructive process. And I might even say that the writing of *Zami* really kept me alive at an exceedingly difficult period of my life. Perhaps that is part of the light that shines from the book; it is a real recollecting, an attempt at getting into the question of "What has helped me to survive the difficult parts of my life from my birth on?" And of course, again and again, this motif returns: it is the love of women, kind as well as cruel, that drives me; not only fantasy relationships but, in fact, all the women who in the course of my life have been involved in strengthening my resolve or have come and helped me in difficult times form the motif. That is one of the strands that became obvious to me during the creation of *Zami*.

It is also an attempt to tell a few stories that are normally not told: what it's like to grow up as a black woman in the New York of the forties and become a lesbian woman. It is an attempt to consider how black women out there in the diaspora raise their children, and it has to do with how we articulate our strength. In addition, it is the opportunity to gather together some of my ideas on how real fiction or types of fiction that are not novels can be created. If I call it a biomythography and not a novel, although it is for me fiction—narrative prose—that's because it embraces so many genres, certainly autobiography, but also history, mythology, psychology, all the different channels through which we, in my opinion, absorb information, process it, and create something new. Though much in *Zami* is autobiographical, it is not an autobiography. . . .

KNF: What does the language in the book have to do with what you express in your poems?
AL: Oh, I love words—and I believe that what makes *Zami* so appealing to many people who might even say, "Oh, I don't like poems," is in fact its lyrical quality. It is a quality that permits feelings to be expressed in words. And that is of course exactly what poems do and what we poets always try to do. If one intends to write creatively, one must always touch people where they live and not where they think . . .

KNF: And in spite of your long, long battles with your family, would you say that their kind of strength has carried over to you?
AL: Yes, that's how I really feel. I believe survival is not something you think about; you do it day by day on the street corner, in the supermarket, in the bus, on the sidewalk—every day is survived. And it's hard to live like that; it is hard to raise your children under such circumstances—but for some of us it's necessary . . . because it's a fact that we are involved in a war. I have tried to train my children as warriors, armed with language and an awareness of the struggles that they will have to face, differently than I did once upon a time.

KNF: *Zami* ends before you resume your dialogue with your mother—didn't that ever happen later? Wasn't she ever interested afterward in your new way of carrying on the struggle?
AL: Yes, my mother is still alive. She is eighty-seven and blind, and she has Parkinson's Disease, but she still lives alone. We have someone who helps take care of her. She is an extraordinary woman. We have made peace—probably shortly before my own children entered the world. For the most part, it's good that I have accepted who she was and what she gave me and what she couldn't give me. I saw life before me clearly, especially after the death of my father, and that made it possible, I think, for her to give up some of her little games. . . .

KNF: People and events are presented very scrupulously in *Zami*, details even down to how the living room floor looked when . . . Does that have a function beyond the relating of personal history?

AL: When I remember, I remember individual details. Perhaps that has something to do with the fact that I was almost blind, but it's also related to my existence as a poet. I construct from details because that's how we build our life, the big picture. It's almost like a kind of impressionistic painting technique . . . I do it too because I think that people will catch on that way, and, if I want to create a scene, then I have to let you know what the tea tasted like and how the floor felt under my feet, and the patterns on the couch, because all of that goes into the "background" for the emotions. One of the methods of presenting "texture," the way things are.

KNF: And an opportunity to trigger associations for those who know their way around New York?

AL: Yes, and for those who don't know New York, I wanted to give an impression of how it was in the streets of Harlem, in the Bagatelle [Club FJD], what the cold-water flats in New York were. That's what I meant by "history." *Zami* should be as much a historical report about a definite time as a story of black lesbians, as the story of Zami. So I have described what young lesbian women in the Village of the fifties wore, and how that differed from other neighborhoods, from Queens or Brooklyn. I wanted things to live on and not get lost.

KNF: In *Zami*, I think the love scenes are among the high points—though they are so disappointing in many books—

AL: I have always been very dissatisfied with most erotic scenes, scenes of lovemaking in the books I read, and especially in books about women. In mine, I wanted to share a sense of joy, tenderness, and poetry. I've re-written them often—deleted many of the clichés . . . I wrote these parts just as I would have written poems . . .

KNF: The mix of sensual experiences, which fuses in your scenes—what does that have to do with what you perceive as the erotic strengths in your writing?

AL: It has a lot to do with that. Because the erotic is not just sexual. I understand the erotic as a force of life which courses through all the ways that we experience life. As I already said, it is an erotic experience to sit on a certain couch and to be aware of how it feels beneath your fingers; to see how the sun shines through that window in a certain way . . .

KNF: Do you see yourself within a tradition of other women writers who experiment with translating myths into fictional works about day-by-day life?
AL: I've always loved mythology. I grew up exclusively with—it's impossible any other way in the white school system—the myths of the Greeks and Romans. And when I later encountered African mythologies, that was very productive and wonderful and very validating. They were full of life; and what I found in West Africa, especially in Dahomey, was that there is a very strong tradition of women—of women who did not draw a line between giving and taking life. In other words, there were women who could be mothers and warriors at the same time. And that re-awakened all that I knew about the black women with whom I had come in contact when I was a child. You know, normally men fight and women plant the ground and give birth, which can only mean that men are stronger and women are nurturing. Well, in Dahomey women are both, and that was a known fact to me from the streets of Harlem . . .

KNF: Do you plan to continue this theme and write a sequel to *Zami*?
AL: I won't write a sequel. Right now, I'm working on a novel; the form will be quite different. The novel deals with a black lesbian mother in the sixties though. And she was married. . . .

KNF: And will the novel be traditional in form—or will it play with forms?
AL: I don't know—I've never written a novel.

KNF: Then it will be Audre Lorde—
AL: Definitely.

Audre Lorde: A Radio Profile

Jennifer Abod / 1987

Recorded as "Audre Lorde: An Audio Profile," Profile Productions, 1988. Program premiere 22 February 1987, WGBH/FM, Boston. Writer, producer, narrator: Jennifer Abod. Associate producer: Angela Bowen. This hour-long profile includes conversations and readings by Lorde; and comments by writers Adrienne Rich, Alice Walker, Angela Bowen, Kate Rushin, Evelyn Hammonds, Mary Helen Washington, John Bracey, the late Joseph Beam, and Calvin Hernton. Excerpts from Lorde's dialogue with Abod transcribed by the volume editor. Printed by permission.

Audre Lorde: My writing is about difference. My writing is about how do we learn to lie down with the different parts of ourselves, so that we can in fact learn to respect and honor the different parts of each other so that we in fact can learn how to use them, moving toward something that needs to be done, that has never been done before. All of my work, if you wanted to put it on a wide enough grid, this is what it's about. It is about surviving and sharing the stories of survival; and who would ever believe our stories unless we tell them?

Jennifer Abod: It would indeed take a wide grid to include the scope of Audre Lorde's work. Lorde, who has been writing since the age of six, is a major American poet, a powerful essayist, and master teacher. She has written thirteen books of poetry and prose, for which she has received international recognition, including a National Book Award nomination. Lorde says that poetry is the way we help give name to the nameless so it can be thought, and it's Lorde's ability to do this that leaves an indelible mark on those who have read her books or heard her speak. In 1987, Lorde was appointed the first Thomas Hunter professor at Hunter College in New York, where she is a professor of English. When students at Hunter College established a women's poetry center, they named it after her. Lorde's influence as a writer, teacher, and philosopher on Black women and men, other people of color, and white feminists cannot be overestimated.

When asked whether she has received the kind of recognition that she would like, Lorde says that to her what is most important is that her work be useful. Many people have found her work useful, including writers Alice Walker and longtime colleague and friend Adrienne Rich. They acknowledge Lorde's stunning ability to honor the differences between people while drawing connections between seemingly disparate groups. They're moved by her generosity, her courage, and shattering honesty, and they admire the elegance and beauty in her choice of words.

AL: I loved words. I used to lie awake at night when I was a child and say words, and I used to picture them as waterfalls of light; and I would say them until the words would literally fracture. I saw things very strangely because I was so nearsighted I was almost blind, and light always broke down into its components. Without my glasses, if I would look at a flame or an electric light, it would break into these wonderful colors. Well, sometimes at night I would lie in bed and I would say these words, and I would image them as pieces of light fracturing, that the word would fracture into its many different sounds and parts, and I would play these games inside my head with words.

JA: Those beautiful fractured forms and tumbling words happened because she could not see; and poor vision, says Lorde, accounts for the intensity with which she has learned to scrutinize things and people. Lorde has a passion for detail and can spend hours walking along a beach in search of shells, making use of them later in one of her necklaces.

AL: I made this necklace. I don't know if you can see the macramé stitches that hold the rocks and shells together, but they're very very fine. I love that kind of work. When I have my glasses off, I'm functionally blind at any ten feet, but I have a focal point that's about three inches in front of my eyes, so I have a very microscopic vision. And I love to do things. I love to see deeply into things, so when I look at *you*, when you said before, I look at you in a way that makes you feel important, it is because I am scrutinizing you, and I am looking carefully at you because I demand of all things that I look at that I *see* them, deeply and clearly; and I look at you the same way I look at the rocks and the shells and the threads and the little miniature things that I put together, the mosaics. I love . . . my eyes are always hungry for detail, and I think this has colored the way I write, and it's colored the way in which I look at the world, and it's colored my life. It is what I come to demand of my seeing.

JA: Audre Lorde began seeing clearly at age four and a half when she received her first pair of glasses. The youngest child in a West Indian household in Harlem, New York, she began speaking about this same time. Those early years of silence still haunt her, and breaking silences is a recurring theme throughout her work.

AL: [reads her poem "A Litany for Survival"]

So much of the theory that I write about, the theory of difference or how differences function and how they have got to be used creatively, comes out of my being, comes out of my living, and of course comes out of the relationship, the eighteen-year relationship that Frances and I have maintained. It's many relationships: it's five three-year or six three-year relationships, you see, because we go through changes over and over again. As we become different people, there is the period of friction and of rearrangement, and then we move on in a different way, and then we change. This is what happens, I believe, in any growing, altering relationship.

Now, to be specific, I would have to say that if I had ever imaged the ideal woman of my dreams, she would not have been blonde and blue-eyed; and so for years I went around denying that Frances was blonde because I had a whole construct of what blondes were about, you see, that of course Frances didn't fit. So for years when anyone said something about, you know, I said, oh, she's not blonde, she's brown. She's got brown hair. I'm using this as just an example of what happens until we begin to really recognize each other's differences and not either explain them away or ignore them. It's only then that we can begin to really use them and deal with what they mean in terms of our living, in terms of our living through each other.

"The Uses of the Erotic," I say, is one of those pieces that speaks so deeply for me because it answers the question that over and over again people say: Well, how did you get to be so—, or how did you know—? And, of course, as I say, hey, I started out like all of the rest of us did, a coward. You know, and these are the things I pulled on inside of me, these are the things you pull on inside of you. You know, we all have them; it's a question of focusing on them. So "The Uses of the Erotic" was—in prose, of course—an attempt to really delineate some of those. And it came about as a response to someone who was finding great fault with me because of a group I was in at the time. I was supposed to present one Sunday—we'd meet every other Sunday—and I was supposed to present, and I was not prepared this Sunday because that night, Saturday night, I had been out dancing. And I had danced my lungs loose. And so I wasn't prepared. And the attitude, of course, was—from the group—not only, well you're not really prepared, but: how could you have chosen dancing rather than doing your presentation? And that's how I really started looking at some of those things in "The Uses of the Erotic." It came out of that, and it does describe in some very very central ways—deep sources of strength for me. [reads from "The Uses of the Erotic"]

JA: Do you ever go back to your own work and read it for enjoyment?

AL: Oh, yes. Yes, I really do. I have to tell you that. I read it not just for enjoyment but sometimes I read it for edification and for strength. I need it sometimes to remind myself, and I sometimes am very surprised. I think: Oh, you see, you knew that! Aha, there it is. I wrote "The Uses of the Erotic" a little while, maybe a month before I had my mastectomy. And when I surfaced from that experience, about six months later, I picked up—when I started looking at my work again—I picked up that piece, and it was, I felt, like when I dig the earth and find a stone, and find some precious stone. It's as if it had been laid down there all of those millions of years, and waited for me to open the earth and find it. Well, when I picked up "The Uses of the Erotic," it was exactly what I needed to read. It was what I needed to say to myself, and I had written it, you see; and I think a lot of our writing, I know a lot of my writing, I write the things that I need to know, that I have not read anywhere else. I write the things that I need to see put down in a certain linear fashion that I haven't seen before. And sometimes I need to go back to it, and it always amazes me. So, yeah, sometimes I do. Mm-hmm, mm-hmm. [reads from "The Uses of the Erotic"]

JA: Has there been anything written about you that you would like to respond to, that you perhaps never have had the chance to?

AL: Oh, my goodness, yes. There is an article in Mari Evans's book, *Black Women Writers*, that I think is the most atrocious set of misunderstandings and trivializations that I have ever read written about me; and I'm just really surprised that she chose to include it. It's by a man who says that the motivating force behind all of my work is the search for the father, and he refers to *The Cancer Journals* as "that brave little book." It is the most trivializing and erroneous piece of writing that I have ever read about me. And I speak about it only because I don't want that to represent me in any form or in any place where, ten or fifteen years from now, people could pick that book up and read about Audre Lorde.

JA: Like Lorde, Alice Walker is one of many Black women writers who tap into their rich African ancestry, which offers them a legacy of strength and spiritual power. Lorde often refers to African goddess images, such as Yemanjá and Mawulisa in her work. And where other people close their correspondence "sincerely" or "with love," she signs hers, "In the hands of Afrekete."

AL: Being raised as a Catholic may have contributed to my being a very spiritual person, but it always feels to me as if they aren't connected; but I suppose a respect for ritual was something that was inbred, although I changed my rituals. The longer I live, the more active I am, the more conscious I become of how important my spiritual life is to me, both in terms of nourishing me and in terms of enabling me to make contact with other people. I think that our spirituality is part of those parts of ourselves that arc across difference, that enable us sometimes to recognize difference and to use our difference. That's one of the functions of spirituality, at least for me. I know that my spirituality has deepened as I have engaged more and more in the work that I came to do. I know it also strengthens me and makes it more and more possible for me to do my work. And I'm not talking about an easy, surface spirituality that comes along with the American desire to trivialize and oversimplify so much of our existence. I'm talking about that very deeply rooted consciousness that we are part of something that didn't start with us, that came from before and will continue after we have gone; but that our piece in it is essential and important.

The word has gone out, of course, that I am in struggle around my health, and there are a lot of people that keep expecting me to lay my magic down. But so long as I'm here, I'm going to be who I need to be, but I can tell you that I have been in very active struggle around my health, that I have been diagnosed as having liver cancer, and I am in the process of saving my own life—or at least fighting very hard to preserve it. So far, I feel very much the victor. I intend, for as long as possible, to go on, waging the kind of war I've been waging for the last few years. In the meantime, I have an enormous amount of work to do; and I have, with the support and good wishes of many, many women who love me and who give me an enormous amount which is not only psychically supporting, but physically supporting too. With the help of that and alternate treatments that I am involved in, I am doing my work. And doing it with style, I hope. So I wrote this poem on the cusp of dealing with a doctor saying to me you have cancer in your liver, and really coming to accept that—and the fury of it and the horror and what it can mean, and also knowing in myself that there is a kind of clarity that it also brought, that I would have to use.

[reads "Never to Dream of Spiders"]

I thought of the image of the civil rights era that has lasted for me all of these years: when they turned the hoses on the children in Birmingham, and they would get up close and they'd turn the fire hoses, and there's one particular picture of a girl in a black skirt and little white blouse with little puff sleeves. And she's holding hands with a young man, and they're running, and they stop and they turn the hoses on them, and it literally bends her in half and sweeps her across the street. That image is imprinted in my eyes—of what it feels like, I felt it, I feel it in my body. That feeling is—like the word. That's why poetry is the most subversive use of language there is because it's about changing feelings. Mm-hmm. Mm-hmm. Mm-hmm.

Of related interest is "The Edge of Each Other's Battles: The Vision of Audre Lorde," a one-hour Profile Productions video by Jennifer Abod about Audre Lorde's social vision and the translation of that vision into a transnational conference celebrating her work and life. Profile Productions, P.O. Box 21387, Long Beach, CA 90801; www.jenniferabod.com; jabod.profile@gte.net.

An Interview with Audre Lorde

Ilona Pache and Regina-Maria Dackweiler / 1987

From *Listen* (Germany), Fall 1987, 27–29. This interview was conducted in
Frankfurt am Main, Germany, and is printed by permission of the interviewers. Ilona Pache consulted her audiotape for the English translation and
has made occasional brief additions to the German text. Trans. Ilona Pache,
with assistance from Wilfried Raussert and Allison Brown.

Question: Ms. Lorde, you emphasize the interrelation of various aspects of
your life: being black, a mother, a lesbian, a feminist, a poet, . . .
Audre Lorde: and a warrior . . .

Q: . . . and a warrior, yes, and you use these various aspects to create power in
your poetry. And you are constantly breaking taboos. Do you see any relationship between the breaking of silence and the creation of power?
AL: Oh yes, I see a very strong connection. I know that I always felt very committed to using my power, committed to change, in the ways that I believed
needed changing, but it was not until I began to break my own silences, to recognize that those silences existed, that they were not serving me, that silence did
not protect me. Therefore, in order to translate that silence first into language
and then into action had to be the point of my empowering myself. So I would
say it is absolutely necessary to break silence, to give a certain form to those
things that we wish, first of all, to change and even more importantly to give
form to those things which we wish to create. In other words, if we are believing
in change, if we are believing in a future that has not yet been, we do not have
templates or patterns for that. We must be able to take out of our desires and
our visions a template or a pattern for the future. I believe that silence is a con-
tract made between the oppressor and my oppression; and that silence is used to
keep me unaware of my power. If I wish to empower myself, as a black woman,
as a mother, as a warrior, as a woman who is committed to change, and to difference. If I am going to identify my power, then I must be able to speak out.

Q: How do you define power?
AL: When I speak of power, I am speaking of personal power on a continuum. That is to say, not merely personal power that concentrates itself *in,*

but personal power which *moves* us. Electrical power runs trains and lights houses. Personal power moves us through the world, whatever we decide that we need to use that power for.

I am interested in women, men too, but in particular in women, because I think so much of female power is wasted. I am interested in seeing women begin to recognize that power is not evil. We have a responsibility, each of us as individuals, to identify what our power is. None of us is all-powerful. But every one of us has *some* power.

We need to identify what that is, and then we need to begin to ask ourselves, how do I use that power in the service of what I believe? Whatever I believe. So I am less interested in making sure *you* believe what *I* believe, as I am in encouraging you to see that you are able to begin using your self to accomplish what you believe. And I will take my chances that we may meet on the battlefield on opposite sides, but I do not believe so . . . because I think in the largest sense, all our futures, our destinies are linked. It may prove otherwise, but I am prepared to take that chance. I am not prepared to have your power wasted.

Because power which is not used doesn't go into a vacuum; it is always used by someone else, and usually against you, and me. Because I am defined by my skin, by my sex, by my age, by my work as not important. You are defined as not important also, because of your sex, but you see there are other stakes involved. As black and white women, African American and German women, we need to identify: where do our visions come together and where are they separate? And where they come together, we need to be able to work together. Not that I will ever be you, or that you will ever be me. We do not have to become each other in order to see that our earth is dying, in order to see that two-thirds of the world's population are people of color and are oppressed by one-third of the world's population which calls itself white.

That is a situation that will damn you and your children, as it will damn me and mine.

Q: You speak of personal power, but you don't speak of institutionalized power. Within the German women's movement, there is heated controversy about the pros and cons as concerns participation in institutional power, for instance, in parliament or academia. How do you compare such controversy about institutionalized power with your concept of personal power?

AL: When I say that we need to identify our power, I don't only mean power in the abstract. Personal power is comprised of social power, political power,

economic power, as well as spiritual and psychic power. We need to see how . . .
you . . . let me use me as an example . . . I need to recognize what powers I have;
I know the powers I do not have. I need also to recognize, for example, that I am
African American and I am black and that puts me outside the pale within a
country that I was born in, which is the United States of America. But still, I am
a citizen of the most powerful country in the world. As such, I have a responsibility as an African American to make cause with, make contact with those
people I am also connected with, with other members of the African Diaspora,
and to speak out of the power I have as an American as well.

I cannot say I am black and so Ronald Reagan has nothing to do with me.
Because it's true, he doesn't have anything to do with me, but I have a certain
amount of power, because for example I can vote, because I can speak to other
Americans. Now most of them, who are white, will not hear me, but some of
them will. That is a responsibility of mine. So that is one kind of power that I
have. In order to recognize that, I must be able to feel strong enough inside of
myself not to give in to the terror of being rejected, being fired, being called
crazy, being called crazy black woman. The personal and the political are
entwined; they are not the same, but they support each other. That lake of
poetry that I spoke of will not empower us if all we do is swim in it. We must
take that—call it nourishment, call it liquid, call it whatever we get there—and
move out into our lives. And each one of us has some effect within our lives.
Now it would be foolish to think that we live in a vacuum. We live in societies
that are permeated with what I call the middle power. It's not the old but it is
the dominant power. It is what runs the political situations in our country.
It is what runs the kinds of ways in which our food is acquired that is killing
us. It is the ways in which the earth is being raped and slaughtered. It would be
foolish to say we can turn our eyes away from that because while we are developing a future we also live within the present. And each one of us has a place
within that present, where we can make ourselves felt. Whether it is demon-
strating, whether it is stopping a child on Kurfürstendamm who calls a black
person "nigger" and saying something so that child knows, even if the parent
does not say something, so the parent and child know there's something wrong
with that, whether it is going into a supermarket as a housewife and saying, as
someone did, "Where did these grapes come from? South Africa? Oh no, I
won't buy things that come from South Africa." Talking loudly enough for
other people in the market to hear and to question: what is she talking about?
But that's hard to do. Each one of us learns to use the big power by learning to
use the smaller, step by step by step. That for me is the way the power that

oppresses us and our personal power come [together]. Each of us has a piece of that huge, monolithic power we fight against. We are taught to see it only in terms of its being so huge that we have nothing to do with it. And that is not true. It is made up in the same way that a portrait is made up, of points of color.

Q: The white women's movement is having trouble recognizing racism as a feminist issue. You once said that white women have the illusion of participating in social power. Do you think that that illusion is a reason for not dealing with racism?

AL: I think that's where it begins. I think it is the people who have the least to lose who begin the fight, and fight the hardest, in the beginning. I think it is true that there are certain temptations facing white women because they are connected to the primary oppressor—who are white men. And sometimes they are deluded into thinking that they *have* a stake in that patriarchal structure, which in fact they do not. But it's harder to see that. In order to recognize that racism is a feminist issue it requires being able to see that racism, sexism, homophobia, elitism, ageism have their root in the same inability to accept difference in a structure that depends for its survival upon profit. That society is so highly structured that someone is on the bottom and those people then generate energy, power, and that power is used by the people on top. If you *believe* that you are towards the top, you are very terrified of being dropped down below. It is essentially divide and conquer. When white women begin to see that it is not altruistic to be involved against racism, but a question of their survival: if they come for my children today, they will come for yours tomorrow. History has taught us that. I am saying that racism is a feminist issue because it is an issue of feminist survival. In the same way that the white women's movement in America will crack and break and fall apart upon their inability to see that, the German women's movement will crack and break apart also if it cannot accept the challenges of racism, anti-Semitism, and all kinds of unacceptable differences.

Q: You have studied the mythologies of Africa very intensively, especially the traditions of the West African Dahomey. According to your depiction, Dahomey women don't see a contradiction between giving life and taking life since they are warriors and mothers at the same time. Does this image stand for some kind of border passing as concerns traditional women's roles?

AL: I found, in Dahomey, images of women that made me feel I was not alone. In many different parts of Africa, there is a division into those who bear and those who bear arms; Dahomey women can be both: warriors and mothers. I thought: Aha! because I know, I feel I am both.

We look for images that make us feel less alone when we are journeying toward that thing that has not yet been. It is affirming to me when I see now images of the Zambian women, the women who fought in Zimbabwe, the Angolan women with a gun on their shoulder and the babies in their arms as they patrol. I would like it not to be so, but if it has to be so, then good, we can do it.

Black women have been doing this for centuries, not only in Africa but certainly in the United States of America, whether it was picking cotton with the children bound on our backs, whether it is heading for freedom with the underground railroad, with the Sojourner Truths. This is part of our history: we know we can bear arms *and* children. This is one of the functions of myth: To underline the fact that even in our dreams and our visions we are not alone. And to have them be black women, because I am tired of seeing only white Christs and white Virgins and white goddesses—all the time I was growing up. I raised a girl child, and I know I wanted to have black images, I wanted to have black queens I could tell her about in her bedtime stories. I wanted to have these images. That is important because that is how we raise children.

Q: In an interview with Adrienne Rich in 1979, you said that poetry is the way for you to express your feelings, while you considered prose a more "strange" medium for analyzing your thoughts. But you were able to write *Zami*, which is prose and seems to be an expression of feelings. Has this relationship between "feeling" and "thinking" changed for you?

AL: It is not only that poetry is merely the way for *me* to express *myself*; it is that poetry *works* by feeling, mine and yours. It is that poetry—and I also think I said this in that article—is the most subversive use of the language because it alters feeling; when it is good it changes the way you feel. I believe that that change in feeling must predate the thinking in order to make the thought truly anchored. I don't think we can have one without the other. That is why I think poetry is the most powerful of the spoken or written parts.

I think that prose reaches, through the left brain, a different part of ourselves, and it certainly engenders thought. I think that there is not complete separation between thought and feeling. That changing our thoughts can affect our feeling, but I think that the course is much longer. I found for myself, when writing prose, I go on and on, with solid blocks of print, and I thought, "it takes so long." One phrase of "ice against the bone" to describe the whole process of what it feels like to be cold. A line of poetry can do that because it alters your feeling, and then you think. I do both, I learned to do both, and I am pleased that I did, I am a poet writing prose, because I am blessed to have had that chaos early enough in my life and to have committed myself to finding what it could teach me. I am pleased to have learned to write prose also, because I think there are many people who refuse to go into that chaotic place of themselves and use poetry. I write prose as a poet would write prose. When I write poetry, I go down into my experience. I take that experience and try to make something through words that will make *you* feel what I want you to feel.

Q: Then it's communication between feelings?
AL: Yes. I cannot do it unless I can touch my own feeling, unless I can touch the experience that that feeling is buried in. And the most important thing is I can take that experience and siphon it through the left brain, language, and make it usable for you. If I open my mouth and scream, that is an expression of feeling, but it's not a poem and it's not really useful to you. I have to take the scream and put words to it in such a way that it will make *you* feel why I was screaming. When I am writing prose, I am trying to make you understand why I am screaming.

Q: The Afro-German movement is still very young. When you were in Berlin in 1984, you gave the impulse for writing a book about the experiences of Afro-German women. In the meantime, Afro-German women have done a lot of work. The book *Farbe bekennen* [*Knowing Our Colors*] was published, anti-racism workshops were held, an Afro-German lesbian group was founded. Where do you see the differences between the tasks of Afro-German women and those of African American women?
AL: I am tremendously excited by meeting Afro-European women, Afro-German, Afro-Dutch, Afro-French, Afro-British, and to look at the ways in which our struggles conform and the ways in which our struggles diverge. Most of all, as an African American woman, I am interested in how much I can learn from my sisters, in other words, how much I do not know as an African American. There are many, many differences—those I am learning. I cannot take the position of an expert, I must go to the Afro-German women and say, "In what way does your experience differ from mine?" One of the differences that is most obvious that I see is that there are so many more of us in the United

States of America, that as African American women we have had a history of recognition of each other, from slavery on, and therefore we have a pool to draw from. I think the Afro-German women have existed in a terrible isolation from each other for so long, and have not had the words sometimes even to identify themselves. They are acquiring this. The effects of tremendous isolation and separation present very different problems. We need to see, and we do, that our oppressor is the same with very different faces.

Frontiers

Pratibha Parmar and Jackie Kay / 1988

From *Charting the Journey: Writings by Black and Third World Women,* ed. Shabnam Grewal, Jackie Kay, Liliane Landor, Gail Lewis, and Pratibha Parmar (London: Sheba Feminist Publishers, 1988), 121–31. Reprinted by permission.

Pratibha Parmar: We are really glad that you're willing to do this interview even though it's trans-Atlantic and on tape. We want to start by asking you about your stay in Berlin, before you came to London in 1984 for the First International Feminist Bookfair. Can you tell us if there was any contrast between your experiences in London and your experiences in Berlin?

Audre Lorde: Well, I was in Berlin for three months before I came to London and there were some very striking differences. To begin with, visually, Berlin is a very calm city. But it is an extremely white city, and the whiteness of it encourages a certain smug assumption that is different from the United States and England. There are few Black people in Berlin, so there's little question of interaction, except on the most objectifying of levels. Being stared at, for instance, if you walk down the street, not always with hostility even, but with curiosity. Landing in London, the first difference is a visual one. So many Black people! There was so much color in the streets, it made my heart sing.

Jackie Kay: Could you talk about the racial tension that you noticed in the streets of London, and how that in fact differed from New York?

Audre Lorde: After having come into the airport and been with you all on the train, and seeing so many Black people I was not prepared for the rather rude level of racism that I met in the streets of London itself. Certainly racial tension is a reality of life in New York and can get really nasty. But this was more personal and immediate. Do you remember, Jackie, when we walked into the bakery to buy some cookies, and the woman came over and said in quite a nasty tone of voice, 'Now, don't touch anything!' As if I would touch her wares! I doubt if I were a white woman who had come into her shop that she would have reacted that way. That's one example. There's a raw frontier quality about the racial confrontations on the streets and in the subways of London that shocked me. And it should not have shocked me because the danger that we experience as Black people in New York cannot be underestimated. White

Berliners are isolated from Black people, and they defend that separation. They are interested in dealing with racism in America, and in England, but are much less prepared to deal with racism in terms of their Turkish and Middle Eastern workers who are the 'Black' people of Germany. That would bring racism too close to home.

PP: You came for the first ever International Feminist Bookfair that was organized in London by a mainly white women's group. First of all in your opinion, how international was that Bookfair? Secondly, you were one of the very few guest Black women writers who played a crucial role in actually confronting head-on the type of racism that we see quite frequently in the white women's movement. The kind where there is a tokenistic gesture for including Black women or, when Black women are included, they are particular Black women who are already quite famous or who are going to be crowd pullers. One of the problems with the organization of that Bookfair was that none of the Black women in London were asked, and furthermore, the way in which it was organized made Black women in Britain feel that it was not something that they could take part in.

You actually refused to take part in the lesbian forum because so many Black women that night were being turned away from hearing you and other Black women speak. Can you say what you felt about that whole experience and where you think that kind of behavior is coming from? Finally, because of your intervention and your support for the Black women who were challenging their right to be able to attend that forum, they were able to participate and it went ahead. But it did leave a very bad taste. Till this day, as far as we're concerned, nothing much has been either written or spoken about what actually happened and what Black women's experiences were at that particular bookfair. So, could you say something about that . . . ?
AL: You're quite right Pratibha, this is a hard one to deal with. It was a very difficult and disheartening situation. I am much more interested in seeing what we—me, you, the Black women of London, even the white women, can learn from that situation. The white women's defensiveness that arose whenever certain questions were raised has to do with the fact that white women hide behind a guilt which does not serve us nor them. I would like to move beyond that guilt. The fact remains: the International Feminist Bookfair was a monstrosity of racism, and this racism coated, distorted, and deflected much of what was good and creative, almost visionary, about having such a fair. Now, if anything

is to be learned from that whole experience it should be so that the *next* International Women's Bookfair does not repeat these errors. And there *must* be another Feminist Book Fair. But, we don't get *there* from *here* by ignoring the mud we have to plod through. If the white women's movement does not learn from its errors it will die by them.

Now, how international was it? I was impressed with the number of Black women invited—Faith Bandler from Australia, Flora Nwapa from Nigeria, and the other African women, as well as women from the United States of America. But it seemed to me that token women had been invited to be showcased, and this always sends off a bell in my brain, even when I myself am one of those women. That awareness did not solidify until I stood up for my first reading to a packed house and saw almost no Black faces, and *that* was the kiss-off! What was going on? I didn't know, but I knew something was up, and the rest, more or less, is history. I was very angry.

I had come to London not because I loved going to bookfairs, but because the idea of a First International Feminist Bookfair excited me. I very much wanted to make contact with Black women in England; I thought, "Well, *this* is the ideal place to do it." I was not well at the time, but I came from Berlin to London despite the strain of travel. What made it worthwhile for me was knowing that I would make contact with a new group of Black women. We could sit down together; and I would find out who you were, listen to you, because I had never met you before. I *knew* that you existed, the Black feminists of England, and I wanted us to share space, to look into each other's faces and explore our similarities and differences, and see what we share and what we don't. That meeting was a major objective for me, but to accomplish it was very difficult because it appeared that the local Black women were not involved. When I raised this question with one of the organizers, I was quite taken aback by her defensiveness. My question was not meant as an attack, certainly not at that time. It was a question, which I have gotten used to having to ask in white feminist circles in the U.S., but which I had not expected to have to ask in London. The aggressive defensiveness that the question aroused, the really hostile, and demeaning responses on the part of some white feminists here got my back up. I was accused of "brutalizing" the organizers by simply asking why Black women were so absent.

I remember some of the earliest tacky battles of the sixties in the white women's movement in the States; a Black woman would suggest that if white women truly wished to be feminist they would have to re-examine and alter their actions, and the whole discussion would be perceived as an attack upon white women's very essence. This is so wasteful and destructive. I realize that the women who organized the International Feminist Bookfair truly believed that by inviting foreign Black women they were absolving themselves of any fault in the way they dealt with Black women. But we should all be able to learn from our errors. They totally objectified Black women by not choosing to deal with the Black women in their own communities.

Channels of communication between Black and white women must be kept open, certainly, but until white women begin to see the results of their blindness and other acts of omission and cancellation, and begin to ask certain questions of themselves, there is a limited input that black women can have into the white women's movement, not because we wish to be separatist, but because trying to raise their consciousness about racism at every turn is just too costly for us. We are not machines, and we have limited sources of energy, and we must choose those areas where that energy will be most effective. Our children are *dying*. All over the world, Black women are in the process of examining who we are: What are our differences? What are the ways in which we do not see each other? How can we operate together better as a unified front? These are questions of survival and we must expend our primary energy upon these questions at the same time as we recognize that without coalition we will always be more vulnerable. However, we *must* be alone at times to build our strengths, rather than siphon off our energies into some vain attempt at connection with a group of women who are not prepared to deal with either their history or ours. Now, your history as Black women in England is a very complex one, and I certainly do not know enough to generalize. I can only react to what I see going on. But it was unfortunate that white women's defensiveness apparently kept them from hearing the questions I tried to raise, because I raised them in the truest spirit of sisterhood, which does not mean without anger. The trivializing and personalizing of this dialogue was yet another attempt to come between the reality of the situation and their responsibility for those realities. The intransigent quality of the organizers' refusal to hear was most oppressive to me.

Unchallenged, racism ultimately will be the death of the women's movement in England, just as it threatens to become the death of any women's movement in those developed countries where it is not addressed. Feminism must be on the cutting edge of real social change if it is to be a true movement. In the same way, unless the German women's movement accepts the fight against anti-semitism as crucial to the survival of that movement *it* is going to die. Whatever the core problem is for the people of a country, will also be the core problem addressed by women, consciously or otherwise. We do not exist in a vacuum. We are anchored in our own place and time and we are part of communities that interact. To pretend that we are not is ridiculous. So I felt enraged by silence and evasion, and I was determined not to have that rage turned either upon myself or upon other Black women. I looked at the source of it and acted to change it. If I altered any consciousness, then it was good. I reacted with anger because sometimes that is the only appropriate response to racist actions. And we all need to be reminded that anger between peers is not fatal, but sometimes silence is.

Also, I wanted to say to the Black women of London, young Black women with whom I was in contact; it is not all in your head. Don't let them muck around with your realities. You may not be able to make very much inroad, but at least you've got to stop feeling quite so crazy. Because, after a while, constantly exposed to unacknowledged racism, Black women get to feeling really crazy. And then, it's all in our heads, the white women say. They say we're being this, we're being that, but they never acknowledge there's a problem and that they are a part of it. When I questioned the social situation at the Bookfair, those women talked double-talk to me. They seemed terrified of Black women, or at least determined not to deal with us.

Rather than keep yelling at the gates, we've really got to begin to look at ourselves in terms of what do we need most, and start to give that to each other. One of the areas that has got to come under scrutiny is how we deal with each other across our own differences as Black women. In other words how do we learn to love each other? And I feel hopeful. I even feel hopeful about the Bookfair because I met you all and that was important to me, really important, to look at your faces, to have questions raised, to have my coat pulled by Black women who could give *me* something to think about too, in terms of a progress and a future. I really value that.

Before we get off onto the next question I want to say, therefore, Pratibha and Jackie, the first International Feminist Bookfair is a landmark for us all. In years to come you may look back at that and see that it was at that point, that you really saw beyond revision, that it was not "all in your head," and that you had to pursue your own interests, because if you waited to build a joint movement, it was not going to happen for a while. If I yelled and screamed and got dirty looks and made women cry and say all kinds of outrageous nonsense about me, nonetheless, I hope it really reinforced for other Black women here that racism in the London women's movement is not an isolated phenomenon, and it doesn't merely exist in their heads. "Hey! She's really saying it too. It's not something that I feel and have got to look away from." And that's always important. I hope a new kind of unity, or a new kind of inquiry between Black women in London will begin. We can worry about exclusion until the fences moulder and rot away and there's nothing left to be excluded from, or we can look at where we are, *who* we are, and begin to build structures and institutions of our own.

JK: You came over for the first International Feminist Bookfair, and as a result of being here, you met a lot of different Black women. We'd like to know what, if any, differences you saw between the Black feminists that you met here, and Black American feminists. Did you feel that there were any differences in the way that we survive, in the way that we confront conflicts? Did you feel that there *was* a movement here of Black women that you could identify? Do you feel that the issues that Black women are dealing with over here are related in any way to the issues that Black women are dealing with in America?

AL: Certainly the issues are very similar. There are issues that we share and there are particular and specific places in which our struggles differ. I felt very very close to you and to the struggles that were going on here. I also felt the weight of the forces against you, and I thought in the light of that, that you were being wonderfully resourceful in maintaining the kinds of connections that you have with each other, the existence of *Sheba*, the way you work together, this very tape, the Brixton Women's Group, the Black women writers. You should be proud of yourselves. You should also recognize how much you've done. Like all of us, you have to ask yourselves, what do you need to become stronger, and then set about giving it to yourselves individually and as a group, these questions of how we attend the differences among us has to become a central question within groups of women of color. We are grappling with many of the same problems and conditions in some similar ways.

In other ways our solutions are different. Take the issue of how we name ourselves, for example. In the United States, Black means of African heritage and we use the term Women of Color to include Native American, Latina, Asian American women. I understand that here, Black is a political term which includes all oppressed ethnic groups, and the term Women of Color is frowned upon.

I love the ways in which you are connected with each other in day to day living; the fact that women live in houses together, or share flats. It feels as if there is, in some ways, much more of a living connectedness here than in the States, and this is one of the ways that we as Black women need to develop. This does not always exist to as large a degree among Black women in the United States. There are many Black women there who are *just* beginning to call themselves feminists, and who vary widely on their definition on what Black feminism *is*. I hope there will soon be some kind of international conference of Black feminists where we can begin to look at who we are, because I believe that the woman who defines herself as a Black feminist living and working in the North-Eastern States as I do, is very different from the woman who lives in rural Georgia, or Kentucky and who calls herself a Black feminist there, and we are both very different from *you*, from the woman who lives in London or Glasgow, the Black woman who was born and bred in Berlin, or Amsterdam, and who also calls herself a Black feminist. I would like to see us get together and discuss who we are, and no doubt if we all desire it enough, it will in fact come about. I look forward to that. In the meantime, these are questions we need to be asking ourselves on a more immediate basis. I love the fact that you get together so often.

JK: We are very concerned at the moment with the right-wing turn this whole country is taking, there is a really threatening feeling in the air, and when I was in New York this summer, I felt that there as well. We're particularly concerned about the growing number of Black women who are disassociating themselves from Black feminism, saying the very same things that white people and Black men would applaud and can use against us. What do you feel are the reasons for Black women treating each other and hurting each other in this kind of way, and how do you think we can constructively do something about this?

AL: You have a right to be angry, but that anger must become articulate. Yes, there has been a very strong right-wing turn. It's not only in England. The racism, sexism and self-hatred that simmer below the surface of any situation of oppression, have now risen to the surface and are being officially sanctioned. That threat that we feel on the streets as Black women, as Black lesbians, is real, and it does increase. As I see it, it is going to get worse before it gets better, and we *must* be able to look that fact in the eye and continue to work and to live and to love, because it *will* get better—and it will get better because you and I and the woman down there across the street are going to keep on doing what we know needs being done. It may not come about in our lifetimes, but what we are doing is invaluable and necessary in the long run—pushing it along. When you say that Black women are beginning to turn away from feminism, you're missing a very important point, which is that, by and large, most Black women, at least in America, have not dealt with issues of feminism as such at all, because they have been reluctant to see the connections between our oppression as Black people and our oppression as Black women.

Much of that reluctance is a result of the rampant racism in the white feminist movements. Our liberations cannot be separated. Some Black women have accepted those intersections and are beginning to say the things that need to be said, within our communities and to each other. That is what is going to have to happen. These women who bad-mouth feminism in our communities are our concern in an immediate and survival way. How do we reach these Black women who belittle and attack us? It is our responsibility and we must do it, but it is not something that happens overnight. We have been raised to work out our pain and frustration on each other, and we do it without thinking, often, for whatever reasons we can find.

Black women mouth the enemies' words against us, Black feminists, because they do not see those words acting against themselves as well. Getting that across to them is one of our most important tasks, and we can only do it on their turf, because they don't come to ours. But we share communities, and there are many places where our lives intersect as Black women, feminist and non-feminist. And those are the places where we need to make contact and coalition. It requires patience and perseverance and the determination to work and identify ourselves in often hostile territory. But all our asses are in the same sling.

How do you think I feel when I hear Alice Walker say "Black feminism sounds like some kind of spray!"? I feel really sad. It hurts me, but it hurts me for Alice too, because I hear her testifying against herself in a way that is painful, and because she does it in a way that also testifies against me. All the time Black women are surrounded by forces that attempt to make us speak out against each other, and all of us have had the experience of opening our mouth and having a frog jump out, but we also have to realize that we are responsible for our own frogs. I know Alice would not attack other Black women in a white women's forum, so I would like to presume that it was not meant as an attack. But the fact remains it was heard as an attack upon Black feminism by many, and it was a very demoralizing statement. I would, in the last analysis, fall back on my mama: her voice saying, "Well honey, sticks and stones can break your bones, but words will never hurt you!," and well, yeah, words do hurt but the fact remains, they don't kill, and I'm interested in getting to action. We make ourselves strong by doing the things we need to be strong for. I want to keep calling us back to a kind of centeredness. I really do like the idea of some day being able to take part in an international conference on Black feminism, a Black women's bookfair, womanist, feminist, whatever you want to call it. And I am planting that vision inside of your heads and hopefully maybe you will take it up and help make it happen.

PP: How do you feel about the need for Black women internationally to make links with each other. We *are* doing that in some ways, but do you feel that what we are doing is enough, and that do we need to do more to actually make an international movement of Black and Third World women? At the moment it seems that we all are working very much in isolation from each other in our different countries, and the need for that international dialogue between us is really crucial. How do you think we could actually strengthen these links?
AL: Pratibha, I think that an international network is absolutely essential, and I think it is in the process of being born, which is what this dialogue is all about. I feel very excited, and very heartened, whenever I think about it, because I feel this is the way it's going to happen. I'm sorry that I was not in Nairobi. It happened there in one way beneath the surface: women making contact with each other over specific areas of our lives that we can fertilize and examine. This is what Black feminism is all about; articulating ourselves, our needs and our resistances as women, and as women within our particular environments. We don't exist in the abstract.

How can we do it? Ah, Pratibha, but we *are* doing it, look, we are sitting here now on both sides of the ocean strategizing. I think about the Black Australian women and their land rights struggles. I think with great excitement about the young Black women I met in Germany, Afro-German feminists. I think of Gloria Wekker in Amsterdam and the Sister Outsider Collective, Timeke and Tania and Joyce. There is a wonderful richness of Black women that I find all around the world. You need to be in touch with those women; they need to be in touch with you. Yes, we all need to see, hey, that there are aspects of our lives that are crazy-making because we are Black women and they happen no matter where we are. What does it mean? What particular ways do we combat that? We need to look at the ways in which we are invited to testify against ourselves, against our beauty, against our daughters. We need to be able to compare notes. How can we do it?

We can do it by finding out who we are and by making attempts to see or to find out who we are not, meeting when we can, and in the absence of that, sharing our work, our thoughts, our letters, our strengths. Trans-oceanic conversations such as this. Maori women in New Zealand. Aboriginal women in Australia. Women in Samoa and Papua and Fiji. *Charting the Journey*, that's what you mean, isn't it? How do we get there from here?

What you chart is already where you've been. But where we are going, there is no chart yet. We are brave and daring and we are looking ahead. Our Black women's vision has no horizon. I would look about me. Where are the places in which Black women are in need? Where are the places in which we can work? Where are those places in our communities? It's long and uphill work, but we *are* part of our communities and we are there as Black feminists and we are an inseparable and integral part of life. So what if some Black women say, "We are not feminists"? That's less important than all of you working together on a project and out of that will come the respect that is inevitable. By their labor, Black feminists help build that dam, win that battle, save that daycare center. That's one way of doing it.

I don't think that we get very far with frontal challenges, although sometimes challenges are absolutely necessary because people have got to be kept on their toes and sometimes you can't just stand around and take that shit without saying *something* because it's bad for the psyche. But, on the other hand you can become so invested in what you're saying that you think talk is the only action necessary. I'm talking from a position of doing both all the time and trying to find some good balance in between. *Charting the Journey*. We are hungry for heroes. To paraphrase June Jordan, we are the women whom we want to become. We can become ourselves. I'm so impressed with *Sheba*, with the press, with how you work together, and with the film. I love to see Black women achieving on so many levels, and you are doing it. That's really wonderful. I would like to inject even more of that into Black women's groups everywhere, where the necessity for being political is often one that's still being discussed rather than assumed. Our lives are political, and our very existence as Black women. Wherever we find ourselves over the earth, a network is being born of Black feminist survival, and I applaud it. We are going to make it, no matter what. I find you very affirming. You bring a lot of joy to me, and therefore a lot of strength. It won't be easy. But all of our strengths together are going to turn this whole world around.

Breaking the Barriers of Silence

Laureen A. Greene / 1989

From *Woman of Power*, issue 14, Summer 1989, 39–41. Reprinted by permission.

Audre Lorde, Black feminist lesbian poet, was born in Harlem in 1934 to Grenadian immigrant parents. Audre describes a life not unsimilar to many African American children born of West Indian parents.

Getting ahead, using discipline, hard work, and education were the values espoused continually and practiced vigorously in West Indian–American households. Children were expected to accept authority without question and to follow the path set out for them to achieve in the land of opportunity—America.

Audre is very much the product of those values. She went to Catholic elementary school and then to Hunter High School, which was known to accept only "smart" and mostly white young women. In New York's Black communities of the fifties, and even to this day, "Hunter girls" were set on a college track and seen as those selected by white people as having potential. This in itself was, and still is, enough to set females apart from the general population in these communities.

The conscious choices that Audre Lorde has made about her life have always been extensions of "The battle to preserve my perceptions—pleasant or unpleasant, painful or whatever" [from her interview with Adrienne Rich]. She makes no apologies for her decisions.

There are things about her life that she clearly has had no input in choosing, such as being Black, female and born in New York City. Her writing, however, reflects a woman who has consciously used who she is to explore the creative use of difference and to encourage the breaking of silences.

In addition to the inherent challenges that come with being Black, female and lesbian in Western culture, Lorde has had to deal with an on-going paradox of acceptance and resistance to cancer. She continues to use the gift of freedom derived from this experience, while consciously working to conquer the "dis-ease."

In this interview, she talked about the conscious choices she has made and is still making about the way she has lived and is living her life.

Laureen Greene: Do you think that if Black people made a conscious decision to stop being oppressed, that it would change the way we live?
Audre Lorde: Not unless it comes along with real determination to use who we are to that end. I don't believe in the spiritual end to oppression. I believe very strongly in the spiritual component to channeling and using one's power to end oppression, but I think it takes work.

LG: Do you think that a first step, or at least a major step, is a conscious decision to say "no more," that when the work comes, and there is a conscious decision, you find a way?
AL: I'll tell you what I do believe: that we have to envision the future we want before we can work to achieve it, and so it must be possible for us to really image what we want; and to image what we want, we have to be able to bear knowing that we don't have it yet, and that's very hard. I think a lot of people are really afraid to believe they can create a better future. They complain and they grouse, but they don't really want to image how the world could be different. I think it's frightening because you have to admit you don't have. It's wanting without having. It's really hard to want without having or even the possibility of getting.

LG: So we stifle our want. We don't even try to want in some ways.
AL: The death of want; killing want, killing conscious desire is one of the primary weapons of oppression.

LG: Surely when you talk about your mother, or I talk about mine, it is clear that there were certain things that they didn't think they were capable of. They felt that one simply lived a good life and worked hard.
AL: Yes, you got a social security job or a civil service job.

LG: You have said your mother approached the world by changing her perception of its reality, if she couldn't change its reality; yet you seem to have chosen to work toward changing the reality of racism, homophobia, sexism and other forms of oppression. Do you think your choice of approach, which clearly differs from your mother's, is a response to, culmination of, or progression of her approach?
AL: I think it's perhaps a progression of her approach. You must understand that my mother was a woman born and raised in Grenada, who came to the United States as a Black woman in the twenties and had many fewer options

than I do. I have, in many ways, been able to articulate my power. Not that I am
more powerful, I think, than my mother was (she died last August, that's why
I'm using the past tense); but I think that I've been able, through many of the
things that I got from her, to articulate my power in more ways than she was
able to articulate hers.

LG: Do you think African American women have more of a stake in stopping
oppression because more of our sons and daughters are dying in the schools
and in the streets?
AL: I think we have more of a stake in changing oppression because we feel
it more. Because our children feel it more, and because we know that survival is
not theoretical, that it is an actual matter of everyday living. It's a decision we
make every day to survive. I think that we have a stake in stopping oppression
more than most people because we're warriors for life; and I think Black women,
particularly those before me, know survival isn't theoretical, we live it everyday.
We live it on the streets, we live it in the banks, we live it with our children.

LG: Since I've had cancer, death is a much more familiar face than it ever was
before. Before, it was something abstract that I would have to do eventually. But
now, it has become something I have been forced to look at and be fearful of. Has
your experience with cancer changed the timbre of your work and its intensity?
AL: Yes, it has.

LG: You say in *A Burst of Light* and in *The Cancer Journals* (and I'm paraphrasing), that facing death has given you freedom from fear. Has that feeling grown
or diminished since 1979, when you signed off on *The Cancer Journals?*
AL: Oh, it's grown.

LG: Would you say that the way we choose to live our lives affects the way
we die?
AL: Yes, exactly so, because any crisis we face in our lives is a composite of
whatever we have done before. We are always in training for the next step.
How we live our lives absolutely will affect how we die, because it will affect
how we view not only what has gone before, but what comes after, and death
is another step, I feel. Now that I have faced my mortality without embracing
it, there is nothing anyone can do to me again.

Above the Wind: An Interview with Audre Lorde

Charles H. Rowell / 1990

From *Callaloo* 14.1 (Winter 1991), 83–95. The interview was conducted on 29 August 1990. © Charles H. Rowell. Reprinted with permission of The Johns Hopkins University Press.

This interview was conducted by telephone between Charlottesville, Virginia, and St. Croix, U.S. Virgin Islands, during the morning of 29 August 1990.

Charles Rowell: Here on the mainland of the U.S.A., there are those of us who miss seeing and talking with you, and hearing you read your work. And we are concerned about you in your new environment. Will you talk about your stay in your new home in the U.S. Virgin Islands. How has it been? Why did you go there? Is being a writer there the same as being a writer on the mainland?

Audre Lorde: Being a poet here is a very different experience from being a poet on the mainland, but poets become part of any community out of which they operate, because poetry grows out of the poet experiencing the worlds through which she moves. St. Croix in the U.S. Virgin Islands is a very different environment from New York City, from Staten Island. Why did I come here? After three separate bouts with cancer it became very clear to me that I had to change my environment, that I needed a situation where I could continue my work for as long as I was blessed to continue it, but without having to face the pressures of New York. I needed to live my life where stepping out each day was not like going to war. Not that we are not always involved in the war which continues; it will continue until we are all free. But on the level of locks on the door, dealing with subways, traffic, winter cold, shoveling snow—I no longer had the physical stamina to do that as well as my own work. These are some of the reasons I had to leave the Northeast.

Coming to the U.S. Virgin Islands was a combination of many things. I was raised, Charles, in a West Indian household; my parents came from Barbados and Grenada. I talk about this in *Zami*. As children, in New York City, we were raised to believe that home was somewhere else. Home was Grenada or Barbados. My parents had planned to come to the U.S.A. for a little while, make some money and then go back home. That dream never materialized for them, but they raised us with the idea we were just sojourners in this place. There was an American culture, there were American people, but they were not us. We were just visitors, and someday we would return home. I think that was both an asset and a liability for me when I was growing up. I have always had this sense that the Caribbean was a place where someday I would live.

A group of Black women called the Sojourner Sisters invited me down to St. Croix in 1980, for a conference on violence against women, and I was instrumental in bringing about the formation of the St. Croix Women's Coalition, a counseling and advocacy community group focused upon domestic violence. I read my poem "Need, a Chorale for Black Women's Voices" at the conference. I returned almost yearly to meet with these women, and then to take part in the First Conference of Caribbean Women Writers, held in 1986 in St. Croix and organized by the Sojourner Sisters. I had a chance to come back here after my second cancer surgery in 1987, and I decided this was where I would like to live and continue my work. God knows the war continues here in many different faces.

This is a Black Caribbean island which exists in a frankly colonial relationship to the United States, and the issues this raises for us as Blacks and as people of color, antiracist and antiimperialist, cannot be underestimated. The Virgin Islands has a considerable, although relative, power that is not being used; at the same time, we need help. That involves strengthening our Caribbean ties, and at the same time, using the fact that we are citizens of one of the most powerful countries in the world, and a country that stands on the wrong side of every liberation struggle on earth! When I say we, I mean the indigenous people of these islands as well as those of us who have chosen to make the Virgin Islands home.

CR: Will you be more specific about how living in the U.S. Virgin Islands differs from living on the mainland?
AL: As a Black woman, an African-Caribbean American woman, there are certain realities of our battles here that are similar to those of many others who are part of the African Diaspora.

The U.S. Virgin Islands is a part of the Caribbean. We are also for better or ill—and for the most part ill—supposedly part of the United States; we are a "territory," which is a polite word for a colony. The U.S. post office, when it's being really honest, refers to us, the Virgin Islands, as "minor outlying islands."

In reality, we exist in a colonial relationship to the States and the benefits which accrue from that relationship must be weighed against the severe alienation and exploitation which occurs.

Those of us who come here to live seeking a Caribbean environment, or a black English-speaking society, have several political and emotional adaptations to make. First, as Black people on the continental U.S., we have become used to considering ourselves part of the mainstream—that is to say, it matters on the national stage, or at least in the national media, what happens in New York or L.A., even to Black people. In September 1989, when Hurricane Hugo wrecked Charleston, S.C., that news hit you, in Kentucky, and in California, and the people in Idaho. That's true for Florida, and Detroit as well. But when Hurricane Hugo smashed the "minor outlying islands" totally destroying the homes and livelihood of 66,000 people, when our communities were in upheaval, that was not of particular interest to Detroit, Chicago, California, or New York. And Black people in those places don't realize that these are Black communities that were decimated.

Now you can say that one of the functions of this is to teach us a certain amount of humility. That may or may not be true. The point is, what happens on these islands is directly involved with what is going on with Black people on the mainland and all over the world. I am speaking politically and economically as well as socially. For example, how many people are aware that on this tiny Caribbean island is the largest oil refinery in the Western hemisphere, Hess Oil of the Virgin Islands? Larger than their refinery in Jersey, larger than the one in Texas. What does that mean? What does it mean that two days after Hugo leveled St. Croix, when there was no electricity, no telephone, no water, no food, no diapers, when 98 percent of the dwellings on this island were totally destroyed, the United States government came onto this island with MPs and U.S. Marshals and the F.B.I., and immediately guarded Hess Oil? What they first brought down were not emergency disaster relief supplies, but M-16s and military personnel. The U.S. military takeover of St. Croix reminded me of nothing so much as the U.S. military invasion of Grenada.

Now Hess Oil is in the process of literally ramming through the territorial government of the Virgin Islands, an okay to build a catalytic cracker on this island. This was first voted down, then re-passed! The reason Hess wants to build a catalytic cracker on St. Croix is because it cannot build it any other place on the continental U.S. at this point, because of the environmental danger and safety concerns surrounding this kind of operation to produce cheap gasoline from crude oil. This island measures twenty-six by seven miles. The last time a catalytic cracker blew, reportedly, it sent up a fireball that traveled 500 miles.

So these are some of the living issues that we deal with on this island. Meanwhile, Hess Oil pays local workers here one-third less than it pays imported continentals for the same job, and there is no labor statute to prohibit them from doing so. And rum is cheaper than fresh milk. Whether it's oil and land in California and Georgia or creating an oil plantation out of St. Croix, the issues of exploitation by a white militaristic economy are essentially the same, although expressed differently in different locales. How can we use our differences to work together better against the exploitation and destruction of our children, our land, our resources, our planet? And, as hyphenated people, and members of the African Diaspora, what is our relationship to the indigenous peoples of those lands we call home?

CR: I want to go back to a part of my first question. Given the context you've described, will you say more about what you've discovered as the differences— and similarities—between being a poet in St. Croix and being a poet on the mainland of the U.S.A. I'm referring largely to audience. What are the collective responses to the poet—or the artist in general—in St. Croix? Does he/she have any special responsibilities to the society? To the people?

AL: Being a poet is not merely a question of producing poems. Being a poet means that I have a certain way of looking at the world, involving myself in the community around me. I am committed to work, and I see myself as a poet moving through all of the things that I do. The Coalition for Equal Justice is a group I am currently working with, trying to focus attention, in the aftermath of Hurricane Hugo, upon some of the very distinct and dangerous trends that are developing within the social, material, and economic structure of these islands, and St. Croix in particular. For example, over-development, increasing racial tensions, what I was just speaking to about the role of Hess Oil—what do these issues have to do with being a poet? There is a poem in everything I lend myself to, and more than one. Poetry grows out of the textures of life. Local workers may or may not read poetry, but they know very, very well what it means to be paid half as much for the same kind of dangerous work as Hess Oil pays white workers sent down from the States. Now, being able to capture the feeling and sense and the experience of that worker and how I feel being part of a community that tolerates that—this is something I can evoke in poetry. That is what I mean when I say poetry is part and parcel of who I am, and how I experience my world around me; it is also part and parcel of the world in which I move. I am now part of the U.S. colonial community, as well as part of the international community of people of color. I am also part of the Black women's community. I am part of many communities. Poetry is a way of articulating and bringing together the energies of difference within those communities, so those energies can be used by me and others to better do what must be done.

This physical material world that I function in right now affects my poetry. I was part of a St. Croix women's art show called "Risking a Somersault." It was arranged by a German woman here who runs a cafe. So many of the white artists who come down here, come with the attitude that "this is American paradise"; they become totally subsumed by the luscious blooms and the sea, the sand, the sunset, the trees. It's a very physically seductive and beautiful place, but until you deal with the realities within the environment (because that's a part of your art) you're really doing something superficial. What Ulla wanted to do with the art show was focus upon some of the real concerns of St. Croix. Now one of the wonderful things about these islands (since the community is smaller) is that if you have an art show everybody comes. Culture is part of life, or the life of your next door neighbor, so you stop by the show. I did a couple of poems out of my experiences here. And I realized as I did them that one of the things about how the poems were becoming was a consideration of size or length. We're going to have poetry in a public place, and this is one of the primary ways in which poetry gets to many people here, because a lot of people don't buy books. I thought: I want these poems taught and read, so I've got to do them, not on four or five or six pages, but literally on the side of a poster. These were my first truly Cruzan poems.

CR: You affixed a note upfront in your *Chosen Poems—Old and New* (1982). You wrote, "Here are the words of some of the women I have been, am being still, will come to be. The time surrounding each poem is an unspoken image." You say so much in that statement. As I read it, part of what you say has to do with what poetry does for you—and, ultimately, for society at large: how poetry functions for you and how it might function for your readers.
AL: I'm so happy to hear those words, Charles. I don't remember writing them, but as I listen to them, they're like an echo that I agree with so much, and I say to myself, "Oh my, did I write like that then?" But yea.

CR: Will you say more about that statement. It is, I think, very important for those of us who study your poetry.

AL: A poem grows out of the poet's experience, in a particular place and a particular time, and the genius of the poem is to use the textures of that place and time without becoming bound by them. Then the poem becomes an emotional bridge to others who have not shared that experience. The poem evokes its own world.

I'm thinking about the poems that I wrote while I was in Germany. I'm involved in an experimental cancer treatment program and it has been quite successful for me. I go regularly to Berlin, every year. One of the things that I've done during those times has been to become actively involved with the Afro-German movement. There are so many people who think "what?" when they hear that. In other words, what do you mean—Black German war babies? That's the whole point; they're not war babies. The recent changes in eastern Europe, the Wall going down—this has very direct implications for Black people, and other people of color in eastern Germany. Afro-Europeans are distinct minorities. We, as African Americans, need to recognize that, and make contact with our brothers and sisters in Europe. We need to begin to ask some very essential questions about where do our strengths and our differences intersect. We need to do this as people in the African Diaspora, and we need to know this as the "hyphenated people" upon whom, I believe, hope for the world's future rests. That is a consciousness that continues, when I am in other places, but it is highlighted when I am operating in Europe.

Here in the Virgin Islands is where I've chosen to live. I feel that the strength, the beauty, the peace of life in St. Croix is part of my defense kit; it's a part of what keeps me alive and able to fight on. Being surrounded by Black people's faces, some of whom I like, some of whom I don't like, some of whom I get along with, some of whom I don't get along with, is very affirming. Basically there is a large and everpresent Black-fullness to the days here that is very refreshing for me, although frustrating sometimes, because as in so many places, we have so many problems with how we treat each other. But that's part and parcel of learning to build for the future.

CR: Will you talk further about your statement, which I quoted above, in relation to some of your poems. Your collection *New York Head Shop and Museum* is one of my favorites. And the two poems from that collection which immediately speak to me are "New York City 1970" (it opens the volume) and "To My Daughter the Junkie on a Train."

AL: "New York City 1970," the poem that begins *New York Head Shop and Museum*, gives me chills. It was so prophetic. You know, Charles, I have done a revision of *Chosen Poems*. I did it by candlelight, partly to keep myself sane during the aftermath of Hurricane Hugo when we had no lights, no power, no water, no contact with the rest of the world. It was life on a very basic and elemental level, compounded by the enormous amount of hostility directed toward this island from both the mainland and the U.S. occupying forces. The revision was an interesting project. I set myself to revising the poems rather than rewriting them, so, of course, I found myself back into the feeling of the time each was written. I had to project myself back into the poem in order to come out with, not the poem I would write in 1990, but "the" poem that Audre wrote in those days, heightened in that person's voice. You see what the literary problem was? I found it a very good exercise. The themes I dealt with then are still pertinent today, and the concrete particulars are illuminating. I wrote the poem you mention in 1970. In re-writing, I remembered the ways in which I felt myself committed to the city then for a period of time. I thought about my children, who I had raised with those hopes. I thought of the anguish of New York City twenty years ago, and the anguish that is still New York City today. But we are developing new ways of handling that anguish, and time will tell whether we are learning fast enough.

"My Daughter the Junkie on a Train" is for me an essential question, still: what is our relationship to our bruised and damaged children? I see crack invading the streets of downtown Christiansted, and our young people kept off-center by the poor quality of the education that is offered them here, and I see how they, too, become "junk." How do we involve ourselves with the young people of our community, of our society? This question is crucial for the survival of ourselves and our kids and our world. Whether that's a question of giving poetry workshops in high schools here, which is what I am trying to do, or whether it involves counseling teen-aged mothers and fathers or taking to the streets for a new high school, it's got to be done. These are our essentials. How do we involve ourselves in the future? It's not as simple as saying, "Oh well, you know, the Black family," because you have to think about how we define, and keep redefining, the Black family, so that concept becomes relative to the needs of *all* the young people growing up in our community.

CR: And then there's "Blackstudies," the poem that ends *New York Head Shop and Museum.* I want to read parts of it: [quotes the poem]. Will you talk about this poem.

AL: Hearing you read that is such a moving experience for me. I have just been reading about some young Black poets in the *Village Voice.* Barbara Smith sent me the clipping. Their work and vision sounds truly exciting. I have not seen these young people, but when I read this article my heart just swelled. One young woman named Malkia is fifteen years old and politically active. She writes, "Who's gonna go to school with me. I'm gonna get beat up tomorrow." And, I'm thinking, that's who I'm talking about in "Blackstudies." These are the poems I'd want to be writing if I were her age today, and I feel like these are my children. Children who are speaking. I believe that I'm part of their consciousness and part of what moves them to where they are. They are beautiful and embattled, and they know it. So that's the kind of thing that I was talking about in "Blackstudies." I'm saying, are you willing to put all of yourself on the line, and let the young people pick up whatever pieces they need, and run with it? The young people don't have to become you, they have to use something you've got that they need. That's what we have to teach them to do. But that requires a commitment (and openness) which, at the time that poem was written, was a very, very difficult one to make.

To say in the early 1970s, about most of Black studies, "so far, what we are considering represents a limited vision, we've got to be more adventurous, more imaginative; we need to teach blackness, not just in terms of history, not just the terms of who did what or when. Blackness is an approach, a way of taking in the world, and a way of giving back what we get. We need to teach Black everything; we need to teach Black mathematics, we need to teach Black cooking, we need. . . . Blackness is an essential way of looking at life. And that's what Black studies should be about from the 'get.'" Nowadays we talk about an Afrocentric epistemology. But in those days it was harder, without the language, only the sense, the feeling. When you said it, it sounded like a much longer journey was going to be necessary, and many of us weren't ready for the long haul. A lot of black people in power were not willing to hear it.

In 1970, some of us in Black studies wanted to discuss the dangers of a limited vision, and the necessity for broadening the definition and scope of Black studies, if we were to make any genuine impact on the lives of our students and our children. We were accused of being too radical, beside the point, not contributing to nation time; we were called traitors or feminists; we were called liars. History has proven that there was something in what we were say-ing. Black *is* Beautiful, but a black machine is still only a black machine, and a Black fascist is a Black fascist.

When I read a poet like Essex Hemphill, my heart just comes up in my mouth and does an African folk-dance on the back of my throat. I think, yea that's what the brother is doing—he's making something that has never been made or said before. He gives me hope and strength. That is what "Blackstudies" is all about. Carrying it forward. I love the sense of continuity and growth, Charles. It's so deeply exciting to me.

There's going to be a conference in October [1990] held in Boston. It's a chance for people to come together and discuss some of the real issues and themes within my work, how they have been touched by them, and how those themes can best be put into practice, in their communities, in their lives. We are, after all, moving into a new century. What new structures can we build? What old ones can we reconstruct?

CR: In *Chosen Poems*, you also tell us that you did not include any poems from your volume entitled *The Black Unicorn* (1978) "because the wholeness of that sequence/conversation cannot yet be breached." Will you explain and illustrate that statement. For example, what makes it more a sequence than *Coal* (1976)—or your more recent volume, *Our Dead Behind Us* (1986). I like your calling the volume, *The Black Unicorn*, a "conversation."
AL: The poems in The *Black Unicorn* have always felt to me like a conversa-tion between myself and an ancestor Audre. The sequence began in Dahomey when I visited that country with my children in 1974, and continued for the next three years, resulting in *The Black Unicorn*.

CR: I want to go back to something you were talking about earlier: about the Black population in Germany. I am not certain that our reading audience on the mainland of the U.S.A. is aware of that population—or of the vast Black population of Europe in general. Will you talk about the Black population in Germany—and about Black writers there? Of course, we'll discover a lot about Black women writers in Germany from your forthcoming essay on the sub-ject. Did you say it will be the introduction to *Farbe Bekennen* [*Showing Our True Colors*], the anthology of black German women?
AL: One of the most interesting black writers that I met in Germany is a woman who was originally from East Berlin, a poet, Raya Lubinetsky. I find her work very, very exciting. She is doing in German what many of the Black poets

were doing in the 1960s with the English language, creating a new Africanized linguistic approach to language that's part and parcel of her poetry. It's not something that translates very easily. I just really enjoy her work. Writing is not easy for a Black poet in Germany. It is very, very difficult to survive and to create as a Black person in a situation where you are not only discriminated against but wiped out in terms of your message and your identity and your consciousness.

CR: In one of your essays in *Sister Outsider*—I think it's called "Eye to Eye"— you say, "We can learn to mother ourselves. What does that mean for the Black woman? It means we must establish authority over our own definition, providing attentive concern and expectation of growth which is the beginning of that acceptance we came to expect only from our mothers." As you talked about African-German women writers, I start thinking about that statement—and its implications, not only for writers, but for Black women and, ultimately, for Black people in general, wherever we are in the world. Will you talk about the statement I quoted from "Eye to Eye"?

AL: Charles, I consider that essay, "Eye to Eye: Black Women, Hatred, and Anger," to be one of the two core pieces of my prose writing. The other one is "Poetry Is Not a Luxury." I think both deal with difficult questions we have got to raise among ourselves. In "Eye to Eye," I started with a question. Why do we allow ourselves to be used as the primary weapon against each other? What is that all about? We know what it's about externally—divide and conquer—but what is it about internally? And we need to look at this dynamic also between Black women and Black men, Black men and Black men. How do we make necessary power out of negative surroundings? How do we define where we want to go? How do we use whatever we have to help us get there? Within the context of a hostile environment, how do we provide ourselves with what we need? How do we, in effect, make ourselves recognize how important we are to each other? How do we kill that little voice that says "no good," planted in us by this society because we were born Black and female, because you were born Black and male, because we were born Black?

CR: Why do you say these two essays, "Eye to Eye" and "Poetry Is Not a Luxury," are central to your prose? What makes them the core of your prose writing?

AL: Because I feel they are. To write each of those essays I went down really deep, and I started with core questions. I had never written prose like that before. I'm not basically a prose writer; I'm a poet. So I've had to teach myself how to write prose, how to think in solid, linear paragraphs. And it has not been an easy task. I have always felt that "poetry is not a luxury" so I began to investigate, exactly what is poetry in my life? I found myself going deeper and deeper, down to my toes, and having to come back up through the writing process. In doing so, I realized how much of my growth and development, my work, my hopes, my fears, my struggles, my triumphs, how much of my personal history was informed and chronicled by the stuff I was dealing with in these two essays. An enormous amount had to be reexamined, rethought, rewritten, rebased and put together, and when the essays finally happened, each one of them felt like a process I think of only in terms of making a poem. I learned an enormous amount in the writing. They felt like black holes— these small, but incredibly condensed pieces of matter. The ideas and the feelings and questions that are raised in each one of them proliferate through everything I have ever written. They serve as a take-off point for later work; my own, and, I hope, other people's.

CR: And, in fact, in "Poetry Is Not a Luxury" you say, "Poetry is not only dream and vision; it is the skeleton architecture of our lives. It lays the foundations for a future of change, a bridge across our fears of what has never been before." I hope you'll comment on that passage.
AL: We live in a society grown hysterical with denial, with contradiction, dishonesty, and alienated values; a society predicated upon white patriarchal thought. We are moving into the twenty-first century, and the primary question is, what is our position in a world that is seven-eighths people of color? How does our Blackness, our Americanness, fit into that world? What is our function in a livable future? Because there has *got* to be a better way. How do we use ourselves to help bring that future into being? What do we salvage from the past? Our visions are essential to create that which has never been, and we must each learn to use all of who we are to achieve those visions. And I am a poet to my bones and sinews.

CR: Do you see a relationship between one's sexuality and/or sexual preference and one's art? I raise this question for many reasons, two of which relate to different important movements in the U.S.A. and to the current political debate surrounding the future of the National Endowment for the Arts. During the 1960s with the Black Arts Movement, Black artists talked about the relationship of one's Africanness to art. The Women's Movement, which talks about the importance of the womanist or feminist component in art, followed. The Gay-Lesbian Movement, commenting on art, continues to be muted by strident, self-righteous voices which try to impose their visions on the rest of the world. Then there is the silence of the so called "liberal" ranks of the intellectual community, in and outside academic institutions in the U.S.A. There has also been a strange silence in the intellectual ranks of the Black community on the issues surrounding the exhibition of the Mapplethorpe photographs. More Black intellectuals have been willing to talk (in public and in private) about the rights of museums and the right of the general public to see the art it elects to see—and let me tell you, during these repressive times in the U.S.A., a defense of human and civil rights is becoming as necessary as air and water. But what has bothered me about the Mapplethorpe situation is the continued silence of the Black community in the face of Mapplethorpe's obvious objectification and commodification of Black men in his photographs. (My judgment here should not in any way be taken as possible support for Jesse Helms's anti-American campaign against art or the fascist vision of the so called "Moral Majority," because neither Helms nor those people give a hoot about black—or Third World—people. Or about the rights of women in general.) I apologize for my long speech. I must not forget: you are the person interviewed, and I am the interviewer. [*Laughter.*] Again, do you see a relationship between art and sexuality? And will you talk about the Gay-Lesbian Movement and the creation and dissemination of art in the U.S.A.

AL: I am a Black, Lesbian, Feminist, warrior, poet, mother doing my work. I underline these things, but they are just some of the ingredients of who I am. There are many others. I pluck these out because, for various reasons, they are aspects of myself about which a lot of people have had a lot to say, one way or another. My sexuality is part and parcel of who I am, and my poetry comes from the intersection of me and my worlds. There is nothing obscene about my work. Jesse Helms's objection to my work is not about obscenity, however; or even about sex. It is about revolution and change. That is what my writing serves. We are living in a sick society, and any art which does not serve change— i.e., does not speak the truth—is beside the point. Jesse Helms represents the primary obscenity that is crushing not only black people but this country and the world into dust. It is called white patriarchal power. There is nothing obscene about my life nor the art that I create out of my experiences. But by the same token Jesse Helms knows that my writing is aimed at his destruction, and the destruction of every single thing he stands for. That is a basic premise of all my work. If that is a reason for the NEA to take back my grant, hey, let them do it. But don't say it's about obscenity. It's about politics and survival: who will survive, and on what terms? The white artistic community has very belatedly seen the handwriting on the wall, which says no society is going to finance its own reorganization or demise, or contribute to a culture bent upon radical change, not for long. I mean, Black people, Black writers, and other artists of color have known that for a very long time.

In the beginning of the 1980s, Judy Simmons and I, along with other artists of color, tried to get an organization together to question the racist distribution of NEA grants; white writers weren't interested in hearing about it, let alone joining. Why should they? So now that the white arts community is beginning to see that there's a real difference between "take-their-money-and-run" and believing that the political structure is quietly going to underwrite or finance its own alteration, the question arises, once again: what is our art about? What is the real function of art, our goals, our visions as creative cultural workers?

The visions that move me through my life and through my work are diametrically opposed to whatever vision moves Jesse Helms. If he approves it, I certainly won't. Of course I believe that art should enjoy public funding in this wealthy country. The NEA should exist. I can devote a certain amount of my energy to fighting for it, but I cannot devote all my energy to that alone. Jesse Helms's real threat is not just because he wants to muzzle artistic culture in this country, which of course he does. His real threat is because he wants to muzzle or destroy any people-centered culture worldwide. I fight Jesse Helms because he wants to destroy Black people in Angola and North Carolina and Cuba and South Africa, and eradicate the babies of the South Pacific Rim, and starve school children to support R. J. Reynolds and the tobacco industry, and deny women control over their own bodies. I mean, I can run right down the line of obscenities Jesse Helms represents and why he must be stopped.

Now, what does my sexuality have to do with my writing? I believe in the power of the erotic. What does my blood, or my heart or my eyes have to do with my writing. They are all inseparable.

CR: And you know the issues surrounding the question of obscenity are couched in terms of pornography. In your essay entitled "Uses of the Erotic," you say that "pornography is a direct denial of the power of the erotic, for it represents the suppression of true feeling. Pornography emphasizes sensation without feeling."

AL: The function of the erotic is to deepen the experience of the life force; the function of pornography is to deaden or destroy what is living. When Jesse Helms reads safe sex pamphlets on the Senate floor and calls them obscene, he is being pornographic. He is taking something whose aim is to preserve life and trying to turn it into filth.

CR: I describe the voice in your poems and essays as powerful (or as Brenda Marie Osbey once said in a poem—and I think I might be paraphrasing her here—"it's called having a commanding air"). But some of your detractors have accused you of being a strident poet. I am suddenly reminded of two words which appear over and over in *The Cancer Journals*: "silences" and "invisibility." Your poetry says to me: "I will not be silent while people die unnecessary deaths." And I mean that in a very large sense; that statement has many implications. It is through those words that I see you as poet, and it is with those words that I read your poems.

AL: Whenever a conscious Black woman raises her voice on issues central to her existence, somebody is going to call her strident, because they don't want to hear about it, nor us. I refuse to be silenced and I refuse to be trivialized, even if I do not say what I have to say perfectly. What I write is important, and I insist that you feel out what you have to say on the subject, and then maybe you can say it better. But it must be heard. I refuse to be silenced, that's right. And I will not allow my work to be trivialized because what I am writing is not only about me, it is about the lives of many voiceless people, and the life of the planet that we share. You can't get rid of me just by saying I'm strident, or I'm too intense, or I'm silly, or I'm crazy, or morbid, or melodramatic: hey, listen, I can be all of those things, and you still must open yourself to what I am talking about, in the interests of our common future. I won't be here 300 years from now, but I hope this earth and others will be, and maybe something I've said will contribute to making that more possible.

CR: Do you want your poems to empower your readers to think the same or to act also after reading your poems?

AL: I want my poems—I want all of my work—to engage, and to empower people to speak, to strengthen themselves into who they most want and need to be and then to act, to do what needs being done. In other words, learn to use themselves in the service of what they believe. As I have learned to use whoever I am in the service of what I believe. As we move toward empowerment, we face the other inseparable question, what are we empowering ourselves for? In other words, how do we use this power we are reaching for? We can't separate those two. June Jordan once said something which is just wonderful. I'm paraphrasing her—that her function as a poet was to make revolution irresistible. Well o.k. that is the function of us all, as creative artists, to make the truth, as we see it, irresistible. That's what I want to do with all of my writing.

CR: Do you think that two of the most recent movements in this country helped people in the same way you speak here? And I think of the Black Arts Movement which was attached to the Black Power Movement. Although Addison Gayle was right when he said that it was a Northern urban phenomenon, the Black Power Movement grew out of the Civil Rights Movement (or some people might argue that it was a response to the failures of the Civil Rights Movement). The other is the Women's Movement.

AL: They're both very important. God knows we would not be talking here without each of them. However, let us not romanticize the truth. . . . Julius Nyerere once said, just before he left office, "all governments by their nature are reactionary." Well, I don't know whether all institutions have to become reactionary when they get large enough, but both the Black Arts Movement and the Women's Writing Movement, although certainly very important to the development of my work, have presented problematic barriers to creativity. For example, the white Women's Literary Movement certainly gave space and voice to many of my concerns. Nonetheless it has not functioned, by and large, always in the best interests of Black writers, because of its reluctance to deal with racism as a core issue.

There's been a long-standing and very aggressive reluctance on the part of many within both these literary communities, to deal with the essential questions of Black women's writing and Black women's work, or to move on the questions we raise, despite the media exploitation of a laudatory few of us. Certainly, in the Black literary community in particular, those of us who are Black Lesbian writers are frequently, as Barbara Smith recently said with her characteristic wit and pointedness, "the 13th Fairy." Who's the 13th Fairy? That is the godmother who is always forgotten, who is not invited to the ball, or invited too late. Black Lesbian writers are very frequently the "13th Fairy" of Black arts. For example, look at the writers invited to present at the recent Black Arts Festival held in Atlanta. Were you there, Charles?

CR: No, I was in Santo Domingo presenting a paper on Derek Walcott before members of the Caribbean Studies Association. I did send some members of the staff there, to Atlanta, to promote *Callaloo*.

AL: Well, that's just an example. The Black Lesbian-bashing that takes place in the Black Arts Movement is notorious, and I don't have to discuss that here, or discuss the origins of it, but the fact that it still exists when our communities need cultural workers of vision so much is terribly wasteful. When I talk about battling silences, battling invisibility, battling trivializations, I am not only speaking about fighting them in the white literary establishment. If establishment Black male writers cannot see that Barbara Smith and Cheryl Clarke and Pat Parker and I are their sisters in struggle, and that we fight on the same side, then the question is, "What are we fighting for?"

Index

Abod, Jennifer, xiv
Abomey, 66
Achebe, Chinua, 76, 96
Afrekete, 149, 162
Africa, viii, 12, 27, 28, 42, 43, 55, 96, 120, 125,
    144, 148–49
African Diaspora, ix, x, 125, 153, 154, 166, 185,
    187, 189
African Women in Urban Societies–Their
    Changing Roles, 44
Aidoo, Ama Ata, 76, 96
Alvin, 10–11
Amazons, xiii, 144, 149
American Medical Association Journal, 135
American Poetry Review, xi, 116
American Theatre, 11
Amsterdam (Netherlands), 179
Angola, 168, 196
Armstrong, Toni L., ix
Austin, Tex., 104
Australia, 153, 173, 179, 180
Awoonor, Kofi, 27

Bagatelle Club, 156
Baker, Augusta, 9–10, 11
Baldwin, James, xiii, 77
Bandler, Faith, 173
Bannon, Ann, 110
Barbados, 120, 125, 184
Beam, Joseph F., xiv, 158
Beat poets, 32, 111
Berlin (Germany), x, xiv, xv, 137, 140, 145, 169,
    171–72, 189
Bethel, Lorraine, 26
Big Apple Dyke News, 108
Bill Cosby Show, xii
Birmingham, Ala., 163
Black & White Men Together, 87, 103
Black Arts Festival (Atlanta), 198
Black Entertainment Television, xii
Black Panthers, 60

Black Scholar, 67, 97
Blackheart Collective, 131
Blacklight, 129, 131
Boston, Mass., 192
Bowen, Angela, 158
Bracey, John, 158
Brixton Women's Group, 176
Broadside Press, 13, 61
Brooks, Gwendolyn, 35
Bush, George, xi
Byron, George Gordon, Lord, 32

California, 53, 69, 104
Callaloo, 199
Caribbean Islands, ix, 89, 125, 143, 144, 146,
    148, 185–86
Caribbean Studies Association, 199
Carnegie Hall, 56
Carriacou, 120, 125, 143, 149
Catholic Church, 13, 14, 15, 162
Cavin, Susan, 26
Celts, 42
Charteris, Leslie, 17
Charting the Journey (Jackie Kay), 180
Chiaramonte, Lee, xiv
Chicago, Ill., 60
Chi-Wara, 43
Christiansted, Virgin Islands, 190
City College, 59, 119
City University of New York, 85
Clarion-Ledger, 56
Clark, Jil, xiii
Clarke, Cheryl, 129, 199
Clarke, John Henrik, 35, 54–55, 126–27
Clayton, Frances (AL's partner), xiii, 31, 33, 39,
    56, 57, 58, 59, 83, 117, 128, 132, 137, 160
Cliff, Michelle, 33, 119
Coalition for Equal Justice, 187
Columbia University, 85
Conditions, 28, 40, 82, 130
Conference of Caribbean Women, 185

Contact, 122
Cook, Blanche, 33
Cornwell, Anita, xi
Cos, Claire, 33
Countee Cullen Library, 9
Crossing Press, 109, 130
Cuba, 196
Cuernavaca, 40, 48, 50
cummings, e.e., 36–37

Dahomey, 27, 44, 144, 149, 157, 167–68, 192
Dallman, Elaine, 45
De la Mere, Walter, 46; "The Listeners," 46
De Veaux, Alexis, xiv; *Poet Warrior: A Biography of Audre Lorde*, xiv
Demby, William, 44
Detroit Public Library, 3
Di Prima, Diane, 11–12, 34, 52
Domini, Rey (AL's pseudonym), 50
Dykes Against Racism, 87, 103

Effeminist, 29
Ekwensi, Cyprian, 76, 96
Eliot, T. S., 35, 36, 126
Ellington, Duke, 56
Ellis Island, 122
Ellison, Ralph, 77, 97
Eshu, 149
Ethiopia, 13
Eudora, 48, 49
Evans, Mari, 161; *Black Women Writers*, 161

Fairchild, Hoxie, 32
Family Protection Act, 79
Farbe Bekennen (*Showing Our Colors*), ix, 169, 192
FBI (Federal Bureau of Investigation), 186
Festac, 44
Fiji, 180
Fleisher, Deanna, 33
Flowers, Yvonne, 33
Free University of Berlin, ix
Freedom Riders, 53

Gay Community News (Boston), xiii
Gay News (Philadelphia), xiv
Gayle, Addison, 198
Georgia, 177

Gerald, Gil, 101
Germany, ix–x, xiii, xv, 134, 165, 172, 174–75, 189, 192, 193
Ghana, 27, 44
Glasgow (Scotland), 177
Gleason, Judith, 27
Glover, Clifford, 67, 76, 96
Gomez, Jewelle, xiv
Goodman, Bernice, 33
Greensboro, N.C., 38
Greenwich Village, 11, 55, 118, 156
Grenada, xiv, 18, 49, 120, 125, 182, 184, 186
Griffin, Ada Gay, xiv
Guevara, Che, 107
Guy, Rosa, 35, 55

Hacker, Marilyn, 45; *Woman Poet: The Northeast*, 45
Hammond, Karla, xi, 124
Hammonds, Evelyn, 158
Harlem, vii, 9, 15, 37, 119, 143, 156, 157, 159, 181
Harlem Renaissance, 28, 86, 125
Harlem Writers Guild, 35, 54–55, 126–27
Harper, Jorjet, ix
Harper, Michael, 40
Helms, Jesse, xi, 195, 196, 197
Helwerth, Ulrike, ix
Hemphill, Essex, 192
Hernton, Calvin, 158
Herskovits, Melville J., 43
Hess Oil Company, 186–87
Home Girls: A Black Feminist Anthology (Bernice Reagon), 130
Honeywell, 56
Hopkins, Gerard Manley, 27
Horton Hatches the Egg (Dr. Seuss), 10
HOT WIRE, ix
House Un-American Activities Committee, 126–27
Houston, Tex., 69
Howard University, xi
Hubert, 10
Hughes, Langston, 126; *New Negro Poetry*, 126
Hull, Gloria, 26, 98, 130
Hunter College, viii, 32, 45, 49, 85, 106, 109, 137, 145, 158
Hurricane Gilbert, ix

Hurricane Hugo, 186–87, 190
Hurston, Zora Neale, 86

International Feminist Bookfair, x, 172–76
Ixtacihuatl, 41, 48

Jackson, Jesse, 105
Jackson, Miss., 53
Jarrell, Randall, 37–38
Jay, Karla, xvi
John F. Kennedy Institute (Berlin), 145
John Jay College of Criminal Justice, 45, 60, 61, 67–68
Johnson, Alicia, 28
Johnson, Joyce, 110
Jones, Gayl, 91
Jordan, June, 180, 198
Joseph, Gloria I. (AL's partner), ix
Juhasz, Suzanne, 29; *Naked and Fiery Forms*, 29

KaDeWe, 142
Kay, Jackie, x, xv
Keats, John, 12, 32
Kennedy, John F., 72, 95
Kentucky, 177
Kerouac, Jack, 110
King, Coretta Scott, 105
King, Martin Luther, 56, 72, 95, 109
Kitchen Table Women of Color Press, ix, 79, 104, 106, 108, 130, 145
KKK (Ku Klux Klan), 108
Kung Fu, xii

La Llorona, 50
Lacy, Leslie, 76, 96; *The Rise and Fall of a Proper Negro*, 76–77, 96
Lambda Rising, 129
Lane, Alycee J., xii
Larkin, Joan, 33
Leakey, Louis, 13
Leakey, Mary, 13
Lehman College, 58–59
Lesbian Herstory Archive, xiii, xvi
London (England), x, xv, 171, 172, 175, 176, 177
Lorde, Audre: on academic structures, 151, 165; on her adolescence, 30, 49, 71, 90, 111, 127; on the African American community, 28, 62, 81, 86, 87, 102–3, 104, 105, 127, 150, 178, 180,

193, 199; on African American stereotypes, 7, 62, 86, 193; on African American writers, 26–27, 29–30, 73, 76, 77, 78, 85–86, 91, 96–97, 100, 125–26, 127, 150–51, 198; on African mythology, 42, 43, 144, 147, 148, 157, 167–68; on African studies, 43; on African writers, 76–77, 96–97; on Africanness and art, 194; on Afrocentric epistemology, 191; on Afro-European women, x, 169, 173, 174, 189; on Afro-German women, ix, x, xv, 152–53, 169–70, 174–75, 179, 189, 192, 193; on ageism, 80, 165, 167; on alternative aesthetics, 3; on amalgamation, 9; on the American dream, xi, 21, 181, 185; on anger, 21, 67, 73, 76, 77, 81, 92, 96, 107, 127, 129, 148, 163, 173, 175, 177, 193; on animism, 125; on anti-Semitism, 81, 167, 175; on articulating her power, 183, 197; on art's function, xii, 3, 27, 44, 74, 76, 92, 108, 131, 147, 151, 187, 195, 196; on Asian American women, 176; on the Atomic Age, 110; on her audience, 78, 88, 152, 187; on awareness, 15, 17; on battles within the Black community, vi–vii, xiii, 28, 54, 61–62, 65, 72–73, 77, 81, 86, 87, 89, 97, 102, 126, 177, 178, 199; on being African American, 15, 34, 42, 60, 65, 69, 72, 102, 146, 164, 177, 185, 188, 197; on being alienated, 71, 90, 123; on being left-handed, 35; on being lesbian, 23, 25, 28, 61, 72, 81, 82, 85, 93, 101–2, 126, 154; on being a librarian, 10, 11, 51, 52–53, 55–56, 66, 72, 94, 133; on being an outsider, 38–39, 71, 86, 120, 127, 129, 143; on being part of a continuum, 124; on being a poet, 56, 82, 111, 146; on biomythography, 99, 109–10, 128, 143, 148–49, 155; on the Black aesthetic, 3; on the Black Arts movement, 194, 198, 199; on Black English, 150–51, 192–93; on the Black experience, 26; on the Black Goddess, 66, 110, 147, 162; on the Black male establishment, 97–98, 126, 199; on the Black mother as poet, 63; on the Black power movement, xiv, 59, 102, 198; on Black Studies, 61, 191; on Black tokenism, 7–8, 129, 172–73, 198; on the body, xiii, 22, 88, 113, 123, 139, 142, 196; on building coalitions, 80, 81, 88, 103–4, 105, 144, 174, 176; on butch-femme roles, 111; on cancer, xiii, 68–69, 73, 83, 89, 99, 113, 132–42,

162–63, 181, 183, 184, 185, 189; on centeredness, 179; on change, 74, 92, 105, 107, 112, 129, 195; on childbirth, 12, 17, 123; on her childhood, xi, 9–11, 18–23, 30, 45–46, 71, 117, 158; on children, x, xiii, 6, 13, 24–25, 50, 81, 83, 124, 142, 165, 174, 183, 190, 191; on the civil rights movement, xiv, 102, 104, 114, 163, 198; on colonialism, 185–87, 188, 190; on connectedness, vii, x, 5, 9, 12, 13, 14, 32, 34, 41, 49, 62, 68, 99, 177; on consumerism, 6–7, 14; on crack cocaine, 190; on creative chaos, 64, 169; on creative use of differences, 86, 144, 153, 158, 160, 162, 175, 181, 188; on her Cruzan poems, 188; on cultural workers, 188, 196, 199; on Dahomean poetry, 27; on dancing, xii, 160; on death, xiii, 8, 13–14, 16, 52, 69, 99, 123, 183; on the Depression, 120; on designing clothes and jewelry, 140–41, 159; on difference, vii, 67, 73, 78, 80, 86, 87, 90, 98, 100, 102, 105, 144, 158, 159, 167, 174, 188; on dreadlocks, xii; on Eastern philosophies, 76, 96; on elitism, 167; on emotions, xi, 3, 18, 19–22, 24, 32, 45, 46, 91, 99, 156; on English as a second language, 39; on the environment, 118, 123, 165, 166, 186–87, 188, 197; on the erotic, xii, 12, 64, 75, 94, 99, 148, 157, 196, 197; on evil, 13, 28, 165; on evolution through women, 63; on factory work, 143; on the family structure, 6, 9, 190; on female friendship, 12, 13, 33, 143–44, 154, 162; on female stereotypes, 62; on feminism, vii, 3, 23, 28, 79, 81, 83, 135, 150, 167, 173, 174, 176–77, 178, 180, 191, 195; on feminist aesthetic, 3; on her financial difficulties, 50, 52; on fishing, 31–32; on her garden, 122; on gay men, 87, 103, 104, 131, 150; on the Gay/Lesbian movement, 103, 129, 195; on gender differences, 91; on grade school, viii, 10–11, 18, 34; on grammar, 57–58; on grassroots organizing, 103, 130; on health issues, 113; on high school, viii, 11, 13, 18, 21, 32, 34, 35, 39, 47, 51, 64, 71, 88, 115, 181; on homophobia, 29, 78, 80, 81, 102, 150, 167, 182; on honors for her writing, 4; on hope, 8, 153; on humanness, 7, 13, 14, 17, 63, 103; on "hyphenated people," 189; on images in poetry, 41–42, 43, 45, 86, 115–16, 118–19, 147, 188; on imaging, 41–42, 46, 86, 136, 160,

168, 182; on imperialism, ix, xi, 185; on impressionistic technique, 156, 167; on indigenous peoples, 180, 185, 187; on insanity, 23, 35–36, 71, 166, 175, 197; on the intellectual community, 195; on an international community, 188; on an international women's network, 169–70, 179, 180; on interracial lesbian couples, 82, 102, 129 (*see also* Clayton, Frances); on interracial marriage, xiii, 54 (*see also* Rollins, Edwin); on intuition, 47, 64–65; on the Jewish community, 62; on justice, 15–16, 71–72; on keeping a journal, 75–76, 95–96, 122; on land rights struggle, 153, 179; on language, 27, 30, 51, 80, 144, 151, 193; on Latina women, 176; on learning to read, 9–10; on learning to talk, 9–10, 45–46, 71, 90, 159–60; on learning to write, 9–10; on lesbianism and lesbians, vii, x, 23, 25, 28, 38, 61, 62, 67, 101–5, 108, 109, 110, 113, 150, 172, 177–78, 198; on liberation, xi, 5, 17, 78, 80, 87, 178, 185; on libraries, 9–10, 11, 45; on literary critics, 26, 71, 88, 98, 146; on the literary establishment, 26, 85–86, 88, 98, 111, 126, 129; on loss, 19, 81, 117; on love, 13, 14, 15, 20, 59, 73, 74, 92, 107, 175; on her love poetry, 74–75, 93–94; on lyricism of her writing, 155; on machine-like behavior, 7, 19, 64, 174, 192; on male competitiveness, 3; on her mastectomy, 77, 83, 133–34, 137, 161; on memorizing poems, 46, 90; on menstruation, 22, 135; on Middle Eastern workers in Germany, 172; on motherhood, xiii, 5, 6, 81, 82, 147, 149, 167–68, 193; on moving West, 117; on music and poetry, 151; on mythology, viii, 40, 144, 157, 168; on her name, 50; on the name Zami, 143, 149; on naming rituals, 143, 149; on nationalism, 65; on Native Americans, xi, 149, 176; on nature, 41, 115, 122–23; on her nearsightedness, 9, 41, 49, 50, 143, 156, 159; on "nigger," 145, 166; on nightmares, 37; on non-verbal communication, 47; on nostalgia for the 1950s, 109–10; on nursery rhymes, 46; on nursing as a career, 49–50; on objectifying Black women, 108, 174; on obscenity, 195, 196, 197; on her operations, 33, 133, 185; on oppression, 8, 21, 26, 28, 54, 59, 62, 77, 81, 82, 112, 118, 144, 153, 164, 170, 176, 177, 182,

183, 193; on pain, 16, 17, 25, 73–74, 89, 92; on patois, 37; on patriarchal thinking, 63, 77, 122–23, 143, 147, 167, 194, 195; on people of color, 40, 79, 87, 102, 106, 111, 121, 124, 130, 145, 165, 176, 185, 188, 194, 196; on the personal and the political, 165–66, 180; on the poet as part of the community, 106, 184; on the poet as possessed, 27; on poetic forms, 35, 40; on poetry and emotions, xi, 3, 32, 36, 37, 48–49, 55, 73, 93, 121, 127, 147, 168–69, 188–89; on poetry as a means of survival, 23, 30, 35–36, 106; on poetry as subversive activity, 23, 109, 112, 129, 163, 168; on poetry readings, 41, 72, 95, 112, 144; on poetry workshops, 52–54, 72, 94, 121, 190; on the poet's responsibility, 30, 44, 80, 92, 109, 112, 187; on the poet-warrior, xi; on political activism, 79–80, 105–6, 107–8, 112–13, 165–66, 196; on pollutants, 135; on pornography, xii, 196, 197; on poverty, 98, 187; on power, xii, xiii, 8, 15, 21, 23, 24, 27, 31, 38, 43, 57, 63, 64, 68, 69, 77, 87, 91, 106, 108, 119, 138, 146, 152, 164–65, 183, 193, 197–98; on prayer, 14; on preserving her perceptions, 45, 65–67, 181; on the profit motive, 167; on prostheses, 139, 141; on publishing her first poem, 40, 71; on race, xi, 15, 26, 28; on racism, ix, 4–5, 7, 15, 18, 21, 29, 58–61, 65, 67, 77–78, 80, 86, 97, 102, 114, 139, 144–45, 150, 167, 171–75, 177, 178, 182, 198; on rationality, 63, 91, 147–48, 151, 168; on reading, 9–11, 19, 32, 35–36, 37, 43, 48; on renewal, 123; on resisting categorization, 71, 82, 87, 88, 128, 143, 146; on her respect for ritual, 162; on her responsibility as a writer, 88–89, 90; on revising her works, 32–33, 39, 75, 95, 156, 190; on revolution, xii, 8, 59, 107, 112, 195, 198; on rhetoric, 33, 148; on rhythms of words, 37; on right-wing politics, x, 79–80, 87, 177; on rituals for writing, 39; on rock-digging, 90; on role models, 28; on sadomasochism, xiii; on the self, 31, 38, 43, 59, 65, 68, 82, 87, 94, 105, 128, 152, 165; on self-acceptance, 193; on self-hatred, 177; on self-help groups, 142; on sexism, 4–5, 7, 29, 59, 86, 126, 167, 177, 182, 195, 197, 199; on sexual violence, 91; on sexuality, 22, 86, 87, 194, 195, 196; on silences, x–xi, xiii, 6, 8, 9, 21,

62, 69, 73, 80, 85, 100, 160, 164, 175, 181, 195, 197, 199; on sisterhood, 13, 174; on her sisters, 9, 10, 18, 20, 22, 34; on slavery, 168, 170; on social protest, 74, 92; on the Space Program, 8–9; on speaking for the voiceless, 145, 197; on speaking in poetry, 46, 71, 90; on spirituality, 123, 162, 182; on her stained-glass apprenticeship, 52; on stories of survival, 158; on stream-of-consciousness writing, 51; on the sun as female image, 42; on support-groups, 6, 33, 34, 35; on the surreal, 41–42; on survival, x, 13, 15, 26, 30, 31, 38, 45, 52, 65, 68, 69, 74, 81, 82, 89, 90, 93, 98, 100, 110, 112, 119, 143, 144, 147, 151, 155, 158, 180, 183, 190, 196; on teaching, 13, 14, 27, 30, 31, 43, 52–54, 55, 57–61, 72, 82, 90, 94, 98, 100, 106, 112, 147, 152, 191; on television, xii, 6, 14; on the tension in her work, 127; on "texture" in her writing, 156; on thinking as a suspect process, 51, 147; on Third World women, x, 79, 152, 179, 195; on the tobacco industry, 196; on tools of survival, 151–52; on trivialization of her work, 161, 174, 197, 199; on Turkish workers in Germany, 172; on the underground railroad, 168; on the unicorn, 43; on urban stress, 117–19, 184; on victimization, 74, 91, 145; on vision for the future, 44, 82, 83, 85, 91, 94, 99, 106, 112, 135, 146, 164, 168, 175, 180, 181, 194, 196; on a vision of completeness, 12–13; on vulnerability, xiv, 31, 38, 62, 86, 120, 140; on a warrior's stance, 118, 142, 144, 149, 152, 155, 157, 164, 167–68, 183; on Western thought, 42, 91; on white America, x–xi, 7, 18, 21, 28, 34, 39, 77, 97, 110, 143, 166; on the white artistic community, 196, 199; on the white female establishment, 5, 167, 172, 174, 175; on the white male establishment, 4–5, 29, 62, 67, 68, 78, 143, 147, 167; on a white militaristic economy, 186–87; on withstanding pressure, 141–42; on womanist art, 195; on women-identified women, 12, 62, 66, 74, 149, 154; on women's communities, 80–81, 82, 124, 130, 144; on the women's literary movement, 157, 198; on the women's movement, 5, 7, 86, 98, 114, 144, 150, 165, 167, 172–73, 174–75, 194, 198; on the women's press, 6, 28, 79, 107, 109, 111, 130,

180; on women's traditional roles, 167–68; on words, xii, 13–14, 30, 35, 36, 37, 41, 47, 48–49, 52, 74, 92, 155, 159; on writer's block, 16, 76, 136–37; on writing as agent of change, 74, 106, 112, 197; on writing as central to her life, 72, 90, 94, 106, 146, 154; on writing as craft, 42, 93; on writing at the edge, 68, 119; on writing fiction, 128–29, 157; on writing poetry, xi, xii, 4, 9, 11, 13, 14, 16, 19, 22, 23, 26, 27, 30, 32, 34, 37, 41, 71, 90, 115, 158, 188, 193–94, 196; on her writing process, 95–96, 193–94; on writing prose, ix, 34, 39, 50, 51, 58, 70, 144, 168–69, 193–94

Works: "The American Cancer Society or There Is More Than One Way to Skin a Coon" (poem), 6, 62; *Auf Leben und Tod: Krebstagebüch (The Cancer Journals)*, 136, 144; *Between Our Selves* (poems), 30, 33, 40, 85; "Between Ourselves" (poem), 30, 43; *The Black Unicorn* (poems), viii, 30, 42, 43, 45, 66, 72, 73, 76, 85, 93, 95, 125, 192; "Blackstudies" (poem), 54, 191, 192; *A Burst of Light* (essays), viii, 183; *Cables to Rage* (poems), 40, 56, 85; *The Cancer Journals* (essays), xiii, xv, 45, 77, 85, 99–100, 113, 123–24, 129, 136–37, 139, 144, 161, 183, 197; "Change of Season" (poem), 42; *Chosen Poems Old and New* (poems), 109, 111, 117, 188, 190, 192; *Coal* (poems), 36, 40, 42, 45, 85, 192; "Coal" (poem), 119; "Coping" (poem), 121; "Dear Toni Instead of a Letter of Congratulation upon Your Book and Your Daughter Whom You Say You Are Raising to Be a Correct Little Sister" (poem), 40; "Equinox" (poem), 57; "Eye to Eye: Black Women, Hatred and Anger" (essay), 129, 193; *First Cities* (poems), 11, 34, 40, 51, 52, 57, 72, 83, 93, 94; *From a Land Where Other People Live* (poems), 3, 4, 5, 13, 30, 36, 61, 62, 85; "From the House of Yemanjá" (poem), 147; "Going Away to San Francisco, I Passed Over You and the Verrazano Bridge" (poem), 122; "Harriet" (poem), 76, 95; "I Am Your Sister: Black Women Organizing Across Sexualities" (speech), vii; "La Llorona" (story), 50, 121; "Letter for Jan" (poem), 93; "A Litany for Survival" (poem), 30, 69, 95, 160; "Love Poem" (poem), 61–62; "The Master's Tools Will Never Dismantle the Master's House" (essay),

151; "Need: A Choral for Black Women's Voices" (poem), 67, 185; "Neighbors" (poem), 13; "Never to Dream of Spiders" (poem), 163; "New York City" (poem), 117, 119, 190; *New York Head Shop and Museum* (poems), 5, 6, 85, 93, 117, 189–90, 191; "One Year to Life on the Grand Central Shuttle" (poem), 8; *Our Dead Behind Us* (poems), 192; "Outlines" (poem), 129; "Outside" (poem), 30; "Poem for a Poet" (poem), 37; "Poetry Is Not a Luxury" (essay), xi, 45, 51, 62, 146, 193, 194; "Power" (poem), 33, 67–68, 76, 96; "Rooming Houses Are Old Women" (poem), 36; "Scar" (poem), 43; "Sequelae" (poem), 76, 95; *Showing Our Colors: Afro-German Women Speak Out* (introduction), ix–x; *Sister Outsider* (essays), vii, x, xi, xii, 128, 129, 193; "Solstice" (poem), 42; "Suffer the Children" (poem), xiv; "Summer Oracle" (poem), 42; "Tar Beach" (prose), 40; "To Girls Who Know What Side Their Bread Is Buttered On" (poem), 121; "To Marie in Flight" (poem), 123; "To My Daughter the Junkie on a Train" (poem), xiv, 190; "To the Poet Who Happens to Be Black and the Black Poet Who Happens to Be a Woman" (poem), 146; "Touring" (poem), 72, 95; "The Transformation of Silence into Language and Action" (essay), x–xi, 69; "The Uses of Anger" (essay), 150; "Uses of the Erotic: The Erotic as Power" (essay), xii, 45, 64, 69, 75, 94, 148, 160, 161, 196; "Walking Our Boundaries" (poem), 93, 121–22; "Who Said It Was Simple" (poem), 4, 30; "A Woman Speaks" (poem), 43; *Zami: A New Spelling of My Name* (biomythography), viii, ix, xiv, 40, 85, 99, 109, 110, 111, 120, 125, 128, 143–44, 148–49, 152, 154–57, 167, 184

Lorde, Frederic Byron (father), xi, 9, 15, 18–25, 120, 125, 144–45, 155

Lorde, Linda Belmar (mother), xi, 9–10, 15, 18–23, 25, 34, 36, 45, 50, 89, 120, 121, 125, 144–45, 149, 154, 182–83

Lubinetsky, Raya, 192

Madeline (Ludwig Bemelmans), 10

Maori, 180

Mapplethorpe, Robert, 195

Margaret, Helene, 35, 36; *Change of Season*, 35

Marlow, Alan, 11
Martin Luther King March on Washington, 101,
   113–14
Mawulisa, 42, 148, 162
McBride, Gertrude, 55
Medea, 50
Medgar Evers College, vii
Metzger, Dina, 141
Mexico, viii, 40–41, 48–49, 120–21, 127, 143
Mexico City, 40, 48
Millay, Edna St. Vincent, 35, 36, 126
Minnesota, 31–32
Mississippi, 53, 94
MLA (Modern Language Association), 27, 69
Montague, Mass., 45
Moral Majority, 79, 195
Morehead, Jeanne, 35
Morgan, Robin, 29
Morrison, Toni, 77, 97, 129; *Song of Solomon*,
   77, 97; *Sula*, 77, 97
Moving Out, 6
Ms. Magazine, 4, 29, 61, 133, 140

Nairobi, 179
National Black Coalition of Gays and Lesbians,
   101
National Book Award, viii, 3–4, 158
National Conference of Afro-American
   Writers, xi
National Endowment for the Arts, 11, 194, 196
National Gay Health Network, 113
National University of Mexico, 48
Naylor, Gloria, 129, 149; *The Women of Brewster
   Place*, 149
Neruda, Pablo, 126
New York City, 9, 38, 41, 59, 85, 115–19,
   121–22, 156, 181, 184, 190
New York Public Library, xvi
New York Times Book Review, 129
New Zealand, 153, 180
Nigeria, 44, 173
Nixon, Richard, 117
Nwapa, Flora, 76, 96, 173
Nyerere, Julius, 198

Oguntoye, Katharina, ix
Olson, Lester C., xvi
Opitz, May, ix

Orlanda Women's Press, ix
Orwell, George, 107; *1984*, 107
Osbey, Brenda Marie, 197
Ozarks, 12

Papua, 180
Parker, Pat, 129, 130, 199
Parkerson, Michelle, xiv
Persephone Press, 109, 111
Pitchford, Kenneth, 29
Poet's Press, 11, 52
Ponsot, Marie, 122–23
Popocatepetl, 48
Prevention, 134
Progressive, xi

R. J. Reynolds Company, 196
Rackham, Arthur, 46
Reagan, Ronald, xi, 79, 80, 166
Reagon, Bernice, 104, 147; *Home Girls*, 104, 130
Reed, Ishmael, 26, 29
Rias-Butts, Yolanda, 11–12, 33, 57, 59
Rich, Adrienne, viii, 3, 33, 116, 119–20, 121,
   158, 159, 168, 181; *Diving into the Wreck*, 3
Risking a Somersault art show, 188
Rollins, Edwin (AL's husband), xiii, 11, 24, 52,
   54, 58, 59, 117
Rollins, Elizabeth Lorde (daughter), xiii, 13–14,
   39, 82, 117–18, 167
Rollins, Jonathan (son), xiii, 13, 24–25, 39, 52,
   82, 83, 102, 118
Romantic poets, 32
Rosenberg, Michaela, 137
Ruf, Waltraut, 136
Rushin, Kate, 158

"Saint, The" (Simon Templer), 17
Samoa, 180
San Diego, Calif., 79
Schmidt, Heidrun, ix
Schomburg Collection, 10
Schultz, Dagmar, ix, xv; *Farbe bekennen
   (Showing Our Colors)*, ix, 169
Scopolamine ("twilight sleep"), 17
Scott, Patricia Bell, 98
Search for Education, Elevation, and
   Knowledge (SEEK), 57, 60

Seventeen, 71, 88
Shakespeare, William, 27, 49
Shakti, Uma Kali, x
Shange, Ntozake, 97, 98; *For Colored Girls Who Have Considered Suicide When the Rainbow Is Enuf*, 97
Shapiro, Karl, 54
Shaughnessy, Mina, 57
Sheba Press, 176, 180
Shelley, Percy Bysshe, 12, 32
Shockley, Ann, 129
Signs, 116
Simmons, Judy, 196
Sister Outsider Collective, 179
Sisters in Support of Sisters in South Africa, ix, 152
Smartt, Dorothea, x
Smith, Barbara, 26, 28, 33, 98, 104, 129, 191, 198, 199; *Some of Us Are Brave*, 98
Sojourner Sisters, 185
South Africa, 103, 122, 166, 196
Spare Rib, x
Spencer, Anne, 28
Spinnboden-Archiv (Berlin), xiii
Spinsters Ink, 45
St. Croix, Virgin Islands, 184, 186, 188, 189
Stamford, Conn., 48
Stanton, Elizabeth Cady, 7
Star, Susan Leigh, xiii
Staten Island, 16, 85, 122, 128
Steif, William, xi
sub rosa Press, ix

Third World Women's Archives, 108
This Bridge Called My Back: Writing by Radical Women of Color, 130
Togo, 44
Tougaloo College, xiii, 52, 53, 55–56, 57, 72, 85, 94–95, 115, 125
Town School, 55–56

Truth, Sojourner, 7, 168
Tutuola, Amos, 76, 96

University of the City of New York, 140

Vendler, Helen, 41
Vietnam War, 8
Village Voice, 191
Virgin Islands, ix, 184–90

W. W. Norton & Company, 45, 109, 111, 130
Walcott, Derek, 199
Walker, Alice, viii, 3, 28, 97, 124–25, 129, 130–31, 158, 162, 178; *The Color Purple*, 97; *Revolutionary Petunias*, 3
Walker, Margaret, 35
Washington, D.C., 15–16, 145
Washington, Mary Helen, 158
Watts, 116
Weeks, Ricardo, 35
Wekker, Gloria, 179
Weleda, 134
West African Market Women Associations, 43–44
West Indies, 18, 21, 37, 49, 109, 125
Williams, Galen, 53
Windsor, Catherine, 19; *Forever Amber*, 19
Women of Tropical Africa, 43–44
Wood, Deborah, xi
Wordsworth, William, 32
World War II, 110, 115
Wylie, Elinor, 35

Yale Series of Younger Poets, 127
Yemanjá, 147, 162
Yoruba, 27, 44, 149

Zambia, 168
Zimbabwe, 168